Lecture Notes in Computer Science 13815

More information about this series at https://link.springer.com/bookseries/558

Asbjørn Følstad · Theo Araujo ·
Symeon Papadopoulos · Effie L.-C. Law ·
Ewa Luger · Morten Goodwin ·
Petter Bae Brandtzaeg (Eds.)

Chatbot Research and Design

6th International Workshop, CONVERSATIONS 2022
Amsterdam, The Netherlands, November 22–23, 2022
Revised Selected Papers

Editors
Asbjørn Følstad
SINTEF
Oslo, Norway

Theo Araujo
University of Amsterdam
Amsterdam, The Netherlands

Symeon Papadopoulos
CERTH-ITI
Thessaloniki, Greece

Effie L.-C. Law
Durham University
Durham, UK

Ewa Luger
University of Edinburgh
Edinburgh, UK

Morten Goodwin
University of Agder
Grimstad, Norway

Petter Bae Brandtzaeg
University of Oslo
Oslo, Norway

ISSN 0302-9743   ISSN 1611-3349 (electronic)
Lecture Notes in Computer Science
ISBN 978-3-031-25580-9   ISBN 978-3-031-25581-6 (eBook)
https://doi.org/10.1007/978-3-031-25581-6

This Springer imprint is published by the registered company Springer Nature Switzerland AG
The registered company address is: Gewerbestrasse 11, 6330 Cham, Switzerland

Preface

Introduction

Chatbots are an object of ongoing researcher and industry interest. As chatbots have increasing relevance for a broad range of users and application areas, the need for research is substantial. As attested by the research presented in this volume, useful chatbot applications span from health care and wellbeing to digital government and customer service. Research areas range from user insight and experience to the design and technological underpinnings of conversational interaction.

To provide a meeting place for researchers and practitioners with professional interest in chatbots, and strengthen research knowledge on chatbots, the international CONVERSATIONS workshop has been organized as a yearly event since 2017. In response to the variation in chatbot research areas, the workshop series is distinctly cross-disciplinary with contributions from computer science, the social sciences and humanities, management and communication research, as well as design research and human-computer interaction.

The CONVERSATIONS workshops are intended as open and inclusive arenas for sharing and discussing chatbot research and design and have since 2019 been conducted as two-day events. Due to the COVID-19 pandemic, the workshops were held online in 2020–2021, but we returned to an on-site format in 2022 to strengthen the opportunity for networking and interaction among workshop participants.

CONVERSATIONS 2022 was the sixth workshop in the series. While being an on-site event, about one-third of the sessions were held in hybrid mode for increased access. The workshop took place on November 22–23, 2022, hosted by the University of Amsterdam in collaboration with SINTEF, the University of Oslo and its Centre for Research on Media Innovations (CRMI), Centre for Research and Technology Hellas, Durham University, University of Edinburgh, and the University of Agder.

In total, 111 participants from 25 countries registered for the workshop – 56 on-site, the remainder online.

Paper Invitation, Review, and Revision

The workshop Call for Papers outlined an interest in chatbot research, design and applications within six key areas – based on the promising directions for future chatbot research identified through earlier editions of CONVERSATIONS. Specifically, we asked for contributions addressing chatbot users and user experience, chatbot frameworks and platforms, chatbots for collaboration and participation, chatbot ethics and privacy, and how to leverage advances in AI technology and large language models.

The Call for Papers was communicated through relevant mailing lists. We also forwarded the Call in the network of researchers and practitioners associated with the CONVERSATIONS workshop series. Four types of submissions were encouraged: Full papers, position papers, project presentations, and groupwork proposals. The project presentations category was new to this year's edition of the workshop, intended as a means for researchers to promote projects of relevance and interest to the CONVERSATIONS audience.

We received 39 submissions, 27 full papers, four position papers, six project presentations, and two groupwork proposals. The full papers, position papers, and project presentations were subject to double-blind review. Each paper was reviewed by two to three independent members of the program committee, with one of the seven workshop organizers serving as review lead and responsible for the meta-review. The program committee members reviewed between two and four submissions. The organizers led the review process for five or six submissions. Decisions on acceptance were made in an organizers' meeting after all reviews had been submitted by the program committee members and summarized by the lead reviewers. Conflicted submissions were processed without involvement of the interested parties. One full paper submission was desk rejected as it was out of scope for the workshop. The two groupwork proposals were assessed by a jury, consisting of the organizers.

In total, 12 full paper submissions were accepted, six after minor revision and six after major revision. Revisions were only accepted following a compliance check by the respective lead reviewer and, if necessary, one or two rounds of additional revisions. In one case, the final decision also required follow-up feedback from reviewers. The acceptance rate for full papers was 44%.

Workshop Program and Outcomes

The two-day workshop program included a keynote speaker, an invited talk, two groupworks, six paper sessions, and a panel discussion.

The keynote speaker was Catherine Pelachaud, Director of Research of the ISIR laboratory, Sorbonne University. Pelachaud presented the development of a socially interactive agent, including work on multimodal interaction and adaptation of conversational strategies to strengthen user engagement.

In the invited talk, Sandro Pezzelle, University of Amsterdam, shared research experiences on adapting state-of-the-art conversational systems, based on pre-trained language models, to different age groups.

The workshop participants could choose between two groupworks. Sviatlana Höhn, Bettina Migge, Doris Dippold and Britta Schneider organized a groupwork on Attitudes, Preconceptions and Practices in Conversational AI Design. Jan de Wit and Anouck Braggaar conducted a groupwork on Platforms for Chatbot Development and Research.

The topic of the panel discussion was evaluation of chatbots in research and practice; specifically, how to do useful and reliable evaluations. The panelists represented research and industry, including Michael McTear (Ulster University), Nena van As (boost.ai), Margot van der Goot (University of Amsterdam), and Elayne Ruane (UCD). The panel provided insight into the complexity of relevant chatbot evaluation criteria, the need to flexibly adapt evaluation design to the specific characteristics of a context of use, and the need for transfer and aggregation of insight across evaluations.

The paper sessions included presentations of accepted full papers, position papers, and project presentations organized in six topical clusters; three of which were on-site only and three in hybrid mode – both on-site and online.

In these proceedings, all the accepted full papers are structured into two overarching themes where each theme includes six papers.

In the first theme, *chatbot users and user experience*, the papers provided new insight and knowledge from a broad range of domains. Leuwis and He presented an investigation of a chatbot for smoking cessation and factors impacting the user experience of such a chatbot. Nordberg and Guribye addressed user experience of news consumption through voice user interfaces. Liebrecht, Kamoen, and Aerts investigated usage and preference of different implementations of conversational agents for voting advice. Silva, de Cicco, Levi, and Hammerschmidt provided new insight into the effect of gamification in chatbots for brand communication. Abbas, Følstad, and Bjørkli presented a study of users' perceptions of chatbots for digital government service provision. Lastly, Henkel, Linn, and der Goot summarized findings from a study of intention to use mental health chatbots among LGBTQIA+ users. The range of the studied application domains provides valuable new knowledge on a variation of specific chatbot use-cases, but also serves to shed light on themes that cut across these domains – for example, related to factors underpinning usage intention and user experience.

The second theme, *chatbot design and applications*, included papers that provided new knowledge on the design of chatbot interactions and dialogue as well as insight on specific implementations. Abbo, Crovari, and Garzotto presented a promising approach to in-app troubleshooting by way of a conversational agent. Van Hooijdonk, Martijn, and Liebrecht provided a novel framework for analyzing a chatbot design aspect of high interest to practitioners, that is, the chatbot's initial self-introduction. Chira, Mathioudis, and colleagues presented a multi-modal chatbot for user-friendly collection of data from specific patient groups. Angenius and Ghajargar provided in-depth reflections on conversation as design material, grounded in a study of a chatbot for journalling. Stolwijk and Kunneman presented their work on integrating chatbot responses on general knowledge and a specific task at hand, through an engaging study of a cooking assistant. Finally, Niederer, Schloss, and Christensen provided insight into their work on a chatbot to help users with product configuration in a conversational manner.

Three of the accepted full papers were nominated for the CONVERSATIONS best paper award. The nominated papers were those with the best average scores from the reviewer feedback. From these three nominees, a jury consisting of the seven workshop organizers selected the winner of the award. The CONVERSATIONS 2022 best paper award was given to Charlotte van Hooijdonk, Gabriëlla Martijn and Christine Liebrecht for their paper *A Framework and Content Analysis of Social Cues in the Introductions of Customer Service Chatbots.* The two runners up were Lotte Leeuwis and Linwei He with their paper *Hi, I'm Cecil(y) the Smoking Cessation Chatbot: The Effectiveness of Motivational Interviewing and Confrontational Counseling Chatbots and the Moderating Role of the Need for Autonomy and Self-Efficacy,* and Giulio Antonio Abbo, Pietro Crovari and Franca Garzotto for their paper *Enhancing Conversational Troubleshooting with Multi-modality: Design and Implementation.*

Upon completing the successful sixth edition of the CONVERSATIONS workshop, we are thankful to all authors, program committee members, presenters, participants, and supporters – all who helped make the workshop a great place for sharing and discussion of chatbot research and design. We are happy that the workshop series serves to strengthen the community of chatbot researchers and already look forward to the next edition of CONVERSATIONS.

November 2022

Asbjørn Følstad
Theo Araujo
Symeon Papadopoulos
Effie L.-C. Law
Ewa Luger
Morten Goodwin
Petter Bae Brandtzaeg

Organization

General Chairs/Workshop Organizers

Asbjørn Følstad   SINTEF, Norway
Theo Araujo   University of Amsterdam, The Netherlands
Symeon Papadopoulos   Centre for Research and Technology Hellas, Greece
Effie L.-C. Law   Durham University, UK
Ewa Luger   University of Edinburgh, UK
Morten Goodwin   University of Agder, Norway
Petter Bae Brandtzaeg   University of Oslo & SINTEF, Norway

Program Committee

Alexander Mädche   Karlsruhe Institute of Technology, Germany
Ana Paula Chaves   Northern Arizona University, USA
Carolin Ischen   University of Amsterdam, The Netherlands
Charlotte van Hooijdonk   Utrecht University, The Netherlands
Christian Löw   University of Vienna, Austria
Christine Liebrecht   Tilburg University, The Netherlands
David Kuboň   Charles University, Prague, Czech Republic
Despoina Chatzakou   Centre for Research and Technology Hellas, Greece
Elayne Ruane   University College Dublin, Ireland
Eleni Metheniti   CLLE-CNRS|IRIT-CNRS, France
Eren Yildiz   Umeå University, Sweden
Fabio Catania   Politecnico di Milano, Italy
Frank Dignum   Umeå University, Sweden
Frode Guribye   University of Bergen, Norway
Guy Laban   University of Glasgow, UK
Jo Dugstad Wake   NORCE & University of Bergen, Norway
Jo Herstad   University of Oslo, Norway
Juanan Pereira   Universidad del País Vasco/Euskal Herriko Unibertsitatea, Spain
Konstantinos Boletsis   SINTEF, Norway
Lea Reis   University of Bamberg, Germany
Leigh Clark   Swansea University, UK
Lorenz Cuno Klopfenstein   University of Urbino "Carlo Bo", Italy

Contents

Chatbot Users and User Experience

Hi, I'm Cecil(y) the Smoking Cessation Chatbot: The Effectiveness of Motivational Interviewing and Confrontational Counseling Chatbots and the Moderating Role of the Need for Autonomy and Self-efficacy

Lotte Leeuwis and Linwei He(⊠)

Department of Communication and Cognition, Tilburg School of Humanities and Digital
Sciences, Tilburg University, Tilburg, The Netherlands
l.he_1@tilburguniversity.edu

Abstract. This study aimed to investigate if and how chatbots can increase smokers' intention to quit, specifically looking into the effectiveness of two communication styles (i.e., motivational interviewing (MI) and confrontational counseling (CC)) and the moderating role of individual differences (i.e., need for autonomy and perceived self-efficacy) that may affect smokers' experience with the chatbot. In an online between-subjects experiment ($N = 233$), smoking participants were assigned to interact with either a MI chatbot ($n = 121$) or a CC chatbot ($n = 112$) for one 8-min session. Their need for autonomy and perceived self-efficacy were measured, as well as their satisfaction with the conversation and pre- and post-test intention to quit smoking. No significant effects of different communication styles were found regarding the outcomes, nor did the need for autonomy moderate these results. However, the effect of MI on user satisfaction was more profound among smokers with higher self-efficacy, and a positive effect of self-efficacy on user satisfaction appeared. Additionally, interacting with the chatbots about one's smoking behavior significantly increased participants' intention to quit, regardless of its communication style. As such, this study sheds light on the potential of conversational chatbots for smoking cessation interventions, as well as pathways for future research.

Keywords: Conversational agents · Smoking cessation · Motivational interviewing · Need for autonomy · Self-efficacy

1 Introduction

For a long time, governments and organizations across the world have tried to increase smoking cessation rates using various interventions [1]. Many of these interventions focus on highlighting the risks associated with smoking, often by using fear and/or emotional appeals [2]. While such heavy messages can be effective for some smokers, others may cope with the messages more defensively, leading to rejection and dismissal

A. Følstad et al. (Eds.): CONVERSATIONS 2022, LNCS 13815, pp. 3–17, 2023.
https://doi.org/10.1007/978-3-031-25581-6_1

of the message [3]. As a result of such individual differences in emotional and behavioral responses toward anti-smoking messages, tobacco use remains a public health problem of a high caliber [4]. Therefore, developing vehicles for individualized smoking cessation communication has been a recent research priority. For that purpose, conversational agents such as chatbots may be well-suited, as they decrease pressure on health care providers by allowing 24/7, low-cost access to individualized counseling for a large portion of the population that wants to quit smoking [5, 6].

Chatbots can be defined as "artificial intelligence programs designed to simulate human conversation" [6] and have seen a rapid increase in their ability to assist in health counseling over the years [5]. The initial effectiveness and acceptability of chatbots for health counseling has been demonstrated in various settings, such as mental health and physical activity [6].

Within the field of individualized smoking cessation counseling, modern chatbots can use various communication styles, such as confrontational counseling (CC) and motivational interviewing (MI). CC focuses on confronting smokers with the consequences of their behavior to counter self-exempting beliefs and increase risk perceptions through direct advice and health-related information [7]. In contrast, MI aims to enhance the client's motivation and belief that behavior change is necessary through self-persuasion [8]. Despite their differences, both MI and CC are client-centered, directive, and effective in facilitating behavior change [7, 9].

The potential of chatbots and their one-to-one nature allows for individualized conversations, and it is important to gain insight into which communication style fits which individual's needs and preferences. Tailoring to such preferences is likely to lead to higher user satisfaction with the chatbots and, by extension, a higher success rate regarding the target behavior [10]. In this context, two factors may be particularly applicable: the need for autonomy as outlined in Self-Determination Theory (SDT) [11] and perceived self-efficacy as outlined in Social Cognitive Theory (SCT) [12]. Specifically, a higher need for autonomy may ask for autonomy-supportive interventions (i.e., MI), whereas a lower need for autonomy may signal a need for explicit directions from an expert (i.e., CC). Thus, meeting a client's need for autonomy may require the chatbot to use different communication styles. Similarly, it is possible that smokers with a higher perceived self-efficacy in their behavior change abilities could be able to cope with the confrontation of CC, whereas those with a lower self-efficacy need the motivational enhancement found in MI to feel capable of behavior change [3, 7].

Although there is a rich amount of research in personalization techniques for health interventions, little research has compared MI and CC directly while taking into consideration the moderating role of individual differences, especially in chatbot-delivered health interventions. Therefore, to fill this gap in the literature and shed light on the use of chatbots in smoking cessation interventions, this study aims to explore the optimal communication style (MI vs. CC) for a chatbot in terms of user satisfaction and quit intention and the role of the need for autonomy and self-efficacy.

2 Conceptual Framework

2.1 Communication Styles for Smoking Cessation Chatbots

Within the substance abuse counseling literature, confrontation is a frequently mentioned practice [13]. Traditionally, CC aims to break through defense mechanisms such as denial and minimization of the problem, by directly confronting the client's resistance to change [13]. Within the smoking cessation field, CC counselors use techniques such as direct education, challenging clients' perceptions of the issue, and providing a treatment plan [14]. Contrary to the common idea that CC leads to a clash between the counselor and the client, research showed that this style positively predicts client involvement, and that CC may even be perceived as genuine and authentic if delivered in an empathetic manner [15]. However, if the client feels threatened by the counselor's pursuit of behavior change, resistance may escalate, leading to less satisfaction among the client and, in turn, a lower intention to change their behavior [8].

In response to the observed potential for client resistance in CC, Miller and Rollnick [8] developed MI: A counseling style for behavioral change by eliciting motivation *within* the client as opposed to imposing motivation *onto* the client [8, 13]. The MI counselor subtly guides the client through this journey by expressing empathy, accepting resistance, encouraging self-reflection, and acknowledging and supporting the client's self-efficacy [8]. Thus, whereas CC relies on directive advice and expert opinions from a professional, in MI, the client is regarded as the expert and the main driving force behind motivating oneself for behavior change [9].

Over the past decades, research on the effects of MI and CC on smoking cessation and other health behavior has yielded mixed and inconclusive results [16]. Some researchers argue that most smokers do not suffer from lack of knowledge about the negative consequences of smoking and do not need to receive information-based expert advice (i.e., CC), but instead a more motivation-based intervention (i.e., MI). However, there is also evidence suggesting that some individuals found MI too paternalistic and thus preferred a CC-resonant approach [17]. Therefore, CC can be effective for smokers who expect the counselor to be the expert rather than themselves [18]. A similar inconclusiveness pertains within the field of MI in smoking cessation interventions. For example, a meta-analysis showed that MI is efficacious for a wide range of problem behaviors (e.g., alcoholism and physical exercise), but not for smoking cessation. Other, more recent meta-analyses did find greater abstinence amongst smokers who received an MI intervention, although the effects were small [9].

Overall, these results illustrate that both CC and MI seem to have the potential to motivate behavior change. However, despite methodological disparities in this line of research, most literature seems to support the notion that MI yields less resistance and is therefore more likely to effectively change behavior, which is especially relevant for addiction where high resistance is common [16]. Secondly, meta-analyses showed that CC may work for a small portion of the population, but that MI works better for a larger group of individuals, making it a more efficacious approach [19]. Lastly, in the context of chatbot-delivered interventions, CC is most likely to be successful when the sender is deemed a legitimate knowledgeable expert and chatbots may not be particularly suited for this communication style as chatbots are usually not considered as medical authorities [5]. On a broader note, it is suggested that people prefer chatbots that offer emotional support (i.e., MI) more than informational chatbots (i.e., CC) [20]. Given that this is likely to lead to increased user satisfaction and a higher intention to adhere to the intervention, it is hypothesized that:

A chatbot employing MI leads to a higher intention to quit (H1) and higher user satisfaction (H2) amongst smokers in comparison to a chatbot employing CC.

2.2 Moderating Role of Need for Autonomy

Whilst there is mounting evidence supporting the effectiveness of MI, most of the studies in this field were conducted in face-to-face clinical settings. Hence, the efficacy of automated MI delivered by chatbots remains inconclusive. In an earlier study [21], we compared an MI-style chatbot with a neutral-style chatbot and found no significant impact of MI. Similarly, recent reviews also acknowledged the inconclusiveness regarding the efficacy of automated MI and, therefore, called for research to further examine human factors that could impact chatbot interventions [22].

Human factors play an important role in the interaction with chatbots, and accounting for individual differences in designing the chatbot can improve user satisfaction and adherence [23]. Specifically in behavior change interventions, need for autonomy is a crucial characteristic that determines users' experience with the intervention. When this need is satisfied, the individual feels that it is intrinsically rewarding to perform the target behavior [24]. On the other hand, when one's need for autonomy is not satisfied, the individual feels pressured to think or behave in a way determined by external others, such as practitioners or interventions (e.g., chatbots) and might engage in defensive responses. Whilst the need for autonomy is universal, the level of this need differs per individual [24]. For instance, 'self-reliers' are individuals with a higher need for autonomy and are less likely to seek external control, whereas 'expert-dependents' are individuals with a lower need for autonomy and tend to depend on external guidance [24]. Therefore, in order to maximize the effectiveness of and user satisfaction with the smoking cessation chatbot, its communication style should be adapted to the client's preference, ranging from autonomy-supportive (i.e., MI) to more directive-confrontational communication (i.e., CC).

Indeed, whereas CC might lead to resistance, recent research [25] contends that this resistance may not be caused by communication style, but by different needs for autonomy among clients. For instance, individuals with a higher need for autonomy feel more satisfied by autonomy-supportive communication (i.e., MI), leading to better health behavior outcomes (i.e., intention to quit smoking). Similarly, clients with a lower need for autonomy were more likely to seek guidance from an expert [24]. It seems plausible that clients with a lower need for autonomy would benefit more from the advice and guidance that CC delivers, whereas those with a higher need for autonomy would benefit more from enhancing intrinsic motivation as done through MI. Coleman et al. [18] provided some evidence for this claim and found that smokers who have a higher need for autonomy prefer a counselor that respects their autonomy (i.e., MI) as opposed to a counselor that gives confrontational advice (i.e., CC). More specifically, smokers with a higher need for autonomy may prefer to act independently, which is facilitated more by MI, whereas smokers with a lower need for autonomy may prefer to receive specific advice, which is facilitated more by CC. As such, it is hypothesized that:

The need for autonomy moderates the relationship between chatbot communication style and smokers' intention to quit smoking and user satisfaction, in that the positive effect of MI (vs. CC) on intention to quit (H3) and user satisfaction (H4) is stronger for smokers with a higher need for autonomy than for smokers with a lower need for autonomy.

2.3 The Moderating Role of Perceived Self-efficacy

In addition to the need for autonomy, self-efficacy is another factor that should be considered when designing a smoking cessation chatbot. Considering smoking cessation is often characterized by hardship and relapse, it is necessary for smokers to have at least some confidence in their ability to quit before they start an attempt. Bandura's SCT [12] states that the higher one's perceived self-efficacy, the more confidence and commitment one feels toward achieving their goal. In smoking cessation research, many studies suggested that self-efficacious smokers often have a higher intention to quit than those with a lower perceived self-efficacy (for a review, see [26]).

There is evidence to suggest that the level of self-efficacy may affect the way clients respond to an intervention. Gaume et al. [27] found that counselors with more CC-styled skills are effective in behavior change for clients who express high levels of confidence in their ability to change. Similarly, Colby et al. [28] found that MI did not lead to increased quitting self-efficacy nor increased smoking abstinence, possibly because participants already had a relatively high level of self-efficacy at baseline. Together, past research suggests the possibility of a ceiling effect, which could mean that smokers with a high level of perceived self-efficacy may not be advantaged by an MI chatbot that specifically aims to raise this level. Additionally, smokers with a high level of self-efficacy may believe that they are able to quit smoking whenever they want and that they are not vulnerable to smoking risks, hereby reducing pressure to quit, and reducing the effectiveness of MI [7]. To counter these self-exempting beliefs, Kotz et al. [7] found that CC is useful in increasing risk perceptions, making cessation more likely. Hence, CC would be more beneficial for smokers with a high level of self-efficacy, whereas MI might be more beneficial for smokers with a lower level of self-efficacy. As such, it is hypothesized that:

Perceived self-efficacy moderates the relationship between chatbot communication style and smokers' intention to quit and satisfaction, in that the positive effect of MI (vs. CC) on intention to quit (H5) and user satisfaction (H6) is stronger for smokers with a lower perceived self-efficacy than for those with a higher perceived self-efficacy.

The conceptual model can be seen in Fig. 1.

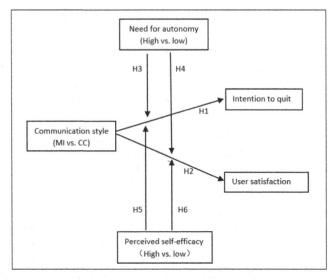

Fig. 1. Conceptual model of the hypotheses

3 Methods

3.1 Participants

An a-priori statistical power analysis using G*Power revealed that a sample size of 158 participants is necessary to uncover small to medium effects (effect size $f = 0.25$, power $= 0.8$), in accordance with previous meta-analyses on the effects of MI on smoking cessation [9]. To be able to partake in the experiment, participants had to be at least 18 years old, proficient in English, and have smoked at least one cigarette in the week prior to participation. As such, from November 23rd, 2021, to December 3rd, 2021, a total of 270 participants were recruited who met the requirements, agreed to the terms of the study, and completed the survey.

Participants who did not finish the chatbot conversation ($n = 37$) were removed from further analysis, leaving a final sample of 233 participants. Among these participants, 147 identified as female (63.1%), 83 as male (35.6%), and three as non-binary or preferred not to say (1.3%). Most participants reported to be between 18 and 25 years old (81.5%, $n = 190$) or 26 to 30 years old (11.2%, $n = 26$), the remaining participants indicated to be over 31 years old (7.3%, $n = 17$).

3.2 Experimental Design and Procedure

The online between-subjects experiment was conducted using Qualtrics for the survey-based part of the experiment and Flow.ai, a chatbot-building platform frequently used by companies and researchers, for the chatbot-part of the experiment. Prior to the commencement of data collection, ethical approval was obtained from Tilburg School of Humanities and Digital Sciences. Additionally, a pre-test was conducted to see whether the two conditions differed significantly using the Client Evaluation of Motivational

Interviewing (CEMI) scale [29]. This proved to be the case in the pre-tested materials ($M_{MI} = 5.1, SD_{MI} = 0.7, M_{CC} = 3.9, SD_{CC} = 0.8, t(22) = 4.00, p < .001$) as well as the materials used in the official experiment, finding that participants in the MI condition perceived the chatbot as more MI-like ($M = 5.1, SD = 0.9$), whereas participants in the CC condition perceived the chatbot as more CC-like ($M = 3.6, SD = 0.8, t(231) = 3.20, p = < .001$). Therefore, the manipulation was deemed successful.

Upon starting the experiment, participants first provided demographic data and information about their smoking status, after which they were randomly assigned to either the MI condition ($n = 121$) or the CC condition ($n = 112$). Participants' need for autonomy and perceived self-efficacy was measured, as well as their intention to quit at baseline. Then, participants were redirected to the Flow.ai environment, where they were asked to engage in one 8-minute conversation with either Cecily the MI chatbot or Cecil the CC chatbot. After the conversation, participants' intention to quit and their satisfaction with the conversation were measured. Finally, the participants were debriefed and thanked for their participation.

3.3 Operationalization

MI Chatbot Condition. MI works through a relational component and a technical component, in which the former focuses on acceptance, collaboration, evocation, and compassion – in other words, the 'MI-spirit' [8]. Within chatbots, the use of natural, person-like discourse and the use of emoticons can enhance this MI spirit, which were incorporated into the MI chatbot's dialogue. The technical component was operationalized by asking open-ended questions, providing reflections and affirmations [8]. During the conversation, the chatbot emphasized that that the participants were the experts rather than the chatbot, engaged the participants in shared agenda-setting to devise a goal for the conversation, encouraged the participant to express their thoughts and feelings about behavior change, helped the participant with identifying goals and barriers to change and setting a quitting plan if the participant wished to do so.

CC Chatbot Condition. The primary aim of the CC chatbot was to make the participant face the issues that their smoking behavior may cause by providing confrontational health information and unsolicited feedback on the participant's behavior [7, 8]. During the conversation, the chatbot directed the participant to talk about their current smoking behavior, after which the participant was told that their behavior is quite worrisome. The chatbot provided advice (without asking for permission) on how to tackle nicotine dependency. Factual data were used to confront minimization of the issue or resistance [7]. Lastly, the chatbot urged for readiness and abstinence by providing advice on how to deal with withdrawal symptoms and encouraging the participant to seek assistance from a medical professional. Examples of both chatbot utterances can be found in Table 1.

The interaction in both conditions took roughly same amount of time. Except for the aforementioned manipulations, the content of the dialogues (e.g., the information provided) was comparable across the two conditions.

Table 1. Example chatbot utterances of the two conditions.

MI chatbot utterances	CC chatbot utterances
"In this conversation, you are the expert on your own situation, smoking behavior, and thoughts." (collaboration)	"It may feel good now, but think about your future self for a second." (directive)
"Could you reflect on how quitting smoking may hinder your progress toward this goal?" (open-ended question)	"Before you can start your quit attempt, you must feel 100% ready. That way, your chances of a successful attempt are higher." (urge for readiness)
"Okay, so if I understand you correctly, your goal is […], but smoking can prevent you from achieving this goal: "[…]"." (reflection)	"That's quite worrisome." (judgement)
"You should definitely be proud of that achievement! ☺" (affirmation)	"I advise you to distract yourself by thinking about your reasons for quitting, and what you're doing all this for." (direct advice)

3.4 Measurements

Nicotine Dependency. The Fagerström Test for Nicotine Dependence (FTND) [30] was administered prior to experimental exposure. This measurement contained six questions, such as "How many cigarettes do you smoke per day?". The total number of points participants received based on their answers ranged from 2 and 12. A higher sum indicated a stronger nicotine dependency ($M = 3.6$, $SD = 2.1$, Cronbach's $\alpha = .72$).

Need for Autonomy. To measure participants' need for autonomy, the Help-Seeking Scale [31] was administered. This scale consisted of fourteen items. An example statement is "Instead of dealing with a problem on my own, I prefer to rely on someone who knows more than I". The questions were presented using a Likert-scale, ranging from 1 (*not at all true of me*) to 7 (*very true of me*). A higher computed mean score indicated a higher need for autonomy ($M = 4.5$, $SD = 0.7$, Cronbach's $\alpha = .71$).

Perceived Self-efficacy. To gain insight in the extent to which participants feel self-efficacious enough to change their behavior, the Smoking Abstinence Self-Efficacy Questionnaire (SASEQ) [32] was administered. This measurement consisted of six 'vignettes', such as "You feel agitated or tense. Are you confident that you will not smoke?". Participants' perceived self-efficacy was then measured using a Likert-scale, ranging from 1 (*certainly not*) to 5 (*certainly*). A higher computed mean score indicated a higher perceived self-efficacy ($M = 2.7$, $SD = 0.8$, Cronbach's $\alpha = .76$).

Intention to Quit. Participants' intention to quit was measured using the Contemplation Ladder [33], a one-item instrument on which participants can rank themselves in terms of their readiness to quit on a scale from 0 (*no thought of quitting*) to 10 (*taking action to quit*). This question was administered prior to experimental exposure to establish a baseline value ($M = 6.4$, $SD = 2.9$) as well as after exposure ($M = 7.2$, $SD = 2.5$) to assess whether the conversation led to an increased intention to quit.

User Satisfaction with the Conversation. Lastly, user satisfaction with the conversation was measured using the Client Satisfaction Questionnaire (CSQ-8) [34]. The CSQ-8 contains eight items, such as "To what extent has the consultation with the chatbot met your needs?", which were measured on a scale ranging from 1 to 4. A higher computed mean score indicated a higher user satisfaction with the conversation ($M = 2.6$, $SD = 0.6$, Cronbach's $\alpha = .93$).

Perception of Motivational Interviewing. Manipulation checks were carried out using a shortened version of the CEMI scale [29]. The scale included statements such as "The chatbot told you what to do" and "The chatbot showed you that it believed in your ability to change your behavior". Scores were measured using a Likert-scale ranging from 1 (*not at all*) to 7 (*a great deal*). A high total mean score indicated that the participant viewed the chatbot as MI-like; a low total mean score indicated that the participant viewed the chatbot as CC-like ($M = 4.3$, $SD = 1.1$, Cronbach's $\alpha = .76$).

3.5 Statistical Analysis

To test the effect of MI (vs. CC) on intention to quit and user satisfaction, taking into consideration of the possible influence of age, gender, and nicotine dependency [35], two one-way ANCOVAs were performed. To test the hypothesized moderating role of need for autonomy and self-efficacy, Hayes' PROCESS model 1 with covariates was used. All analyses were performed with SPSS 27.

4 Results

4.1 Main Analysis

Main Effects. H1 posited that an MI chatbot would lead to a higher intention to quit in comparison to a CC chatbot. A one-way ANCOVA showed that the covariates age ($F(1, 228) = 1.37$, $p = .243$), gender ($F(1, 228) = 1.38$, $p = .241$), and nicotine dependency ($F(1, 228) = 3.52$, $p = .062$) were not significantly associated with the intention to quit, although nicotine dependency was only marginally insignificant. No significant effect of chatbot communication style on one's intention to quit was found, $F(1, 228) = 0.97$, $p = .325$. Thus, H1 could be rejected.

H2 posited that an MI chatbot would lead to higher user satisfaction with the conversation in comparison to a CC chatbot. Similarly to H1, the covariates age ($F(1, 228) = 0.26$, $p = .613$), gender ($F(1, 228) = 0.15$, $p = .700$), and nicotine dependency ($F(1, 228) = 0.01$, $p = .253$) were not significantly associated with user satisfaction. A significant effect of chatbot communication style on user satisfaction could not be uncovered, $F(1, 228) = 1.31$, $p = .253$. Therefore, H2 could also be rejected.

Moderating Role of Need for Autonomy. Taking the analyses one step further, H3 posited that smokers' need for autonomy would moderate the relationship between chatbot communication style and intention to quit, in that the positive effect of MI (vs. CC) on intention to quit is stronger for smokers with a higher need for autonomy than for smokers with a lower need for autonomy. Results from Hayes' PROCESS model 1 showed that need for autonomy did not moderate the relationship between chatbot communication style and intention to quit ($b = -.15$, $t = -.32$, $p = .746$). The main effect of need for autonomy on intention to quit was also insignificant ($b = -.11$, $t = -.16$, $p = .876$). None of the covariates (i.e., age, gender, nicotine dependency) were significant either. Thus, H3 could be rejected.

Similarly, H4 hypothesized the moderating role of need for autonomy in the relationship between chatbot communication style and user satisfaction with the conversation. Results showed that the interaction was not significant ($b = -.03$, $t = -.25$, $p = .806$), nor was the main effect of need for autonomy on user satisfaction ($b = .12$, $t = .64$, $p = .520$) or any of the covariates. H4 could also be rejected.

Moderating Role of Perceived Self-efficacy. Similar procedures with PROCESS model 1 were carried out to test the proposed moderating effect of perceived self-efficacy. H5 posited that the positive effect of MI (vs. CC) on intention to quit is stronger among people with lower self-efficacy. The moderation was not significant ($b = -.09$, $t = -.23$, $p = .822$), nor was the main effect of perceived self-efficacy on intention to quit ($b = .81$, $t = 1.25$, $p = .213$). None of the covariates (i.e., age, gender, nicotine dependency) were significant either. H5 was therefore rejected.

Lastly, H6 proposed the moderation of self-efficacy in the relationship between chatbot communication style and user satisfaction. Results revealed a significant moderation ($b = -.21$, $t = -2.09$, $p = .038$). However, simple slope analysis showed that the effect of MI is stronger among individuals with higher self-efficacy, which is opposite to what was hypothesized. Additionally, a main effect of self-efficacy appeared ($b = .40$, $t = 2.42$, $p = .016$), such that higher self-efficacy predicts higher user satisfaction with the chatbot. No significant covariates were found (i.e., age, gender, nicotine dependency). Therefore, H6 was rejected. The results of the hypothesis testing are visualized in Fig. 2.

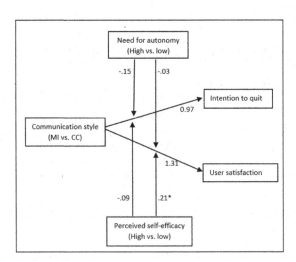

Fig. 2. Test results as integrated in the conceptual model. *$p < .05$

4.2 Secondary Analysis

A repeated measures ANCOVA was carried out to test whether conversing with the chatbots raised participants' intention to quit. The covariates age ($F(1, 229) = 1.45$, $p = .229$), gender ($F(1, 229) = 2.34$, $p = .136$), and nicotine dependency ($F(1, 229) = 2.98$, $p = .086$) were not significantly associated with participants' post-test intention to quit. No significant effects of chatbot communication style on intention to quit were found, $F(1, 228) = 0.78$, $p = .379$. However, a large significant effect was found of chatbot interaction in general on intention to quit, $F(1, 232) = 59.20$, $p = < .001$, $\eta_p^2 = .20$. Smokers' intention to quit after exposure was significantly higher ($M = 7.2$, $SE = 0.2$) than at baseline ($M = 6.4$, $SE = 0.2$, $M_{difference} = 0.8$, $SE = 0.1$, $p < .001$). Thus, conversations with a chatbot about smoking – no matter what communication style is used – seem to be effective in raising smokers' intention to quit.

5 Discussion

5.1 Main Findings

This study aimed to uncover the potential of conversational chatbots in motivating smoking cessation. Specifically, the study investigated the effectiveness of chatbot-delivered MI and CC in raising one's intention to quit, which communication style led to higher user satisfaction with the conversation, and to what extent these outcomes were moderated by individuals' need for autonomy and perceived self-efficacy. Overall, results show that chatbot interaction about smoking cessation – regardless of the communication style used by the chatbot – does lead to a significant increase in one's intention to quit smoking. However, intention to quit and user satisfaction with the conversation did not differ between participants in the MI condition and participants in the CC condition, nor were these outcomes moderated by participants' need for autonomy or perceived self-efficacy. Thus, all hypotheses were rejected.

It was hypothesized that MI (vs. CC) as a communication style would lead to a higher intention to quit and higher user satisfaction among smokers. Participants' intention to quit did significantly increase after the chatbot interaction, regardless of their assigned condition. An explanation for the insignificant results may be found in the conceptualization of MI and CC in this study. An analysis of the subscales of the manipulation check revealed that the technical skills of both the MI chatbot ($M = 4.8$, $SD = 1.3$) and the CC chatbot ($M = 4.3$, $SD = 1.4$) were perceived to be quite MI-like. Thus, participants in the CC condition still found that the chatbot helped them to feel confident about their ability to quit by discussing the need for behavior change, despite its confrontational approach to the conversation. This resemblance was not the case for the relational subscale, on which the MI chatbot ($M = 5.3$, $SD = 1.3$) was perceived as more MI-like than the CC chatbot ($M = 2.9$, $SD = 1.1$). This echoes previous research demonstrating that people appreciate empathic communication from a chatbot, compared to purely informational chatbots [20]. In addition, Lundahl et al. [16] found that the effect of MI is subject to a dosage effect, meaning that more treatment time using MI may lead to better outcomes. Considering that this study consisted of a single 8-min session, it could be that the duration of the exposure was too short for the expected effects of MI to occur.

Future research should investigate whether multiple sessions and/or longer exposure to an MI chatbot could provide stronger effects on intervention outcomes. Additionally, future research may investigate whether a distinctively CC-based approach – without MI-related elements, as found in this study – can be effective to begin with in chatbot-delivered counseling, since chatbots may never possess the legitimate expertness of a medical professional that usually makes clients more receptive to professional health advice [5].

We attempted to examine whether the main effect of MI could be explained by considering participants' need for autonomy. No significant results were found with this regard. However, albeit insignificant, results showed that participants with a higher need for autonomy had a lower intention to quit than participants who had a lower need for autonomy, regardless of the communication style of the chatbot. This finding may illustrate that smokers with a higher need for autonomy may benefit less from smoking cessation chatbots *precisely* because of their desire to make decisions without interference from others or persuasive technologies [24]. It is, therefore, essential that the chatbot is presented in a non-intrusive way, allowing people to interact with the chatbot at their own choice and own pace. Research on persuasive chatbots has shown that perceived intrusiveness negatively predicts people's perception of the chatbot and the persuasiveness [36]. In this study, due to the relatively short interaction time, it is likely that the purpose of the conversation (i.e., motivating smoking cessation) was introduced early without enough initial engagement, which resulted in threats to one's autonomy. Since these results illustrate that the opportunity to act autonomously is relatively important to most people, future (qualitative) research could shed light on how people with varying levels of need for autonomy could benefit from health-related chatbots – if people with a high need for autonomy can benefit from such interventions at all. These results could show how interventions should be designed in order to be need-supportive and effective in facilitating behavior change.

Self-efficacy was proposed as a moderator in the relationship between chatbot communication style and intention to quit and user satisfaction. We found that self-efficacious smokers were more satisfied with the interaction, and that the effect of MI on user satisfaction was more profound among people with higher self-efficacy. Perhaps, smokers with a lower self-efficacy may prefer to receive information about how to sustain a quit attempt (i.e., CC) while MI works better with already self-efficacious smokers by encouraging them to reflect on their own beliefs and facilitate action planning. Addiction researchers have categorized interventions on a continuum, ranging from more self-help approaches (e.g., mobile app, booklet) to more intensive care (e.g., nicotine replacement therapy) [37]. It could be that an MI chatbot falls on the self-help end and is more suitable for people with higher self-efficacy. However, this study investigated self-efficacy as a trait and did not investigate whether an MI chatbot could effectively raise one's perceived self-efficacy during the process. A potential proposition to be considered in future research is whether an increase in perceived self-efficacy after conversing with a conversational chatbot could mediate – rather than moderate – the relationship between chatbot communication style and intervention outcomes.

5.2 Limitations and Suggestions for Future Research

The present study sheds some light on the use of chatbots for smoking cessation, however, there are several limitations that warrant consideration in the interpretation of the findings. First, this study did not gather any information regarding participants' race or education, even though past research has found that such factors may influence one's communication preferences and experience with digital interventions such as chatbots [38]. Future research considering these traits could yield some additional insight in the potential and effectiveness of chatbots in health counseling, for example, how chatbots could convey a higher trustworthiness or legitimacy and therefore lead to higher user satisfaction and better intervention outcomes.

Second, we did not measure participants' perception on the quality of the interaction and the chatbot, while such perception might have played a role in user satisfaction and the intention to quit. To have more experimental control and to ensure that the chatbot in both conditions delivered the content in a structured and consistent manner, we created the chatbots with constrained capability. Participant input was limited to mostly predetermined keywords, and the chatbots used little natural language processing and generation. Although constrained chatbots are commonly used in the healthcare domain to ensure controllability and avoid unwanted harm [39], it might limit the variability and quality of the interaction, and hinder user experience. Future research is encouraged to explore the potential with more advanced chatbots and find the balance between controllability and user experience.

6 Conclusion

This study set out to explore the effectiveness of conversational chatbots using two different communication styles – MI and CC – on smokers' intention to quit and user satisfaction with the conversation, and the moderating role of smokers' need for autonomy and perceived self-efficacy. No significant effects of MI (vs. CC) on intention to quit and user satisfaction emerged, nor were these effects moderated by need for autonomy or perceived self-efficacy. However, results did show that a higher perceived self-efficacy translates into a higher user satisfaction, as well as modest evidence that chatbot interaction about smoking cessation effectively raises intentions to quit. As such, practical implications of this study include that health professionals may consider developing chatbots in order to keep up with clients' demands regarding cessation help whilst simultaneously decreasing the pressure on health care systems. Still, more research is needed into what exactly smokers desire when it comes to counseling chatbots to elevate the success of such tools. This study aims to provide a steppingstone for further research into this topic, which is currently more important than ever.

References

1. Zhu, S.-H., Lee, M., Zhuang, Y.-L., Gamst, A., Wolfson, T.: Interventions to increase smoking cessation at the population level: how much progress has been made in the last two decades? Tob. Control **21**, 110–118 (2012)

2. Thompson, L.E., Barnett, J.R., Pearce, J.R.: Scared straight? Fear-appeal anti-smoking campaigns, risk, self-efficacy and addiction. Health Risk Soc. **11**, 181–196 (2009)
3. Witte, K., Meyer, G., Martell, D.: Effective Health Risk Messages: A Step-By-Step Guide. Sage, New York (2001)
4. Organization, W.H.: WHO Report on the Global Tobacco Epidemic, 2021: Addressing new and emerging products. World Health Organization (2021)
5. Palanica, A., Flaschner, P., Thommandram, A., Li, M., Fossat, Y.: Physicians' perceptions of chatbots in health care: cross-sectional web-based survey. J. Med. Internet Res. **21**, e12887 (2019)
6. Milne-Ives, M., et al.: The effectiveness of artificial intelligence conversational agents in health care: systematic review. J. Med. Internet Res. **22**, e20346 (2020)
7. Kotz, D., Huibers, M.J., West, R.J., Wesseling, G., van Schayck, O.C.: What mediates the effect of confrontational counselling on smoking cessation in smokers with COPD? Patient Educ. Couns. **76**, 16–24 (2009)
8. Miller, W.R., Rollnick, S.: Motivational Interviewing: Helping People Change. Guilford Press, New York (2012)
9. Heckman, C.J., Egleston, B.L., Hofmann, M.T.: Efficacy of motivational interviewing for smoking cessation: a systematic review and meta-analysis. Tob. Control **19**, 410–416 (2010)
10. Strecher, V.J., Shiffman, S., West, R.: Randomized controlled trial of a web-based computer-tailored smoking cessation program as a supplement to nicotine patch therapy. Addiction **100**, 682–688 (2005)
11. Deci, E.L., Ryan, R.M.: Self-determination theory: a macrotheory of human motivation, development, and health. Can. Psychol. **49**, 182 (2008)
12. Bandura, A.: Regulation of cognitive processes through perceived self-efficacy. Dev. Psychol. **25**, 729 (1989)
13. Schneider, R.J., Casey, J., Kohn, R.: Motivational versus confrontational interviewing: a comparison of substance abuse assessment practices at employee assistance programs. J. Behav. Health Serv. Res. **27**, 60–74 (2000)
14. Francis, N., Rollnick, S., McCambridge, J., Butler, C., Lane, C., Hood, K.: When smokers are resistant to change: experimental analysis of the effect of patient resistance on practitioner behaviour. Addiction **100**, 1175–1182 (2005)
15. Moyers, T.B., Miller, W.R., Hendrickson, S.M.: How does motivational interviewing work? Therapist interpersonal skill predicts client involvement within motivational interviewing sessions. J. Consult. Clin. Psychol. **73**, 590 (2005)
16. Lundahl, B.W., Kunz, C., Brownell, C., Tollefson, D., Burke, B.L.: A meta-analysis of motivational interviewing: twenty-five years of empirical studies. Res. Soc. Work. Pract. **20**, 137–160 (2010)
17. Ahluwalia, J.S., et al.: The effects of nicotine gum and counseling among African American light smokers: a 2 × 2 factorial design. Addiction **101**, 883–891 (2006)
18. Coleman, T., Cheater, F., Murphy, E.: Qualitative study investigating the process of giving anti-smoking advice in general practice. Patient Educ. Couns. **52**, 159–163 (2004)
19. Miller, W.R., Rollnick, S.: Meeting in the middle: motivational interviewing and self-determination theory. Int. J. Behav. Nutr. Phys. Act. **9**, 1–2 (2012)
20. Liu, B., Sundar, S.S.: Should machines express sympathy and empathy? Experiments with a health advice chatbot. Cyberpsychol. Behav. Soc. Netw. **21**, 625–636 (2018)
21. He, L., Basar, E., Wiers, R.W., Antheunis, M.L., Krahmer, E.: Can chatbots help to motivate smoking cessation? A study on the effectiveness of motivational interviewing on engagement and therapeutic alliance. BMC Public Health **22**, 1–14 (2022)
22. Shingleton, R.M., Palfai, T.P.: Technology-delivered adaptations of motivational interviewing for health-related behaviors: a systematic review of the current research. Patient Educ. Couns. **99**, 17–35 (2016)

23. De Vreede, T., Raghavan, M., De Vreede, G.-J.: Design Foundations for AI Assisted Decision Making: A Self Determination Theory Approach (2021)
24. Smit, E.S., Bol, N.: From self-reliers to expert-dependents: identifying classes based on health-related need for autonomy and need for external control among mobile users. Media Psychol. **23**, 391–414 (2020)
25. Altendorf, M.B., van Weert, J.C., Hoving, C., Smit, E.S.: Should or could? Testing the use of autonomy-supportive language and the provision of choice in online computer-tailored alcohol reduction communication. Digital health **5**, 2055207619832767 (2019)
26. Hyde, J., Hankins, M., Deale, A., Marteau, T.M.: Interventions to increase self-efficacy in the context of addiction behaviours: a systematic literature review. J. Health Psychol. **13**, 607–623 (2008)
27. Gaume, J., Gmel, G., Faouzi, M., Daeppen, J.-B.: Counselor skill influences outcomes of brief motivational interventions. J. Subst. Abuse Treat. **37**, 151–159 (2009)
28. Colby, S.M., et al.: Enhanced motivational interviewing versus brief advice for adolescent smoking cessation: results from a randomized clinical trial. Addict. Behav. **37**, 817–823 (2012)
29. Madson, M.B., et al.: Measuring client perceptions of motivational interviewing: factor analysis of the client evaluation of motivational interviewing scale. J. Subst. Abuse Treat. **44**, 330–335 (2013)
30. Heatherton, T.F., Kozlowski, L.T., Frecker, R.C., Fagerstrom, K.O.: The Fagerström test for nicotine dependence: a revision of the Fagerstrom tolerance questionnaire. Br. J. Addict. **86**, 1119–1127 (1991)
31. Komissarouk, S., Harpaz, G., Nadler, A.: Dispositional differences in seeking autonomy-or dependency-oriented help: conceptual development and scale validation. Personality Individ. Differ. **108**, 103–112 (2017)
32. Spek, V., Lemmens, F., Chatrou, M., van Kempen, S., Pouwer, F., Pop, V.: Development of a smoking abstinence self-efficacy questionnaire. Int. J. Behav. Med. **20**, 444–449 (2013)
33. Biener, L., Abrams, D.B.: The contemplation ladder: validation of a measure of readiness to consider smoking cessation. Health Psychol. **10**, 360 (1991)
34. Larsen, D.L., Attkisson, C.C., Hargreaves, W.A., Nguyen, T.D.: Assessment of client/patient satisfaction: development of a general scale. Eval. Program Plann. **2**, 197–207 (1979)
35. Shiffman, S., Brockwell, S.E., Pillitteri, J.L., Gitchell, J.G.: Individual differences in adoption of treatment for smoking cessation: demographic and smoking history characteristics. Drug Alcohol Depend. **93**, 121–131 (2008)
36. Van den Broeck, E., Zarouali, B., Poels, K.: Chatbot advertising effectiveness: when does the message get through? Comput. Hum. Behav. **98**, 150–157 (2019)
37. Secades-Villa, R., Alonso-Pérez, F., García-Rodríguez, O., Fernández-Hermida, J.R.: Effectiveness of three intensities of smoking cessation treatment in primary care. Psychol. Rep. **105**, 747–758 (2009)
38. Kontos, E., Blake, K.D., Chou, W.-Y.S., Prestin, A.: Predictors of eHealth usage: insights on the digital divide from the health information national trends survey 2012. J. Med. Internet Res. **16**, e3117 (2014)
39. Safi, Z., Abd-Alrazaq, A., Khalifa, M., Househ, M.: Technical aspects of developing chatbots for medical applications: scoping review. J. Med. Internet Res. **22**, e19127 (2020)

Interacting with the News Through Voice User Interfaces

Oda Elise Nordberg$^{(\boxtimes)}$ (iD) and Frode Guribye (iD)

University of Bergen, 5007 Bergen, Norway
{oda.nordberg,frode.guribye}@uib.no

Abstract. A key application area for voice user interfaces (VUIs) is news consumption, and there is a need to explore how such interactions are performed
in practice. This paper presents a study exploring how novice users navigate the
news through VUIs and what interactions point to users' expectations beyond the
VUIs' current capabilities. A field trial with seven participants in five households
and follow-up in-depth interviews with six of the participants were conducted.
The analysis provides a detailed picture of how such interactions are practically
accomplished and offers insights into the participants' perspectives on their experiences. The participants had some expectations when interacting with the news
through VUIs, but many of these were not met. This paper identifies three key challenges: 1) lack of interactional guidance in news contexts, 2) limited navigation
capabilities in news sources, and 3) insufficient support for in-depth exploration of
the news, with accompanying design implications for more engaging interactions
with VUIs for news purposes.

Keywords: Voice interactions · Voice user interface (VUI) · Journalistic design

1 Introduction

How people consume news has changed over the last decades. We have shifted from
reading printed newspapers, listening to the news on the radio, and watching it on TV
to reading it on the web and interacting with news on social media. With these changes,
news audiences' engagement has become a key part of news companies' business models
[1]. Incorporation of chatbots is one strategy used to create engagement with the news.
Chatbots utilize a technology that gives users access to data and services through dialogue
[9, 13]. In theory, interactions with chatbots can be either written or spoken dialogue, but
the term is usually associated with written interactions [10]. In this article, we focus on
spoken dialogue chatbots and use the phrase voice user interfaces (VUIs) to emphasize
this aspect. Even though both text-based and voice-based conversational technologies
are categorized as chatbots, it is important to recognize that these have distinct types of
interactions, possibilities, and challenges.

There has been considerable research on text-based chatbots for news purposes, in
areas such as design and implementation [17, 19], the chatbot persona and relationships
with news audiences [8], users' experiences and expectations [34], news recommendations [4], and people's perceptions of chatbots and information credibility [33]. There

A. Følstad et al. (Eds.): CONVERSATIONS 2022, LNCS 13815, pp. 18–33, 2023.
https://doi.org/10.1007/978-3-031-25581-6_2

have been a few studies on VUI and news, focusing on news quality [6], potential benefits of a self-disclosing VUI for news consumption [26], and the exploration of interactive news stories [16]. However, the field remains underexplored.

Recent advances in natural language processing have led to the widespread adoption of VUIs. VUIs, such as Amazon Alexa, Apple's Siri, and Google Assistant, are currently present in many people's lives, either as services on their smartphones or as physical smart speakers in their homes. VUIs are increasingly used for news consumption [22], and the so-called digital news leaders argue that audio is becoming more important [8] and will "transform the way audiences discover media over the next few years" [23, p. 35]. The progress in natural language processing solutions offers new possibilities for interactions with the news, where users can take a more active role. The current VUIs have some obvious limitations, and there exists a mismatch between users' expectations and technological capabilities [18]. There is a need to better understand how users interact with VUIs and what expectations they have for such encounters. Most research on VUIs has been conducted in laboratories and not in users' natural settings, with some exceptions [e.g., 25, 31].

In this study, we aim to explore how novice users interact with the news using VUIs and what interactions point to their expectations beyond the VUIs' current capabilities. This study is anchored in a tradition—within human–computer interaction (HCI)—of studying and analyzing naturally occurring interactions with technology [3, 7, 24], which has also been used for studying VUIs [25]. Inspired by interaction analysis [15], we assume that to understand the current practice of utilizing VUIs for news consumption and to gain knowledge about users' expectations, it is valuable to examine interactions between VUIs and people in their everyday lives. The social and ecological aspects of everyday lives provide us with realistic and detailed data that we can analyze to obtain a better understanding of these interactions and expectations.

We present the results of a seven-day field trial in five households where the participants were tasked with regularly using a VUI to consume news content. These interactions were recorded and later analyzed, inspired by interaction analysis [15]. We conducted interviews with the participants to evaluate their experiences and gain insights into their perspectives. Our study contributes to research on chatbots by exploring how people interact with VUIs, that is, spoken dialogue chatbots, for news purposes. Our study aims to provide a better understanding of the limitations of VUIs for news purposes and to suggest how these interactions can be improved. Our work offers the following contributions to the field. 1) We present a detailed analysis of six types of interaction requests relating specifically to the VUI news domain: *initiating news interactions, navigating between different news sources, navigating within a news source, accessing specific genres of news, requesting explanations related to elements in the news, and seeking additional information and reports.* 2) We describe three key challenges in interacting with news content via VUIs, with accompanying design implications: *lack of interactional guidance in news contexts, limited navigation capabilities in news sources, and insufficient support for in-depth exploration of the news.*

2   Background

In this section, we present related work on VUIs and conversational interactions with the news.

2.1   Voice User Interface

VUIs are technologies where spoken words are the main input and output. Other terms used to describe similar voice technologies include (intelligent) personal assistant, smart speaker, conversational agent, and conversational user interface. The last term has been widely debated, and it is argued that such an interaction is not truly conversational [5, 25, 27, 28]. On one hand, using speech as the main form of interaction offers many possibilities: it is natural and intuitive, making the interaction easier and possibly more inclusive [9]. On the other hand, people with hearing or speech impairments may be excluded by VUIs. Compared to graphical user interfaces (GUIs) and text-based user interfaces, VUIs can decrease the cognitive effort spent on tasks [30]. Speaking is usually faster than typing, which may enhance task efficiency and user satisfaction. VUIs are hands-free technologies, giving users the possibility to multitask, and can be beneficial for people with some physical disabilities. When engaged in text-based interactions, users can quickly browse through content and focus on reading the relevant parts. In contrast, VUIs can be less efficient in this sense, as users must listen to the full answer to obtain an overview of the content [30]. In some VUI systems, such as many smart speakers, speech is the only type of input and output. The lack of visual cues and affordances can make it difficult to know the full extent of the VUIs' capabilities [32].

Fueled by the imagery of a future powered by artificial intelligence, a certain hype has surrounded the use of VUIs, portrayed as naturally integrated into everyday conversations. Empirical studies of this phenomenon paint another picture and point out the normal, natural troubles with such interactions [25]. Rather than being understood as full-fledged conversations, interactions with VUIs often have a transactional purpose, meaning that they are goal-oriented and often involve users gathering the information required to complete a task or attain an objective [18]. In everyday use, VUIs are commonly embedded in complex settings with multiple participants, and users often encounter problems [29]. Myers et al. [21] find four categories of problems faced by users when interacting with unfamiliar VUIs: *unfamiliar intent* (the person utters a command the VUI do not support or phrases the query in such a way that the VUI cannot parse it), *natural language processing errors* (the VUI "mishears" what the person says), *failed feedback* (the VUI provides feedback, but it may be ambiguous, or the person misinterprets it), and *system error* (technical bugs). Users respond to these troubles in different ways, for example, by simplifying or adding more information to the utterance, make a different request, restarting the interaction, settling, or quitting [21].

Lugar and Sellen [18] find that users' expectations of conversational agents' capabilities and their *actual* capabilities are highly imbalanced. They argue that users have difficulties in visualizing how the conversational agent works and that the agent reinforces this incomprehensibility by not revealing necessary information about its capabilities and (lack of) intelligence. Sciuto et al. [31] point out that it is difficult for users to discover new features, as they usually explore the functionality of the VUI the first time they interact with it. To overcome the problem with VUIs acting as black boxes, Porcheron et al. [25] suggest that designers should follow Dourish and Button's [7] advice on "observable-reportable abstractions", by presenting information and signals regarding what the system does, why it does so, and what is likely to be done next.

2.2 Conversational Interactions with the News

Traditional journalism can be described as having a lecture-like and monologue form. In contrast, conversational journalism aims at presenting news in a conversational manner [20]. News organizations have explored the use of text-based chatbots as a way of attracting news audiences by offering a more conversational form of journalism. By operating on a personal messaging platform with a conversational and informal tone, a chatbot secured the participation of niche audiences that were previously not engaged in news consumption [8]. In a user study of international, well-known news chatbots, Zhang et al. [34] find advantages and challenges of current news chatbots. On one hand, they make it easy to search for news information, and interactive and personal content can be engaging. On the other hand, current news chatbots still have limitations in terms of their effectiveness, informativeness, efficiency, and human-like attributes.

The most notable contribution to VUIs in the news domain comes from the study of Dambanemuya and Diakopoulos [6], who evaluated smart speakers for information quality in news queries. They found that Alexa had a high response rate of 90%, of which 70% were considered relevant to the questions asked. How the users phrased their query affected the results: "Can you tell me about…?" and "What happened?" resulted in more relevant responses compared to "What is going on?" and "What is new?" The authors speculated that this may be due to the first two queries referring to static events (often associated with Wikipedia pages), whereas the latter two pertained to evolving events. In many cases (60.4%), the sources of Alexa's information were not specified. When sources were known, they were usually Wikipedia pages, and only 1.4% of the responses came from news sources.

3 Methods

In this section, we describe the methods used in this study. First, we outline how we conducted a field trial to examine how the participants interacted with the news through VUIs. Second, we explain how we used interviews to better understand the participants' experiences and expectations. Lastly, we describe our analysis process.

3.1 Field Trial

We began this project by conducting a field trial [3] in April 2021 to explore how novice users interacted with VUIs in their everyday lives to be updated on the news. Field trials are often used in HCI to explore new technologies and use cases in a more natural setting than laboratory experiments. By undertaking a field study "in the wild," we could obtain information on the actual use of the system, including the possibility of "unanticipated use," and more detailed data on what works and what does not [3].

Participants. In the study, we recruited novice users who were inexperienced with VUIs for news purposes as we aimed to explore participants' initial expectations and experiences. Based on convenience sampling and our personal network, we recruited a total of 7 novice users (4 women and 3 men) from 5 households. Their ages ranged from 26 to 66 years. See Table 1 for an overview of the households and the participants. All participants had some knowledge of VUIs; for example, they had tried a personal assistant on their smartphone. However, none of the participants had used it to be updated on the news. Six of the participants were Norwegian and interacted with the VUIs in Norwegian, while one participant, Ben, interacted with his chosen VUI, Amazon Alexa, in English.

Table 1. An overview of the participants of the field trial. The names are pseudonyms. GA = Google Assistant; Alexa = Amazon Alexa

Household	Name	Age	Gender	VUI
1	Amy	62	Female	GA
1	Alf	66	Male	GA
2	Ben	27	Male	Alexa
3	Cat	26	Female	GA
3	Cal	26	Male	GA
4	Deb	51	Female	GA
5	Eva	32	Female	GA

Organization The participants explored and interacted freely with a physical VUI in their homes but were given instructions to use it to be updated on the news twice a day for a week. The participants who did not own a physical VUI (all, except Ben) each received a Google Home Mini device for the study period. We helped the participants in setting up the VUI, and they chose their preferred news sources. They recorded their interactions with the news using a voice recording app on their phones and sent these recordings to us through an encrypted transfer page. This resulted in a total of 70 voice recordings, lasting between 13 s and 10 min and 14 s, with a total duration of 6.3 h. All recordings were transcribed. Before the field trial was carried out, a one-day pilot study was conducted with one participant to ensure that the instructions were clear and that we would gather usable data. The research project was reviewed and approved by the local research ethics committee.

3.2 Interviews

After completing the field trial, all participants were asked to participate in a follow-up interview regarding their experiences. A semi-structured interview protocol, which was reviewed in the pilot study, was followed. In the households that consisted of two members, both were asked to participate in the same interview. In Cal's and Cat's case, Cal could not participate. The interviews lasted between 21 min and 1 h and 15 min, with a total duration of 3.2 h. The interviews consisted of four main topics: the participants' news habits prior to the field trial (e.g., how they normally got updated on news, different news preferences), how they interacted with the VUI to be updated on the news (e.g., a typical scenario; their goals, utterances, expectations), how they experienced these interactions (what they liked and disliked, errors they encountered, their overall experience), and speculations on how these interactions could evolve in the future (how these could be improved, possible roles of the VUI).

3.3 Analysis

Our analysis was inspired by interaction analysis [15], which examines how humans interact with one another and with artifacts and tools, in our case, VUIs. In interaction analysis, the data are found in the details of naturally occurring, everyday social interactions between human and technological actors, as well as their surroundings. These include talk, non-verbal interactions, and the use of artifacts and technologies [15]. Our analysis was based on audio recordings from the field trial, which provided rich data from natural, everyday interactions with the VUI, and the interviews offered additional descriptions and explanations. The first author categorized the materials from the field trial and the interviews. From these first annotations, we inductively identified the themes presented in this paper. The talk and the interactions with the VUI were assessed to identify routine practices, accompanied by subsequent challenges and solutions. The interviews were used to supplement these findings and to gain an understanding of the participants' accounts of their experiences. In the analysis, we paid particular attention to the factors pointing beyond the VUIs' current capabilities.

4   Results

In this section, we present the results of the field trial and the interviews. Subsection 4.1 provides an overview, while Subsects. 4.2, 4.3, 4.4, 4.5, 4.6 and 4.7 focus on each of the six distinct interaction requests of the participants, relating specifically to the VUI news domain.

4.1   Overview

The participants obtained news updates through the VUI twice a day, as the assignment specified. They mainly did so once in the morning and once in the evening. Most participants performed this task while alone, but sometimes, the participants who lived together used it jointly or with the other person present. The participants sometimes did other things simultaneously with using the VUI for news, for example, eating or cleaning. Based on the analysis, the current situation of obtaining news updates through a VUI is quite simplistic and limited. The process starts with a person saying the VUI's wake word, usually followed by a command or a question about the news. The VUI then finds the news sources that the person follows and presents them one by one. These sources are specified in the Google Home app or the first time the user asks about the news (Alexa). Each source has a pre-recorded audio file, similar to or the same those on radio, that is played from start to end. These audio files do not seem to facilitate interactions other than those related to traditional audio files, such as pause and play.

During the interviews, all participants stated that it was easy to ask the VUI to present them with news and that they felt updated, but none of them wanted to continue using the VUI for news purposes. The participants attempted to interact with the news in different ways, which normally led to errors, in agreement with the descriptions by Myers et al. [21]. The participants expressed uncertainty about the VUI's capabilities. They explained that it was difficult to know which functions were available in the VUI and what information the VUI based its actions on. Even when a command succeeded, the VUI usually provided limited information, leaving the user confused:

"I asked her to turn on podcast once, and then she just turned on a random podcast, and I kind of did not know. She probably said in the end that it was Aftenposten's podcast, but where she found it, I don't know." (Eva)

All participants explained that the technology and the interaction needed improvements, but they believed that it had potential for the future. As demonstrated in the following subsections, the participants attempted to interact with the news in six distinct ways that relate specifically to the VUI news domain: initiating news interactions, navigating between different news sources, navigating within a news source, accessing specific genres of news, requesting explanations related to elements in the news, and seeking additional information and reports. As we shall demonstrate, most of these interaction requests were beyond the two VUIs' capabilities to fulfill.

4.2 Initiating News Interactions

The VUIs used in this study were smart speakers with many different roles, such as presenting news. The news initiation usually started right after activating the VUI. These first interactions with the VUI for news were usually successful, except for a few instances with system errors [21]. What the participants said when they wanted news updates varied, but it was usually phrased as a request or a short command, as shown in the excerpts below. The following excerpt presents a typical successful interaction in which a person wants to be updated on the news.

```
(GA = Google Assistant)
Alf: (00:07) OK Google, what's the latest news?
GA: (00:10) This is the latest news. NRK Nyheter 22:03 today.
```

As shown here, Alf asks for the news. The VUI presents the news source NRK Nyheter, and at 00:18, the pre-recording from NRK Nyheter starts. While Alf politely *requests for* the news, his wife, Amy, uses a *command* instead:

```
Amy: (00:14) OK Google, the news.
```

4.3   Navigating Between News Sources

All participants followed several news sources on their VUI. Navigation between the different sources was one of the most successful types of interactions in this study. The participants could specify which source they wanted to listen to, and the VUI would find the mentioned source. They could also navigate between sources by telling the VUI to "skip," leading to the VUI presenting the next source in line, as shown below:

```
(00:11) [VG Nyheter starts]
Cat: (00:51) Okay Google, next.
GA: (00:56) Finansavisen at five today.
(00:59) [News from Finansavisen starts]
```

4.4   Navigating Within a News Source

All participants, except Deb who did not interact notably with the news, tried to navigate within news sources. The VUIs in our study lacked the capabilities for this navigation, making this an unfamiliar intent problem [21]. If a user told the VUI to skip a current story, the whole news segment from that source was skipped by Google Assistant. Several commands were tested, such as *next* and *forward*, without any success.

```
Alexa: (00:28) From CNN. [CNN news starts]
[News about activism and the president (US)]
Ben: (00:59) Alexa, eh, skip.
["Dang-dang" sound [neutral] from Alexa]
Alexa: (01:04) This update is not available right now.
```

In the preceding excerpt, Ben tries to skip a specific news item, but Alexa informs him that this action is not yet possible. Compared to Google Assistant, Alexa does not skip the whole news segment. From the way that Alexa answers, "skip" is recognized as an action, but it is still considered an unfamiliar intent problem [21] as the command is not supported. Cat tried several different commands, but none was recognized by Google Assistant. The following excerpt shows how Google Assistant links the command *forward* to music streaming services. It takes 47 s from Cat's first attempt to skip a news story until she ends up back to the same story.

```
Cat: (00:28) OK Google, [VG Nyheter stops] can I listen to
the next news item?
GA: (00:32) Sorry, I didn't understand.
(00:34) [VG Nyheter continuous]
Cat: (00:40) OK Google, forward.
Cat: (00:45) OK Google ... [VG Nyheter stops] forward.
GA: (00:49) Song selection is only available for YouTube Mu-
sic Premium subscriptions, but you may like this station. .
(00:58) [Music starts to play]
Cat: (01:00) [Laughs a bit] Okay Google ... [music stops] Can
you turn back to the news?
GA: (01:06) To listen to the news, just say "give me the lat-
est news" ...
Cat: (01:09) Give me the latest news.
GA: ... You can also request news from specific ...
Cat: (01:11) OK Google.
GA: ... sources or best ....
Cat: (01:13) Give me the latest news.
GA: (01:15) Here is the latest news. Resumes VG at 22:17…
```

Alf explained that he tried several different ways to navigate within one source, but he never figured out what he needed to say. This experience was consistent among most of the participants. In the interview, Alf explained his experience:

> *"What I found troublesome was if... Let's say you were on NRK Nyheter and didn't want to hear more about Corona. You want to hear the next news item from NRK. If you then say "Next," then she is done with NRK. Then, she jumps directly to the next news source."*

4.5   Accessing Specific Genres of News

Sometimes, the participants wanted a specific genre of news, for example, local news, international news, or culture-related news. When asked about specific genres of news, the VUIs could not provide a result, causing unfamiliar intent problems [21].

```
Alf: (05:51) OK Google, update me on sports from NRK.
GA: (05:57) I cannot play sports news from NRK yet.
```

As shown in the preceding excerpt, Alf's command to the VUI is somewhat complex, as he wants a specific genre of news from a specific source. The VUI recognizes *sports* as a genre but explains that it is unable to perform this action. The *"yet"* at the end of its response indicates that this is a function that may be available in the future.

4.6 Seeking Additional Information and Reports

Occasionally, the participants interrupted the news sequence to ask the VUI for more information about the news being presented or to know what other sources mentioned about the topic. The VUI did not understand these questions, as demonstrated below:

```
[News story about the murder of lawyer Kjærvik]
Alf: (02:51) OK Google, update me on the Kjærvik murder.
GA: (02:56) I'm sorry; I didn't understand that.
(02:58) [The news continues]
Alf: (03:06) OK Google, can you tell me what VG says about
the murder of Kjærvik?
GA: (03:12) Sorry, I do not understand what you mean.
(03:16) [The news continues]
```

The example above shows that Alf interrupts the news sequence because he wants more information about the news story being presented. Google Assistant does not understand his request (unfamiliar intent) [21] and continues. Alf interrupts again, specifically asking what another news source reports about the said case. Google Assistant still does not understand and continues with the news segment once again.

4.7 Requesting Explanations Related to Elements in the News

Sometimes, the news included information or topics that the users wanted to know more about. This typically comprised topics or elements that the participants were not very familiar with, making it difficult to follow the current news item. This required the VUI to stop the segment and "search" for an answer to give the user. Such questions were often difficult for the VUI to answer, but sometimes it came up with a relevant answer:

```
[News about inspection of trucks at the borders]
Cat: (03:11) OK Google. [NRK Nyheter stops] What are the
rules of entry into Norway?
GA: (03:16) At regjeringen.no, it says: "Only foreigners who
are resident in Norway can travel into Norway now. [...]
(03:38) [NRK Nyheter continues]
```

The excerpt above shows a successful interaction in which the VUI answers the participant's question. However, there are also unsuccessful interactions in which the VUI answers but misunderstands the context, as seen in the excerpt below:

```
[News about the new, European football league "Super League"]
Eva: (01:33) Okay Google ... [NRK Nyheter stops] What is the
Super League?
GA: (01:38) This is what Wikipedia can tell: "The Super
League is the highest level in Danish football. The winner
will be the Danish champion. [...]
Eva: (01:49) Okay Google ...
GA: ... the championship was decided ..."
```

Eva understands that the answer is incorrect and tries to be more specific:

```
Eva: (01:51) What is the Norwegian Super League?
GA: (01:55) Sorry, I do not understand what you mean.
```

In Eva's example, her husband later told her what the Super League was. A consequence of the VUI not taking the context into account and providing the wrong information is that the users might believe it and possibly spread misinformation.

5   Discussion

Engagement is considered key in the competitive news market [1]. There are expressed expectations in the industry [22, 23] and among researchers [8, 14] that conversational interfaces, such as VUIs, will influence future news practices and possibly enhance news engagement [12]. For these expectations to be realistic, the experience of interacting with VUIs in news settings needs improvement. We argue that it is necessary to better understand how users interact with VUIs in news contexts, as well as identify their expectations, needs, and preferences. Our research is a step in this direction. Our study's results showed how the participants had concrete expectations of the capabilities of VUIs in news settings, but most of these were not met. The participants expected to be able to navigate between and within news sources, access specific genres of news, receive explanations related to elements in the news and obtain additional information and reports. In addition to their unmet expectations, the participants encountered problems that aligned with those reported in previous research on VUIs [18, 21, 25].

The conversational format of VUIs offers new possibilities to interact with content, and as our analysis indicates, people have many expectations in this regard. In news contexts, the VUIs in our field trial used traditional concepts and formats from the radio, where the users were passive listeners. The role of VUIs when interacting with the news was mostly limited to finding the different sources and presenting them, but the news sources did the actual presentations through pre-recorded audio files. If the technology worked properly, the process was straightforward. If the users wanted to listen to a sequence of several different radio-like news segments (often with repetitive news items across different news sources), it worked well. However, if the users wanted to interact by navigating the content or were seeking more in-depth knowledge by asking questions, they would most likely encounter problems. When the users engaged in these types of actions, the VUI had to pause the news segment and try to identify the users' aim. However, the current VUIs lacked the capability to take into account the context that initiated the users' interaction (e.g., a topic presented on the news that led them to ask a question). In our field trial, the participants consistently tried (and most often failed) to interact with the news through the VUI, and their expectations and VUI capabilities were mismatched in this application area, too [18]. The fact that it was easy to access the news and that the participants then considered themselves updated on the news was not enough for them to keep wanting to use VUIs for news after the study. All participants agreed that the technology and the interactions needed improvements.

Text-based news chatbots play a more distinct role compared to the VUIs explored in our research. Such news chatbots are developed purposely to convey news information in a conversational manner [e.g., 8, 17, 33], while the VUIs explored in the study are intelligent assistants with multiple roles where news distribution is just one of them. As with news chatbots [34], it is easy to use VUIs to find news, but the interactive and personal content that engages news chatbot users is absent in these VUIs. In the future, it could be valuable to explore how features from text-based news chatbots could be transferred to VUIs. In relation to previous research on information quality in VUI news queries [6], our research also indicates the relevance of how people frame their queries. Research on naturally occurring interactions with VUIs has highlighted the normal, natural problems that people encounter when interacting with VUIs [21, 25]. Our study has identified specific problems related to the VUI news domain. We claim that not all VUI problems can be solved on a general level alone and that there is a need to examine the difficulties experienced in certain VUI domains, such as news. Based on our results, we argue that VUIs' capabilities are not fully utilized in news settings. We have identified three main issues when using VUIs for news, accompanied by design implications to improve this experience.

5.1 Interactional Guidance in News Contexts

The first issue that we want to highlight is the users' uncertainty about the VUIs' capabilities when interacting with the news. Currently, users are accustomed to playing a passive role when consuming news, such as when reading online newspapers or listening to news podcasts. VUI technology offers new opportunities to interact with the news, but this may be an unfamiliar experience for users, and they may have a limited understanding of what the VUIs' capabilities are. Our study's participants wanted to interact with the news by asking questions and trying to navigate the content, but they experienced difficulties in doing so. They tried but failed, and they used different responses to meet these troubles, consistent with the findings reported by Myers et al. [21]. The users wanted to interact with the news but did not know *how* to do it. Even after a week, the participants were unsure of the VUIs' capabilities. This gap between the users' expectations and the VUIs' capabilities could be reduced if the VUIs would guide the users on possible, *relevant* interactions. We think that there is a need to develop customized guidance and tailored fallback, both on a general and domain specific level. Both Google Assistant and Alexa had some interactional guidance for the news domain, but it came quite sporadically and was too generic.

In the future, research should focus on how to better convey relevant VUIs' capabilities in different, typical use settings. A VUI could explain its capabilities in a given application area and offer the users further clues, for example, about how to navigate within the news content, in line with Porcheron and colleagues' [25] suggestion to follow the advice on "observable-reportable abstractions" [7]. By presenting more feedback and guidance, the VUI can assist users in exploring and understanding its existing capabilities. Further, users may acquire more insights and knowledge about VUI processes in both successful and unsuccessful interactions, which may give them a more realistic understanding of how the VUI operates.

5.2 Navigation *Between* and *Within* News Sources

One of the main issues encountered by the participants involves navigating the news content. The VUI lets them navigate *between* different sources but not *within* a specific source. There is a need to create vocabulary that facilitates the navigation of news content. In the future, research should explore how people envision the news presented through VUIs and the kinds of utterances used when they want to navigate news content. As demonstrated in Dambanemuya and Diakopoulos' study [6], the way that people phrase their queries to the VUI influences the relevance of the information they receive. For example, some standardized expressions—such as "Give me the next story," "Skip this story," or "What does another source say about this topic?"—could be established to guide both user expectations and VUI capabilities.

This might require the existing news audio files to be tagged or labeled with metadata so that the VUI can differentiate between the separate stories. This will need work from news agencies when they prepare their contents to be accessed through VUIs. Another solution could be for the VUI to use text-to-speech technology and read directly from online newspapers, in the same way that it reads from Wikipedia, among others. Using text-to-speech functionality might influence the experience. It would be a tradeoff between having a professional journalist read the news—using the prosody and intonation expected of this "radio-talk" genre [11]—and the limitations in this regard when a story is read by a machine.

5.3 In-Depth Exploration of the News Through VUIs

As Ford and Hutchinson [8] discussed concerning news chatbots, VUIs could deliver news in a more conversational format, where users could have more advanced interactions and ask questions, if this is considered in the design process of such systems. The VUIs' conversational format suggests the possibility to interact with the news in a more conversational manner compared to more traditional news media, such as newspapers or radio broadcasts. We argue that VUIs have an unexplored interactive potential in news settings and that our findings encourage the development of more advanced interactions. Our study's participants frequently tried to interact with the news through the VUI in advanced ways but were seldom successful. They also attempted to educate themselves and explore the topics presented on the news with a more in-depth approach by asking related questions and trying to navigate the content. When they asked the VUI questions related to the news, it rarely gave a good answer. The VUI should be aware of the topics of the news items being presented, including knowledge of the main entities (e.g., characters, settings, and phenomena). By having some sort of awareness, the VUI will more likely respond with relevant information when questions are raised. Similar to the previously mentioned design implication, this could be addressed by adding tags and metadata to the audio files.

6 Conclusion

In this paper, we have presented our findings from a seven-day field trial, followed by interviews, where we explored how novice users interacted with the news through VUIs and what their expectations were. Some of our findings align with those of previous research on news chatbots and VUIs, while others are specific to the VUI news domain. We have demonstrated how users have specific unmet expectations for the VUIs' capabilities in the news context, related to navigation and in-depth explorations.

Our study also has some limitations; the most notable is its limited context—it was conducted on a small sample of participants in Norway, and mainly in Norwegian (one participant did the task in English, with American news sources). Only two types of VUIs were used: Google Assistant and Amazon Alexa. Thus, the findings regarding VUIs' functionalities may not be applicable to other contexts, VUIs, or languages. As all participants were novice users, it could be beneficial to also conduct research involving users experienced in using VUIs for news purposes. As this was a field trial aiming for natural settings, the participants freely chose which news sources they wanted to interact with. It is therefore possible that our findings may be relevant to some but not all news sources on VUIs. The participants recorded their own interactions using their phones, making the interactions less natural. It is also possible that not all interactions were recorded. However, we have found that our collected data are rich enough to provide us with valuable insights into how novice users interact with the news through VUIs and to obtain a clearer picture of what their expectations are.

Our study demonstrated how interactions with VUIs for news purposes were unsatisfactory and how the participants had several unmet expectations. In the analysis, we present six distinct types of interaction requests relating specifically to the VUI news domain: *initiating news interactions, navigating between different news sources, navigating within a news source, accessing specific genres of news, requesting explanations related to elements in the news, and seeking additional information and reports.* Based on these interaction attempts, we highlight three main problems with accompanying design implications: *lack of interactional guidance in new settings, limited navigation capabilities in news sources,* and *insufficient support for in-depth exploration of the news.* The design implications point to how it is possible to provide support for a better experience when interacting with the news through VUIs and take advantage of the potential that pertains to the interactions. We encourage future research to focus on VUIs for news purposes, especially on establishing a vocabulary for news interactions and the exploration of designing more advanced interactions.

References

1. Batsell, B.: Engaged Journalism. Columbia University Press, New York (2015)
2. Brown, B., McGregor, M., Laurier, E.: iPhone in vivo. In: Proceedings of the 2013 Conference on Human Factors in Computing, CHI 2013, pp. 1031–1040. ACM Press, New York (2013). https://doi.org/10.1145/2470654.2466132
3. Brown, B., Reeves, S., Sherwood, S.: Into the wild: challenges and opportunities for field trial methods. In: Proceedings of the 2011 Conference on Human Factors in Computing, CHI 2011, pp. 1–12. ACM Press, New York (2011). https://doi.org/10.1145/1978942.1979185
4. Chen, L., et al.: A pilot study for understanding users' attitudes towards a conversational agent for news recommendation. In: Proceedings of the 4th Conference on Conversational User Interfaces, CUI 2022, pp. 1–6. ACM Press, New York (2022). https://doi.org/10.1145/3543829.3544530
5. Clark, L. et al.: What makes a good conversation? Challenges in designing truly conversational agents. In: Proceedings of the 2019 Conference on Human Factors in Computing, CHI 2019, pp. 1–12. ACM Press, New York (2019). https://doi.org/10.1145/3290605.3300705
6. Dambanemuya, H.K., Diakopoulos, N.: "Alexa, what is going on with the impeachment?" Evaluating smart speakers for news quality. In: Computation + Journalism Symposium, pp. 1–4. The Brown Institute for Media Innovation, New York (2020)
7. Dourish, P., Button, G.: On "technomethodology": foundational relationships between ethnomethodology and system design. Human-Comput. Interact. 13(4), 395–432 (1998). https://doi.org/10.1207/s15327051hci1304_2
8. Ford, H., Hutchinson, J.: Newsbots that mediate journalist and audience relationships. Digit. J. 7(8), 1013–1031 (2019). https://doi.org/10.1080/21670811.2019.1626752
9. Følstad, A., Brandtzaeg, P.B.: Chatbots and the new world of HCI. Interactions 24(4), 38–42 (2017). https://doi.org/10.1145/3085558
10. Følstad, A., Skjuve, M., Brandtzaeg, P.B.: Different chatbots for different purposes: towards a typology of chatbots to understand interaction design. In: Bodrunova, S.S., et al. (eds.) INSCI 2018. LNCS, vol. 11551, pp. 145–156. Springer, Cham (2019). https://doi.org/10.1007/978-3-030-17705-8_13
11. Goffman, E.: Forms of Talk. University of Pennsylvania Press, Philadelphia (1981)
12. Gómez-Zará, D., Diakopoulos, N.: Characterizing communication patterns between audiences and newsbots. Digit. Journal. 8(9), 1093–1113 (2020). https://doi.org/10.1080/21670811.2020.181648
13. Gorwa, R., Guilbeault, D.: Unpacking the social media bot: a typology to guide research and policy. Policy Internet 12(3), 1–30 (2018). https://doi.org/10.1002/poi3.184
14. Jones, B., Jones, R.: Public service chatbots: automating conversation with BBC news. Digit. Journal. 7(8), 1032–1053 (2019). https://doi.org/10.1080/21670811.2019.160937
15. Jordan, B., Henderson, A.: Interaction analysis: foundations and practice. J. Learn. Sci. 4(1), 39–103 (1995). https://doi.org/10.1207/s15327809jls0401_
16. Jung, H., et al.: Tell me more: understanding user interaction of smart speaker news powered by conversational search. In: Proceedings of the 2019 Conference on Human Factors in Computing, CHI 2019, pp. 1–6. ACM Press, New York (2019). https://doi.org/10.1145/3290607.3312979
17. Laban, P., Canny, J., Hearst, M.A.: What's the latest? A question-driven news chatbot. In: Proceedings of the 58th Annual Meeting of the Association for Computational Linguistics: System Demonstrations, pp. 380–387 (2020). https://doi.org/10.18653/v1/2020.acl-demos.4
18. Luger, E., Sellen, A.: Like having a really bad PA: the gulf between user expectation and experience of conversational agents. In: Proceedings of the 2016 Conference on Human Factors in Computing, CHI 2016, pp. 5286–5297. ACM Press, New York (2016). https://doi.org/10.1145/2858036.2858288

19. Maniou, T.A., Veglis, A.: Employing a chatbot for news dissemination during crisis: design, implementation and evaluation. Future Internet 12(12), 1–14 (2020). https://doi.org/10.3390/FI1207010

20. Marchionni, D.: Conversational journalism in practice: a case study of the Seattle times' 2010 Pulitzer prize for breaking news reporting. Digit. J. 1(2), 252–269 (2013). https://doi.org/10.1080/21670811.2012.748513

21. Myers, C., et al.: Patterns for how users overcome obstacles in voice user interfaces. In: Proceedings of the 2018 Conference on Human Factors in Computing, CHI 2018, pp. 1–7. ACM Press, New York (2018). https://doi.org/10.1145/3173574.3173580

22. Newman, N.: Journalism, media, and technology trends and predictions 2018. Digital news report, Reuters Institute (2018)

23. Newman, N.: Journalism, media, and technology trends and predictions 2019. Digital news report, Reuters Institute (2019)

24. Pizza, S., et al.: Smartwatch in vivo. In: Proceedings of the 2016 Conference on Human Factors in Computing, CHI 2016, pp. 5456–5469. ACM Press, New York (2016). https://doi.org/10.1145/2858036.2858522

25. Porcheron, M. et al.: Voice interfaces in everyday life. In: Proceedings of the 2018 Conference on Human Factors in Computing, CHI '18, pp. 1–12. ACM Press, New York (2018). https://doi.org/10.1145/3173574.3174214

26. Rao, S., et al.: Ethical self-disclosing voice user interfaces for delivery of news. In: Proceedings of the 4th Conference on Conversational User Interfaces, CUI 2022, pp. 1–4. ACM Press, New York (2022)

27. Reeves, S.: Some conversational challenges of talking with machines. In: Companion of the 2017 ACM Conference on Computer Supported Cooperative Work and Social Computing, CSCW 2017, pp. 431–436. ACM Press, New York (2017)

28. Reeves, S.: Conversation considered harmful? In: Proceedings of the 1st Conference on Conversational User Interfaces, CUI 2019, pp. 1–3. ACM Press, New York (2019). https://doi.org/10.1145/3342775.3342796

29. Reeves, S., Porcheron, M., Fischer, J.: "This is not what we wanted": designing for conversation with voice interfaces. Interactions 26(1), 46–51 (2018). https://doi.org/10.1145/3296699

30. Rzepka, C., Berger, B., Hess, T.: Voice assistant vs. Chatbot–examining the fit between conversational agents' interaction modalities and information search tasks. Inf. Syst. Front. 24, 1–18 (2021). https://doi.org/10.1007/s10796-021-10226-5

31. Sciuto, A., et al.: "Hey Alexa, what's up?" In: Proceedings of the 2018 Designing Interactive Systems Conference, DIS 2018, pp. 857–868. ACM Press, New York (2018). https://doi.org/10.1145/3196709.3196772

32. Valério, F.A.M., et al.: Here's what I can do: chatbots' strategies to convey their features to users. In: Proceedings of the XVI Brazilian Symposium on Human Factors in Computing Systems, IHC' 2017, pp. 1–10. ACM Press, New York (2017)

33. Zarouali, B., et al.: Overcoming polarization with chatbot news? Investigating the impact of news content containing opposing views on agreement and credibility. Eur. J. Commun. 36(1), 53–68 (2021). https://doi.org/10.1177/0267323112094090

34. Zhang, Z., Zhang, X., Chen, L.: Informing the design of a news chatbot. In: Proceedings of the 21st ACM International Conference on Intelligent Virtual Agents, IVA 2021, pp. 224–231. ACM Press, New York (2021). https://doi.org/10.1145/3472306.347835

Voice Your Opinion! Young Voters' Usage and Perceptions of a Text-Based, Voice-Based and Text-Voice Combined Conversational Agent Voting Advice Application (CAVAA)

Christine Liebrecht[(⊠)] [iD], Naomi Kamoen[iD], and Celine Aerts

Tilburg School of Humanities and Digital Sciences, Department of Communication and Cognition, Tilburg University, Tilburg, The Netherlands
{C.C.Liebrecht,N.Kamoen}@tilburguniversity.edu

Abstract. Conversational Agent Voting Advice Applications (CAVAAs) are chatbot-based information retrieval systems for citizens who aim to inform themselves about the political issues at stake in times of political elections. Previous studies investigating these relatively young tools primarily focused on the effects of CAVAAs that include a text-based chatbot. In order to further optimize their design, current research compared the effects of CAVAAs with a text, voice, and combined chatbot. In an experimental lab study among young voters ($N = 60$) these three modalities have been compared on usage measures (the amount of information retrieved from the chatbot, and miscommunication), evaluation measures (ease of use, usefulness, and enjoyment), and political measures (perceived and factual political knowledge). Results show that the three CAVAA modalities score equally high on political measures and the perception of enjoyment. At the same time, the textual and combined CAVAA outperform the voice CAVAA on several aspects: the voice CAVAA received lower ease of use and usefulness scores, respondents requested less additional information, and they experienced more miscommunication when interacting with the voice chatbot. Analyses of the usage data also indicate that in the combined condition users hardly use the voice-option and instead almost exclusively rely on text-functionalities like clicking on suggestion buttons. This seems to suggest that using voice is too much of an effort for CAVAA users; we therefore recommend the usage of text-bots in this specific usage context.

Keywords: Voting advice applications · Conversational agents · Chatbot modality · Usefulness · Ease of use · Enjoyment · Political knowledge

1 Introduction

While Cava is Spanish sparkling wine, CAVAA is the abbreviation for Conversational Agent Voting Advice Application. Like Voting Advice Applications (VAAs) that are very popular in elections times [10], such as the Dutch *Stemwijzer*, German *Wahl-O-Mat*, and Swedish *Valkompassen*, CAVAA users answer political attitude statements

© The Author(s), under exclusive license to Springer Nature Switzerland AG 2023
A. Følstad et al. (Eds.): CONVERSATIONS 2022, LNCS 13815, pp. 34–49, 2023.
https://doi.org/10.1007/978-3-031-25581-6_3

about relevant political issues (e.g., 'Taxes on housing should be increased') and receive a voting advice based on their answers [6, 19]. In contrast to a regular VAA, however, a CAVAA has an integrated chatbot functionality that users can address if they experience comprehension problems when answering the political attitude statements. The chatbot in a CAVAA is trained to provide information relevant for solving frequently occurring comprehension problems (also see [13]); it can for example provide information about the definition of political terms ('What is taxes on housing?'), or about the current state of affairs with respect to the political issue ('How high is the taxes on housing at the moment?'). In contrast to other chatbots in the political domain that provide subjective information about the standpoints of a single candidate running in the elections [17], a CAVAA hence aims to provide objective information voters can use to form a well-considered answer to the political attitude statements, which should ultimately lead to a valid voting advice.

Research demonstrates that CAVAAs are valuable information retrieval systems for citizens, as these tools receive better user experience scores than regular VAAs without a chatbot functionality [14]. Moreover, citizens score higher on political knowledge measures after having worked with a CAVAA than after working with a regular VAA [14]. In light of these positive findings, it is now time to further optimize the design of the chatbot in a CAVAA. Since the young audience that forms the prime user group of (CA)VAAs is becoming more and more experienced with voice technology in their daily lives [7], the current study will explore the effects of different chatbot modalities for young voters (aged 18–25), comparing a text-based CAVAA to a voice-based CAVAA and a CAVAA that combines these two modalities.

The three CAVAA versions are compared with respect to three types of outcome measures. First, we compare the tools with respect to a set of usage measures (the number of questions asked to the system, and the amount of miscommunication occurring) to get an idea of how modality might affect the extent users feel invited to ask questions to the chatbot (compare [14]). Second, we include subjective tool evaluation measures (ease of use, usefulness, enjoyment) that are commonly used in the field of chatbot research to evaluate a chatbot's design characteristics (compare [32]). Finally, we compare the three versions with respect to political knowledge measures (perceived and factual political knowledge) that are common outcome measures in studies on VAAs (compare [15]), which ultimate goal is to boost the user's political knowledge in order to increase the chance of casting a vote [11].

In comparing these three chatbot modalities on a range of dependent variables in a specific goal-oriented usage context and for a homogeneous group of young voters, current study will not only contribute to research on (CA)VAAs, but also to chatbot research in general. This is because in chatbot research there has been a call for studies on specific chatbot design characteristics in specific domains and across specific user groups [8], and also for an investigation of modality effects across usage contexts [27]. A final reason why current research is of added value to chatbot research, is because not only a full text-based version and a voice-based version are compared, but also a third version combining text and voice; there has been a call for such a version in previous chatbot modality studies [18, 27]

1.1 Modality

Text-based and voice-based chatbots each have their own distinctive qualities. For example, typing a question in a text-based chatbot allows users to check their input for correctness before sending a message to the system [2, 18]. Moreover, a chatbot's written response can be read at the user's own pace [18], which might increase the user's perception of control over the interaction [30]. Finally, in situations where users are not able – or not willing – to use speech, a text-based tool is more accessible [24].

By contrast, voice-based chatbots are easier to use in situations where users cannot type messages themselves or cannot read the chatbot's written answers, for example when using a chatbot while cooking or driving [24]. Furthermore, voice-based technology is generally more intuitive and speaking is also faster than typing [2, 26]. This, however, does not imply that using a voice-bot is more efficient than using a text-based bot, as in a voice-context the user is forced to listen to the full output of the chatbot whereas in a text-based chatbot the user can skim or even skip information efficiently [26]. A final advantage of voice-based chatbots is that voice interaction promotes human-like perceptions, which may result in more enjoyment [25, 33].

While both text and voice have their distinctive qualities, or perhaps, *because* both modalities have their own distinctive qualities, neither can be seen as superior. Several studies show that user perceptions of a chatbot's modality depend both on characteristics of the task and characteristics of the user working with the application. This for example shows from [5], who found voice interaction to lead to more positive attitudes than text interaction, but only in utilitarian tasks (e.g., 'When is Father's Day in 2017?') and not for hedonic ones (e.g., 'Tell me a bedtime story'). Moreover, [27] compared a text and a voice-based chatbot in two task contexts: a goal-directed information search task (i.e., searching for a restaurant with predefined instructions) and an experiential search task (i.e., searching for a restaurant without predefined instructions). Results of that study show that only in the goal-directed task users of the voice-based chatbot experienced more cognitive workload and more enjoyment, though perceptions of efficiency were not affected. Finally, [26] established that there are correlations between certain user characteristics and the preference for a text or voice modality, consequently extending prior studies that focus on demographic characteristics such as age [28].

The Task-Technology Fit theory (TTF; [12]) can be used to explain these differences in the usage and perception of text-based and voice-based chatbots dependent on characteristics of the task and the user. The theory postulates that the task, the individual user, and the functionalities of the technology should match to result in positive performance outcomes. If individuals perceive a high fit between the task and the technology, they experience the technology to be more effective and efficient. By contrast, in case of discrepancies between the user, the task and the technology, the system will receive less good evaluations [12].

In light of TTF, it is relevant to explore how user, task and technology interact in the specific context of CAVAAs. This context can be regarded as utilitarian and goal-directed, since the user wants to gather information about politics and ultimately aims to receive a concrete voting advice from the application. Compared to previous chatbot modality studies that were mainly conducted in (fictitious) customer service contexts (e.g., [20, 26, 27]), the CAVAA context can hence be seen as more cognitively demanding since users try to solve their (real) comprehension problems about political issues by asking questions to the chatbot. As for user characteristics, it is known that CAVAA users make only a minimal effort to actually gather the required information before answering the political statements (see the findings of [13, 14]). Hence, our study can be seen of a study on modality effects in a cognitively demanding context where users make a minimal effort.

It is hard to predict how a text-based, a voice-based and a combined chatbot will be used by young voters in the specific usage context of CAVAAs. On the one hand, reasoning from the TTF, one might expect that a combined CAVAA leads to most intensive usage, and hence, to users asking most questions to the system. This might be expected because users can decide themselves which modality they use, and they might even switch between modalities during the interaction. On the other hand, since (CA)VAA users have been shown to make only a minimal effort when working with the tool [13, 14], it might also be the case that switching between modalities is too much an effort and that users keep working in one of the two modalities in the combined version. For the CAVAAs that contain one modality (voice versus text), it can be reasoned on the one hand that the voice-based chatbot will lead to more information requests, since this modality is more intuitive to use and speaking is faster than typing [2, 26]. On the other hand, interpreting voice-output correctly is harder than interpreting text-output that users can process at their own pace [18, 26].

In light of these different possible scenarios it is hard to formulate a concrete hypothesis about the effect of modality on usage measures. As how users evaluate the tool and also to how much political knowledge they retain are expected to be the result of the actual usage of the tool, we will also refrain from formulating concrete hypotheses about these dependent variables. Instead, we will explore the differences between the three CAVAA modalities for the usage measures, the evaluation measures, and the political measures.

2 Method

2.1 Design

In a between-subjects experimental study, we compared a CAVAA with a text-based chatbot, a voice-based chatbot, and a combined chatbot on several outcome measures. In the experiment, the CAVAAs were distributed in a laboratory setting to a homogenous group of eligible Dutch young voters. Each participant worked with only one of the three CAVAA versions, and subsequently filled out a survey in which the evaluation measures (perceived ease of use, usefulness, enjoyment), and political measures (perceived and factual political knowledge) were measured. In addition, the actual usage of the chatbot modalities was measured by analyzing the chatlogs of participants' CAVAA conversations on the types of information requested, the usage of predefined buttons or free input to obtain information, and the appearance of miscommunication with the chatbot. On December 16, 2021, the research project received ethical approval from Tilburg University's Ethics Review Board (TSHD_RP174).[1]

---

[1] Data collection was initiated prior to final approval, following liaising with the ethics board.

2.2 Participants

We recruited a convenience sample of 60 young Dutch voters between 18 and 24 years old via the participant pool of our university (M_{age} = 20.3 years; SD = 1.88). Of them, 13 participants (21.7%) identified themselves as male, 46 as female (76.7%) and 1 participant (1.7%) identified outside the gender binary. All participants had Dutch as a native language and were registered with a Dutch municipality, and hence eligible to vote. Of the participants, 11 (18.3%) had never voted before, 37 participants (61.7%) had voted in one previous election and 12 participants (20%) had voted in multiple previous elections.

We compared participants in the text (N = 19), voice (N = 20) and combined (N = 21) condition with respect to the above mentioned demographic characteristics and found no differences in prior voting experience (χ^2 (4) = 2.02, p = .73), gender (χ^2 (4) = 3.52, p = .48) and age (F (2, 57) = 3.70, p = .36). This implies that there is no reason to assume that there were *a priori* differences between the participants in the text condition, the voice condition, and the combined condition.

2.3 Materials

Development Process. The three CAVAA versions were developed in collaboration with chatbot developer Genius Voice (geniusvoice.nl). This company designed the look and feel of the chatbots, and trained them to improve intent recognition. To check the functionalities, we pretested our three CAVAA versions among nine participants (three per version). Based on these pretests, several improvements to the CAVAAs were made. Below we will describe the experimental materials as they were used in the final experiment. All experimental materials can be found in Dataverse (https://doi.org/10.34894/MNMLAT).

Modality. In the text-based condition, users could interact with the chatbot either by clicking on suggestion buttons, or by typing in their messages in an open chat window themselves. They hence always used typed text or clicking to consult the chatbots, and they always received an answer in written text in return.

In the voice-based condition, the user and the chatbot communicated via speech. Just like in the text condition, users in the voice condition were shown suggestion buttons in written indicating the types of information they could request, but these buttons were not clickable; instead, users had to read the suggestion buttons out loud to activate them. Moreover, they could also formulate questions themselves by means of free speech, comparable to the open chat function in the text condition. When the user asked a question in the voice condition, the chatbot displayed the answer in text on the screen and also read out the answer aloud.

In the combined condition, users could communicate with the chatbot via both modalities and were able to switch between text and voice during the conversation. This means that they could activate the suggestion buttons by either clicking on them, or by using the voice functionality to activate the content. Moreover, the chatbot's answers were visible on the screen, and when users would activate the sound button, the chatbot answers were also read out loud. Only in the combined condition it was hence possible to switch between the two modalities during the course of filling out the CAVAA. Figure 1 provides an example of the combined condition and describes the look and feel of this condition related to the other two conditions.

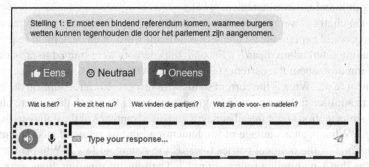

Fig. 1. Screenshot of the combined CAVAA showing the first statement, the three answer options, and four suggestion buttons. Below the suggestion buttons, there are two icons (marked with a dotted line in the figure) that could be used to turn the sound (for output) and microphone (for input) on and off. Moreover there is an open text field to enter a question in written (marked with a dashed line in the figure). In the voice-condition, the open text field was not present and the sound and microphone icons were always on, as in this condition voice was the only modality that could be used to control the CAVAA; in the text-based condition the open text field was visible and the icons to turn the sound and microphone on/off were not displayed, as this CAVAA could only be controlled by using text.

Statements. The CAVAAs' content and conversational flow were based on the experimental materials of [15], who developed a CAVAA for the Dutch National Elections in 2021. In total, 16 political attitude statements from that study were also included in the current research, as they were still topic of debate at the time we developed the materials for the current research. We added two new statements to come to 18 political attitude statements in total, which is the minimal number of VAA statements identified in a corpus study analyzing VAAs in national elections [31]. A (translated) example of a statement is 'There should be a binding referendum with which citizens can stop laws being implemented'.

Users could indicate their opinion towards each statement by answering 'agree', 'neutral' or 'disagree'. These answer options were visualized with a green ('agree'), grey ('neutral'), and red ('disagree') button below each statement (see Fig. 1). After answering all attitude statements, the CAVAA provided the user with a personalized voting advice in which the user's standpoints were matched with the standpoints of the eight most prominent political parties of the Netherlands (similar to [15]).

Information Types. The chatbots were developed with conversational framework Rasa (rasa.com) and trained to recognize the intents of the users on the basis of an extensive list with potential questions users could ask per attitude statement, including synonyms (e.g., 'disadvantages', 'downsides', 'cons') and abbreviations (e.g., 'Partij van de Arbeid',

'PvdA'). These training data led to a NLU-model; the intent-entity combinations subsequently determined the chatbots' output to the user. Based on the user's input, the chatbots provided users with four types of information for each attitude statement in the tool; these types of information were based on the types of questions users have when answering political attitude statements [13].

First, the chatbots were trained to provide semantic information, which means that the chatbots could explain the meaning of a difficult word in the statement (e.g., 'What does a binding referendum mean?'). Second, the chatbots were trained to provide pragmatic information about the current state of affairs with respect to the political issue in the statement (e.g., 'What is the current status with respect to referendums in the Netherlands?'). In addition to semantic and pragmatic information, the chatbots were also able to provide information about the advantages and disadvantages of the policy in the statement (e.g., 'What is an advantage of implementing binding referendums?'), and about the standpoints of the political parties towards the statement (e.g., 'What is the standpoint of the PvdA on binding referendums?'). The four information types were shown below the statement by means of four suggestion buttons, but users could also access information by phrasing questions themselves. The information the chatbot provided in response to users' questions was preformulated by the researchers and always based on reliable resources, such as government websites, online dictionaries, news articles, and existing voting aids (similar to [14, 15]).

Conversation Flow. The conversation between the CAVAA and the user started with the chatbot greeting the user. Thereafter, the first statement was shown. The user could choose to either respond directly to the statement, or to ask for additional information first.

To enhance the dialogical character of the chatbot, we added conversational sentences in three different ways. First, an information request was always introduced with a conversational sentence (e.g., 'Thanks for your question', 'I looked it up for you'). Second, after showing the additional information, the chatbot repeated the statement preceded by a conversational sentence (e.g., 'So, the statement was ...', 'Is there anything else you'd like to know before answering the statement?'). Third, the transition between statements was marked with a conversational sentence (e.g., 'I have registered your answer, let's move on to the next statement'). In all three chatbot versions, the chatbot randomly selected conversational sentences from a list, so that the three experimental conditions contained the same variation in conversational elements.

The chatbots were also equipped with a set of error responses in case they did not understand the user's input or could not find a fitting answer. These responses consisted of an error notification (e.g., 'Sorry, I don't understand your question') and a repair strategy (e.g., 'Could you reformulate it in different words?'). In case miscommunication still occurred, the chatbot's error response hinted on the four types of information that could be requested by the user (e.g., 'Unfortunately, I cannot answer that question. I can give you some information on ...'), which is proven to be a successful recovery strategy in chatbot conversations [3, 4].

2.4 Usage Measures

For the usage measures we analyzed a sample of 60 (participants) * 18 (statements) = 1,080 respondent and item combinations. This sample was coded on the types of information requested by the participants, and whether miscommunication occurred between the user and the chatbot. For the combined condition, we also scored which modality the participants used to request information. A second coder coded a random subsample of 17 chatbot conversations (28%), divided across the three CAVAA versions. The intercoder reliability was always acceptable (semantic information $\kappa = 0.97$, pragmatic information $\kappa = 0.96$, party standpoints $\kappa = 1.00$, (dis)advantages $\kappa = 0.95$; miscommunication $\kappa = 0.76$).

2.5 Evaluation Measures and Political Measures

In an online survey, the evaluation measures were examined first, followed by the political measures. Except for the factual knowledge questions, all survey questions could be answered on a seven-point scale ranging from 'fully disagree' to 'fully agree'.

Enjoyment. The questionnaire started with three statements to measure participants' enjoyment while using the CAVAA. The three items were adapted from a survey in an earlier study by [21] and modified to fit the context of the current study (e.g., 'I found using the chatbot a pleasant experience'). The three items showed to group well together ($\alpha = .88$).

Ease of Use. The ease of use of the chatbot was measured with five items, adapted from the study of [1] (e.g., 'I found this chatbot user friendly'). The five items clustered well together ($\alpha = .81$).

Usefulness. Usefulness was measured with four items based on [1] and modified to fit the context of the current study (e.g., 'Using this chatbot enabled me to answer the statements better than a regular voting aid'). The four items provided a reliable measure ($\alpha = .73$).

Perceived Political Knowledge. Participants' perception of political knowledge after using the CAVAA was measured by adapting four statements from a study by [29] (e.g., 'By using this chatbot, I gained more knowledge about the political landscape'). The four items showed to group well together ($\alpha = .69$).

Factual Political Knowledge. Eight true/false statements were presented on topics related to the political attitude statements in the CAVAA. Participants answered these statements with either 'true', 'false' or 'I don't know'. The latter answering option was included to avoid guessing behavior of participants that could affect the reliability. For the data analysis, the answers to the eight knowledge questions have been recoded. The correct answers have been coded with 1 and both the incorrect answers and the 'I don't know' answers have been coded with 0. This led to a factual political knowledge score between 0 and 8 for every participant.

2.6 Procedure

The study was conducted in December 2021, approximately three months prior to municipal elections in the Netherlands. All participants were recruited via the Human Subject Pool of our university and took part in the experiment in the lab (taking the Corona measures at the time into account). Before starting the experiment in one of the sound proof cabins, participants were given a brief instruction on what Voting Advice Applications are and how to specifically use the CAVAA in the current study. Subsequently, they started the study and were asked to provide informed consent for the usage of their data. It was stressed that participation was completely voluntary and participants could stop at any point in time. After having provided informed consent, participants answered several questions about demographic variables. Next, participants could click on a link that directed them to one of the three CAVAA versions that opened in a new window. After having answered all 18 political statements in the CAVAA, a voting advice was provided. Thereafter, the participant was redirected to the online survey that included the evaluation measures and the political knowledge measures. The questionnaire ended with a debriefing in which the participants were informed about the purpose of the study. In total, the experiment took approximately 20 minutes and all participants received a partial course credit in return.

3 Results

3.1 Usage Measures

The means and standard deviations for the usage measures are shown in Table 1. Across all four types of information a respondent could request, there was a difference between the chatbot conditions: in both the text condition and the combined condition respondents more frequently requested at least one of the four forms of information than in the voice condition (text vs. voice: $\chi^2 = 4.52, p = .03$; combined vs. voice: $\chi^2 = 6.76, p = .009$). There was no difference between the text and combined condition ($\chi^2 = 0.03, p = .86$).

If we split out this analysis per type of information, it can be seen that in the voice condition less information about the advantages and disadvantages of a certain policy was requested compared to the combined condition ($\chi^2 = 7.28, p = .007$), and also that in the voice condition less information was looked up about the party stances compared to the text condition ($\chi^2 = 5.76, p = .02$). All other contrasts failed to reach significance. Also, no significant differences between the three CAVAA conditions were found with respect to the retrieval of semantic and pragmatic information (in all cases: $\chi^2 < 3.55, p > .06$), although the tendencies for differences (p-values between 0.06 and 0.1) indicate that in a larger sample there may be more information requests found for both the text and the combined condition compared to the voice condition.

Table 1. Proportion of times a type of information was requested (Logit and SE between brackets), and the accompanying variances (in Logit) (M) for each experimental condition.

	Semantic	Pragmatic	(Dis)advantages	Party Stances	Total
Text	20.8% (-1.34; 0.33)	19.6% (-1.41; 0.25)	29.7% (-0.86; 0.24)	19.0%* (-1.45; 0.32)	59.2%* (0.38; 0.30)
Voice	15.3% (-1.71; 0.33)	12.2% (-1.97; 0.26)	21.7% (-1.29; 0.23)	7.2% (-2.55; 0.33)	43.1% (-2.76; 0.27)
Combined	21.4% (-1.30; 0.34)	18.8% (-1.46; 0.19)	40.1%* (-0.40; 0.25)	11.4% (-2.05; 0.32)	60.6%* (0.43; 0.26)
$S^2_{resp.}$ Text	0.12	0.46 (0.27)	0.86 (0.34)	1.67 (0.64)	0.83 (0.35)
$S^2_{resp.}$ Voice	0.04	0.50 (0.32)	0.78 (0.32)	1.45 (0.68)	0.54 (0.25)
$S^2_{resp.}$ Comb	0.29	0.07 (0.13)	1.05 (0.37)	1.67 (0.66)	0.51 (0.23)
S^2_{items}	1.51	0.31 (0.14)	0 (0)	0 (0)	0.57 (0.22)

* indicates a significant difference ($p < .05$) with the voice condition.

Table 2. Proportion of times that miscommunication occurred (Logit and SE between brackets), and the accompanying variances (in Logit) (M) for each experimental condition.

	Miscommunication
Text	1.4%* (-4.21; 0.69)
Voice	12.8% (-1.92; 0.18)
Combined	0 (0)
$S^2_{resp.}$ Text	5.49
$S^2_{resp.}$ Voice	0.20
$S^2_{resp.}$ Comb	0
S^2_{items}	0

* indicates a significant difference ($p < .05$) with the voice condition.

We also run a Loglinear Multi-level model similar to [14] to compare the number of times a respondent experienced miscommunication. There was no miscommunication observed in the combined condition (0%), only very little miscommunication in the text condition (1.4%), whereas in the voice condition in about 12.8% of the respondent and item combinations some form of miscommunication occurred. The differences between the text and voice condition were indeed found to be significant ($\chi^2 = 3.20, p < .001$;

see Table 2). The combined condition could not be included in the analysis due to a lack of variance.

As there was no miscommunication in the combined condition and quite a lot of miscommunication in the voice condition, a relevant question is as to how frequently users used the voice option in the combined condition. The combined condition contained 21 participants and they all responded to 18 statements about politics, so there were 378 respondent and item combinations. In only 12 of these cases (3.2%) respondents used their voice to request information. This means that the voice functionality was hardly used and respondents used the text option even if they had the possibility to control the chatbot with their voice.

3.2 Evaluation Measures and Political Measures

In the survey, participants evaluated the CAVAA's enjoyment, ease of use, and usefulness. Furthermore, both perceived and factual political knowledge were measured. The means and standard deviations of all dependent variables can be found in Table 3.

Table 3. Means (M) and standard deviations (SD) between brackets per dependent variable and per experimental condition.

	Enjoyment	Ease of Use	Usefulness	Perceived Knowledge	Factual Knowledge
Text ($N = 19$)	5.60 (1.09)	6.13 (0.68)*	6.12 (0.80)*	4.91 (0.85)	5.11 (1.79)
Voice ($N = 20$)	5.40 (1.12)	5.21 (1.30)	5.34 (1.11)	5.14 (0.93)	5.25 (2.00)
Combined ($N = 21$)	5.63 (0.49)	6.18 (0.53)*	6.01 (0.70)	5.11 (0.86)	5.57 (1.40)

* indicates a significant difference ($p < .05$) with the voice condition.

For each dependent variable, a Factorial ANOVA was conducted to examine whether this variable was dependent on the modality of the CAVAA. For ease of use, there was a modality effect ($F (2, 57) = 7.38, p = .01$). A post hoc test (Bonferroni) indicated that both the text and the combined condition were easier to use than the voice condition ($p = .007$ and $p = .003$ respectively). Also, a modality effect was found for usefulness ($F (2, 57) = 4.55, p = .02$). A post hoc test (Bonferroni) indicated that in the text condition the CAVAA was evaluated to be more useful than in the voice condition ($p = .02$), and that there was also a tendency ($p = .05$) for the CAVAA to be evaluated as more useful in the combined condition than in the voice condition. For enjoyment and the two political knowledge measures, no modality effects were observed (enjoyment: $F (2, 57) = 0.37, p = .70$; perceived political knowledge: $F (2, 57) = 0.39, p = .68$; factual political knowledge: $F (2, 57) = 0.38, p = .69$).

4   Discussion

We explored the effects of chatbot modality (text, voice, or combined) in the specific usage context of Conversational Agent Voting Advice Applications (CAVAAs). In contrast to earlier chatbot studies on modality effects in customer service contexts (e.g., [20, 26, 27]), the current usage context in which users tried to understand political attitude statements can be seen as more cognitively demanding and goal-oriented. In our study, we focused on a homogeneous group of young voters (aged 18-25), who are known to expose satisficing behaviour when working with a CAVAA, which means that they are only willing to make a minimal effort to find information [13, 14].

Results show that users' perceptions of ease of use and usefulness of the tools differ: both the text and the combined condition scored higher on these measures than the voice condition. From the results of our content analysis, two possible explanations can be formulated for these findings. First, users experienced more miscommunication when they used speech input. This miscommunication sometimes occurred when the user tried to request additional information, e.g., when the chatbot did not understand a question like 'Wait are the advantages' when the user probably meant '*What* are the advantages'. Most miscommunication, however, occurred when the user tried to answer the political attitude statements saying 'Agree', 'Neutral', or 'Disagree'. The voice bot for example sometimes thought the user said 'Eend' (the Dutch word for 'Duck') or 'Aids' ('Aids') when the user probably wanted to say 'Eens' (the Dutch word for 'Agree'). Similarly, the chatbot sometimes understood 'Centraal' ('Central') when the user probably meant 'Neutraal' ('Neutral'), or 'Online' ('Online') when the user meant 'Oneens' ('Disagree'). These different forms of miscommunication probably caused the user to feel less in control in the voice condition [30], which may have led to lower scores for ease of use and usefulness.

A second explanation for the lower scores on ease of use and usefulness for the voice condition is that in this condition users felt less invited to ask questions to the chatbot, which may have lowered the perception of ease of use and especially usefulness. A relevant question therefore is as to *why* users file less information requests in the voice condition. One explanation may be related to the previous point suggesting that users were afraid to experience miscommunication. However, as miscommunication was more frequently occurring when the user answered the political attitude statement rather than when asking a question to the system, an alternative explanation, is that users, who are known to make only a minimal effort to request information [13, 14], found using their voice a too big an effort. In our view, this explanation is very plausible especially in light of our finding that in the combined condition users first and foremost used text (clicking) to request information and not voice. The occurrence of miscommunication does not count as an alternative explanation for the reliance on text in the combined condition, as we observed no miscommunication whatsoever in the combined condition. In our view, it is therefore likely that a textual communication mode simply fits the user better in the specific usage context of CAVAAs. To be more certain of what has caused the lesser amount of information requests in the voice condition, and therefore probably the lower scores on usability measures, however, it would be worthwhile to conduct a replication study with an improved version of the voice-based chatbot. This chatbot should then be trained better to recognize respondents' answers to the political attitude statements. In addition, it would be valuable to combine such an experimental study with a cognitive interview afterwards asking users to indicate explicitly how much an effort they thought asking a question was.

Another result of the current study is that no differences between the three CAVAA versions were found for perceived enjoyment. This finding is in contrast with earlier studies showing that users of voice-based chatbots frequently enjoy the interaction [25, 33]. It seems that in the current study users overall enjoyed working with all three CAVAA versions a lot, showing from the relatively high mean scores for enjoyment (around 5), as well as the open comments users made at the end of the survey, such as: 'I really liked using the chatbot!', 'The chatbot helped me to understand the topics in the voting advice application; I really enjoyed using a chatbot in a voting advice application' and 'It felt naturalistic to talk to the chatbot. It is much nicer and more personal to do than just answering questions'. A possible explanation for as to why not just the voice-based CAVAA but all three versions received high scores for enjoyment, might be that CAVAAs are relatively new tools in general. Therefore, a novelty effect [9, 16] may have occurred across all three versions since experiences of enjoyment and novelty are closely related [23].

A final results of the current study is that we found no differences between the three modalities for perceived and factual knowledge. As we expected the effects of the political measures to be the result of the actual usage and evaluation of the tool, and as we did find modality effects for these latter measures, the absence of differences for the political measures may be unexpected. In all three conditions relatively high scores on perceived (means around 5 on a 7-point scale) and factual (means around 5 on an 8-point scale) knowledge were obtained. This may suggest that answering political attitude statements in a CAVAA, irrespective of modality, leads to relatively high scores on these political measures. To further understand this finding it would therefore be interesting for a future study to include not only a post-CAVAA measure of perceived and factual knowledge, but also a pre-CAVAA measure. This way the delta of these two measures can be calculated and used as a more fine-grained measure of perceived and factual knowledge.

5   Conclusion

The goal of this study was to explore how people use and perceive chatbots that differ in modality in the cognitively demanding context of Conversational Agent Voting Advice Applications. The participants' scores on perceived and factual political knowledge, as well as their perceived enjoyment scores did not differ between the chatbot conditions. However, differences were found for usefulness and ease of use: the voice-based CAVAA was both considered less easy to use and less useful than the other two modalities. The content analysis of the chatlogs revealed that users request more information in both the text condition and the combined condition as compared to the voice condition. Moreover, more miscommunication occurred between the tool and the user in the voice condition than in the other two conditions. Finally, results showed that in the combined condition users hardly used the opportunity to control the chatbot using voice and they relied on the type and click functionality in most of the cases. All in all, these results suggest that the combined condition in practice resembled the text condition and that these two conditions outperformed the voice condition in various respects. In order to achieve an optimal fit between users, task, and technology – as formulated by the TTF theory – chatbot developers in the context of political CAVAAs could best develop text-based chatbots, since such chatbots do not only avoid miscommunication, but also stimulate users to request more information in an easy way. This way CAVAAs can best help citizens to find political information. This should ultimately lead to more voters actually casting a vote in real-life elections and to a stronger democracy.

Acknowledgements. The authors would like to thank Tilburg University's Fund (project number ESF2021–2) for the financial support to develop the CAVAAs. A summary of the results of this study has also been published in the Dutch popular-scientific magazine *Tekstblad* [22].

References

1. Ahn, T., Ryu, S., Ahn, T., Ryu, S., Han, I.: The impact of Web quality and playfulness on user acceptance of online retailing. Inf. Manage. **44**(3), 263–275 (2007). https://doi.org/10.1016/j.im.2006.12.008
2. Angga, P.A., Fachri, W.E., Elevanita, A., Agushinta, R.D.: Design of chatbot with 3D avatar, voice interface, and facial expression. In: 2015 International Conference on Science in Information Technology (ICSITech), pp. 326–330. IEEE, October 2015
3. Ashktorab, Z., Jain, M., Liao, Q.V., Weisz, J.D.: Resilient chatbots: Repair strategy preferences for conversational breakdowns. In: Proceedings of the 2019 CHI Conference on Human Factors in Computing Systems, pp. 1–12, May 2019
4. Bohus, D., Rudnicky, A.: Sorry and i didn't catch that! An investigation of non- understanding errors and recovery strategies. In: Proceedings of the 6th SIGdial Workshop on Discourse and Dialogue, pp. 128–143, September 2005
5. Cho, E., Molina, M.D., Wang, J.: The effects of modality, device, and task differences on perceived human likeness of voice-activated virtual assistants. Cyberpsychol. Behav. Soc. Netw. **22**(8), 515–520 (2019)
6. De Graaf, J.: The irresistible rise of Stemwijzer. In: Cedroni, L., Garzia, D. (eds.) Voting Advice Applications in Europe: The State of the Art, pp. 35–46. Scriptaweb, Napoli (2010)
7. Direct Research: De Nationale Voice Monitor 2021 (2021). https://www.directresearch.nl/blogs/de-nationale-voice-monitor-2021/. Accessed 8 Feb 2022
8. Følstad, A., et al.: Future directions for chatbot research: an interdisciplinary research agenda. Computing **103**(12), 2915–2942 (2021). https://doi.org/10.1007/s00607-021-01016-7
9. Fryer, L.K., Ainley, M., Thompson, A., Gibson, A., Sherlock, Z.: Stimulating and sustaining interest in a language course: an experimental comparison of Chatbot and Human task partners. Comput. Hum. Behav. **75**, 461–468 (2017)
10. Garzia, D., Marschall, S.: Voting advice applications under review: the state of research. Int. J. Electron. Govern. **5**(3–4), 203–222 (2012)
11. Gemenis, K., Rosema, M.: Voting advice applications and electoral turnout. Elect. Stud. **36**, 281–289 (2014)
12. Goodhue, D.L., Thompson, R.L.: Task-technology fit and individual performance. MIS Q. **19**(2), 213 (1995). https://doi.org/10.2307/249689
13. Kamoen, N., Holleman, B.: I don't get it. Response difficulties in answering political attitude statements in Voting Advice Applications. Surv. Res. Methods. **11**(2), 125–140 (2017). https://doi.org/10.18148/srm/2017.v11i2.6728

14. Kamoen, N., Liebrecht, C.: I need a CAVAA: how conversational agent voting advice applications (CAVAAs) affect users' political knowledge and tool experience. Front. Artif. Intell. **5**, 835505 (2022). https://doi.org/10.3389/frai.2022.835505

15. Kamoen, N., McCartan, T., Liebrecht, C.: Conversational agent voting advice applications: a comparison between a structured, semi-structured, and non-structured chatbot design for communicating with voters about political issues. In: Følstad, A., et al. (eds.) Chatbot Research and Design: 5th International Workshop, CONVERSATIONS 2021, Virtual Event, November 23–24, 2021, Revised Selected Papers, pp. 160–175. Springer International Publishing, Cham (2022). https://doi.org/10.1007/978-3-030-94890-0_10

16. Kanda, T., Hirano, T., Eaton, D., Ishiguro, H.: Interactive robots as social partners and peer tutors for children: a field trial. Human-Comput. Interact. **19**(1–2), 61–84 (2004)

17. Kim, Y., Lee, H.: The rise of chatbots in political campaigns: the effects of conversational agents on voting intention Int. J. Human–Comput. Interact. 1–12 (2022).https://doi.org/10.1080/10447318.2022.2108669

18. Kocielnik, R., Avrahami, D., Marlow, J., Lu, D., Hsieh, G.: Designing for workplace reflection: a chat and voice-based conversational agent. In: Proceedings of the 2018 Designing Interactive Systems Conference, pp. 881–894, June 2018

19. Krouwel, A., Vitiello, T., Wall, M.: The practicalities of issuing vote advice: a new methodology for profiling and matching. Int. J. Electron. Govern. **5**(3–4), 223–243 (2012)

20. Le Bigot, L., Jamet, E., Rouet, J.-F., Amiel, V.: Mode and modal transfer effects on performance and discourse organization with an information retrieval dialogue system in natural language. Comput. Hum. Behav. **22**, 467–500 (2006)

21. Lee, M.K., Cheung, C.M., Chen, Z.: Acceptance of Internet-based learning medium: the role of extrinsic and intrinsic motivation. Inf. Manage. **42**(8), 1095–1104 (2005)

22. Liebrecht, C., Kamoen, N.: 'Hey Siri, wat is de hondenbelasting?': Voicebots en tekstbots in een politieke context. Tekstblad **27**(1), 22–24 (2022)

23. McLean, G., Osei-Frimpong, K.: Hey Alexa… examine the variables influencing the use of artificial intelligent in-home voice assistants. Comput. Hum. Behav. **99**, 28–37 (2019)

24. Nass, C.I., Brave, S.: Wired for Speech: How Voice Activates and Advances the Human-Computer Relationship. MIT Press, Cambridge (2005)

25. Pal, D., Arpnikanondt, C., Funilkul, S., Chutimaskul, W.: The adoption analysis of voice-based smart Iot products. IEEE Internet Things J. **7**(11), 10852–10867 (2020)

26. Riefle, L., Brand, A., Mietz, J., Rombach, L., Szekat, C., Benz, C.: What fits Tim might not fit Tom: Exploring the impact of user characteristics on users' experience with conversational interaction modalities. In: Wirtschaftsinformatik 2022 Proceedings, vol. 13 (2022)

27. Rzepka, C., Berger, B., Hess, T.: Voice assistant vs. chatbot: examining the fit between conversational agents' interaction modalities and information search tasks. Inf. Syst. Front. **24**(3), 839–856 (2022)

28. Schroeder, J., Schroeder, M.: Trusting in machines: how mode of interaction affects willingness to share personal information with machines. In: Proceedings of the 51st Hawaii International Conference on System Sciences, Hawaii, USA (2018)

29. Shulman, H.C., Sweitzer, M.D.: Advancing framing theory: designing an equivalency frame to improve political information processing. Hum. Commun. Res. **44**(2), 155–175 (2018). https://doi.org/10.1093/hcr/hqx006

30. Sundar, S.S.: The MAIN model: a heuristic approach to understanding technology effects on credibility. In: Metzger, M.J., Flanagin, A.J. (Eds.). Digital Media, Youth, and Credibility. The John D. and Catherine T. MacArthur Foundation Series on Digital Media and Learning, pp. 73–100. The MIT Press, Cambridge (2008). https://doi.org/10.1162/dmal.9780262562324.073

31. Van Camp, K., Lefevere, J., Walgrave, S.: The content and formulation of statements in voting advice applications. In: Garzia, D., Marschall, S., (eds.) Matching Voters with Parties and Candidates. Voting Advice Applications in Comparative Perspective, pp. 11–32. ECPR Press, Colchester (2014)
32. Xu, J.D., Benbasat, I., Cenfetelli, R.T.: The nature and consequences of trade-off transparency in the context of recommendation agents. MIS Q. **38**, 379–406 (2014)
33. Yang, H., Lee, H.: Understanding user behavior of virtual personal assistant devices. IseB **17**(1), 65–87 (2018). https://doi.org/10.1007/s10257-018-0375-1

Value Creation in Gamified Chatbot Interactions and Its Impact on Brand Engagement

Susana C. Silva[1], Roberta De Cicco[2,3,4(✉)], Maria Levi[1], and Maik Hammerschmidt[5]

[1] Católica Porto Business School, Universidade Católica Portuguesa, Porto, Portugal
[2] Department of Neuroscience, Imaging and Clinical Sciences, University of Chieti-Pescara, Chieti, Italy
roberta.decicco@unich.it
[3] CAST, Center for Advanced Studies and Technology, Chieti, Italy
[4] Department of Economics, University of Molise, Campobasso, Italy
[5] Faculty of Business and Economics, Smart Retail Group, Georg-August-Universität Göttingen, Göttingen, Germany

Abstract. Gamification is a powerful instrument to motivate consumers to intensify their brand relationships. Though this potential, the effects of enriching chatbot interactions with gameful experiences on brand engagement has not been studied. To fill this gap, this study tries to understand how gamification contributes to customers' value creation in a gamified conversational context and how this value creation relates to brand engagement. Specifically, we investigate whether and to what extent the hedonic and utilitarian values provided in interactions with gamified chatbots affect cognitive, emotional, and behavioral brand engagement. Based on an empirical study involving a fully functional gamified chatbot, we show that the perceived hedonic value has a major impact on all three brand engagement dimensions, and especially the cognitive dimension. Utilitarian values, though not related to the cognitive dimension of brand engagement, significantly boost the emotional and the behavioral engagement dimensions. These findings point to the potentials of extrinsic and utilitarian motivations for boosting brand engagement also in entertainment-oriented settings like gamified chatbot interactions.

Keywords: Chatbots · Gamification · Utilitarian value · Hedonic value · Consumer-brand engagement

1 Introduction

Chatbots are disembodied conversational agents that communicate with humans through text-based chats or voice commands to address a variety of requests and customer needs [2, 22]. So far chatbots are primarily deployed as non-human versions of frontline service employees resolving simple, standardized tasks in a highly efficient way. Correspondingly, prior research has focused on examining users' engagement with the conversational agent like satisfaction with chatbot interaction [37], intention to use the chatbot again [12] or likelihood of recommending the chatbot [68]. What has been widely neglected so far is whether conversational agents have the potential for engaging customers with

A. Følstad et al. (Eds.): CONVERSATIONS 2022, LNCS 13815, pp. 50–65, 2023.
https://doi.org/10.1007/978-3-031-25581-6_4

brands [38]. Such an augmented view of conversational-based agents for triggering customer engagement beyond solving single service issues has been frequently called for
in current literature [35]. In the new digital society, understanding how to engage and
establish powerful connections between consumers and brands has never been so important, as a new "experience economy" is taking over with consumers starting to highly
value dematerialized interactions [42], and previous engagement strategies based on
monetary rewards failing their purpose [15]. Since individuals play games for intrinsic,
almost addictive reasons [23], using game design elements as an approach for engagement stimulation is an emerging trend in the marketing field (e.g. [16, 61]). This activity
for engagement stimulation, known as "gamification" [36], that involves applying game
elements to non-game related contexts, has been extended to the marketing field where
the use of game design elements in nongame contexts is becoming popular [66]. Augmenting chatbots through game elements is becoming increasingly possible as major
technological advancements give computer agents the ability to interact with users in
a much wider variety of contexts [1, 40]. To get customers to engage with the brand,
however, chatbots have to integrate elements that have a unique power for unfolding
consumers' motivational energy to interact with a brand [42]. We argue that infusing
gamification into chatbot interactions could be such an approach for turning chatbots into
"engagement machines". Integrating game elements into chatbots could have the potential to elicit experiences that are similarly powerful as those instilled through gameplay
and hence can effectively motivate engagement responses [16]. A gamified interaction
detaches individuals from their surroundings and immerses them in the experience thus
provoking a sense of natural flow [9]. Therefore, combining the immersive and motivational power of gamification in human-chatbot interactions could be a strategy for
revolutionizing the way brands engage consumers.

In this study, by using a real-life chatbot interaction, we empirically investigate
how interacting with a chatbot featuring a gamification design affects consumer-brand
engagement. We argue that infusing a gamified experience into a chatbot generates not
only hedonic but also utilitarian value for users, which in turn strengthens cognitive,
emotional, and behavioral engagement with the brand. The empirical findings provide
nice contributions to the recently emerging research on the intersection of gamification
and conversational technologies. We shed light on the mechanisms that enable gamified
chatbots to effectively boost brand engagement by identifying two opposing psychological processes (utilitarian vs. hedonic value). We show that embedding gamification in a
given system is effective when the game elements can impact the targeted users in terms
of what they personally value [19, 62].

2 Theoretical Framework and Hypotheses Development

2.1 Chatbots and Gamification

Due to the explosive proliferation and technological advancements of artificial agents, for
many firms, chatbots have become the dominant interface when it comes to communicating with consumers. It is not surprising that firms see chatbots also as a potential means
to enhance firm and brand engagement. Companies are heavily investing in conversational agents to engage their customers better, and the use of these agents is predicted to

increase by 241% in the travel and hospitality industry and by 187% for consumer good [39].

Gamification is an emerging technology process that enables to mimic the entertaining experiences that games are all about, by using game elements just like playful design does, while having rules, goals, and feedback systems [36]. Literature on gamification applications in marketing stresses that brand engagement occurs mostly because of interactive and challenging experiences and that game elements can facilitate such experiences [6, 36]. There are many types of game components, such as avatars, points, badges, levels, gifting, levels, as well as leaderboards [59], that are more likely to be recognised by users and better integrated into chatbots [44]. This makes the integration of such gamification elements into chatbots a clear option for engagement stimulation. Despite this, no study so far has examined how gamified chatbots enhance brand engagement. Our suggestion to combine chatbots and gamification principles, borrowed from the Werbach and Hunter's Dynamics-Mechanics-Components Pyramid (DMC Pyramid) [59], addresses studies that lament that many gamification applications do not work as intended [40], as well as practitioners and researchers' need to look at appropriate technological systems in which game elements can be embedded to make them (more) impactful.

2.2 Consumer Engagement

Consumer engagement is a positive motivational state that a consumer might experience when interacting with a specific object [33], which is affected by the context and conveyed through cognitive, emotional, or behavioural expressions [14]. Consumers' engagement with the brand is a crucial construct to be investigated because it is a key aspect of company equity and capital [64] as individuals who have a higher engagement with a brand are more satisfied and exhibit higher loyalty [60]. As a result, since in the marketing domain a lot of attention has been cast on how consumers can be triggered to become more aware of and engage more intensively with the brand, marketing practitioners have recently started seeking new solutions to overcome consumer engagement hurdles by using insights from the research on games [29, 36, 61]. Since consumer-brand engagement occurs due to interactive and co-created customer experiences with a brand, it is expected that brand engagement may increasingly occur when iteratively using a gamified service [30].

While some researchers consider engagement to have one dimension, namely behavioural [54] some others believe engagement to be a complex state hanging on several dimensions that deserve further understanding [33] with a one-dimensional concept not fully reflecting its complex scope [32]. Based on this, the present study includes all three main dimensions, i.e. cognitive, emotional, and behavioural, so that a broader and more detailed perspective can be given. Cognitive engagement is the psychological investment or degree of interest [58] when interacting with a brand. Emotional engagement is related to the development of emotional connections and affection towards a brand [33]. Behavioural engagement represents consumers' level of participation and positive involvement in the experience [21]. The examination of these three different foci of brand engagement is important for several reasons. While these different foci often coexist in a given consumption context [14], one focus might prevail over another in the formation of relevant consumer relationship outcomes according to the context and the different foci may play various and variable roles in shaping engagement in terms of the underlying psychological processes that may be activated.

2.3 Utilitarian and Hedonic Values

Högberg et al. [30] propose that consumer-brand engagement is positively reinforced by consumers' perceived values towards a gameful experience. This is in line with [55] who believe that knowing consumer values is essential to support information systems since they heavily influence internet users' perceptions [45] and guide behaviour [48].

According to Means-Ends model by Woodruff and Gardial [62], which is one of the most prominent value models in the literature, consumers act according to what might produce desired benefits and avoid negative consequences. Consumers' engagement towards a given object should thus be influenced by their personal values and own beliefs. In other words, consumers make a self-evaluation of the correlation between what they value from different perspectives and the perceived value offered by the experience, and in case the experience supports them, engagement behaviours are expected [13]. Therefore, personal values work as antecedents of consumer engagement [69], meaning that when aiming at engagement outcomes, managers must understand how consumers perceive value so they can develop experiences that outperform the ones from competitors [63]. Generally, various types of value are taken into account and depending on what is expected from an experience, consumers are contemplated as either problem-solvers or as individuals that seek emotional stimulus [28]. Babin et al. [3] pinpoint the relevance of both utilitarian values including economic and functional aspects, and hedonic values including emotional and social aspects, which respectively reflect Holbrook's [31] extrinsic and intrinsic values. In previous research, Carpenter et al. [7] proved that, rather than one form of motivation being overriding, both hedonic and utilitarian elements are crucial in the retail experience, although one may be more dominant than the other depending on the context. So, there is room to believe that, ideally, both types of value should be considered for consumer engagement creation, especially in case of new technologies.

Perceived utilitarian value refers to the utilitarian outcome resulting from some type of conscious pursuit of an intended consequence [3], which is defined as a way of assessing the functional and economic benefits that consumers receive for choosing a product or service [45]. In general, utilitarian value has been considered to be driven by the desire to fill a basic need or to accomplish a functional task [11]. Overall, when considering utilitarian value, consumers assess the perceived value of an experience through a more cognitive perspective [52], which is recognized as a determinant of consumer engagement as well as behavioural intention [57], reflecting judgments of time-saving, function, and convenience, that relate to a more task-oriented and rational form of evaluation [47]. Utilitarian value has a marked influence on the attitude toward Internet users [18], while showing direct positive effects on consumer satisfaction and word-of-mouth [4].

Based on the above we propose that in a gamified human-chatbot interaction:

H1: Utilitarian value is positively related to cognitive engagement with the brand
H3: Utilitarian value is positively related to the emotional engagement with the brand
H2: Utilitarian value is positively related to behavioural engagement with the brand

Overby and Lee [45] define perceived hedonic value as an assessment of the experimental benefits of choosing a specific product or service, such as the enjoyment, the fun, and the excitement perceived when consuming [28], meaning that an activity that offers these hedonic elements should motivate users to engage in the experience [55]. Being hedonic value intrinsically motivating, this should drive higher levels of engagement in the interaction and equally reflect the positive experience to who conceived such activity [30]. Overall, when considering hedonic value, consumers assess the perceived value of an experience by evaluating emotional and affective factors [34]. From this perspective, if the experience provides a relevant hedonic benefit for consumers, like gamification should do due to its inherent nature, this should drive continuing engagement behaviours (e.g. [13]) and intentions [57]. Like the utilitarian value, the hedonic value was also found to have a positive effect on preference, satisfaction, and behavioural intention [56]. As found in Chan et al. [8], the positive emotions and level of satisfaction provided by the experience increase and contribute to allowing more interactions and behavioural intentions towards the brand. Following this rationale, we expect that, same as utilitarian values, hedonic value is positively associated with consumers' engagement in all its three dimensions when interacting with the gamified chatbot. According to Cronin et al. [10], value judgment has a positive impact on preference, which is the propensity of a shopper to favor a particular retailer. According to Batra et al. [5], a brand must be highly appreciated for a person to experience engagement. Since for more hedonic-oriented users, pleasure and fun are primary benefits while for more pragmatic-oriented users, utilitarian benefits, such as reaching a goal should be more reasoned, brand engagement may be impacted by hedonic elements of extrinsic attributes in all contexts where a utilitarian benefit, such as a discount, might be achieved. Thus, in keeping with the above rationale, we propose that in a gamified human-chatbot interaction:

H4: Hedonic value is positively related to the cognitive engagement with the brand
H5: Hedonic value is positively related to the behavioural engagement with the brand
H6: Hedonic value is positively related to the emotional engagement with the brand

The proposed model would then be the one depicted in the next figure.

3   Research Method

3.1 Study Design

The study aimed to apply real chatbot interactions to enhance external validity to the study. This is less likely to happen when scenarios or screenshots are used, which happens in most of chatbots studies.

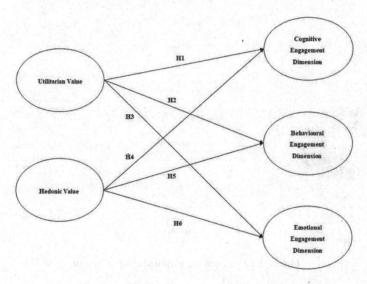

Fig. 1. Research model

A pilot study was run on 60 participants to understand what elements and gamification strategies revealed more relevant results when applied to human-chatbot interaction. These game elements were retrieved from the DMC Pyramid by Werbach and Hunter [59] and included three categories: 1) game dynamics, in the form of emotions, narrative, progression, and constraints; 2) game mechanics, in the form of challenge, reward system, and feedback; 3) game components, in the form of points and badges. Based on the results from the GAMEX scale, developed by Eppmann et al. [17] and the qualitative comments made by participants, the element of the gamified activity for the main study was a challenge in the form of a quiz that consisted of four questions about the brand and its products and a "can you spot the differences" game to win a discount. Each question had three alternative answers for participants to choose from and was related to a different level of difficulty, to give them a sense of progression and challenge. Progression to the next game level was rewarded with a discount of 10% to spend on any product of the brand, and with a symbolic badge to visually recognize the achievement. Badges were used as the main game elements in the interaction, as in Hamari [25]. Participants received instant feedback about whether they answered questions correctly and about their progression in the game. If the answer was correct, participants received a recognition badge and were able to progress to the next level to achieve the highest discount possible. If their answer was wrong, participants would be given the code for the discount associated with the reached level. The conversational design was associated with a fictitious brand page created on Facebook, named "Rainbow Packing" and the chatbot was created using Chatfuel (https://chatfuel.com/), which allow to develop rule-based chatbots using tree-like flows and pre-defined structures to help users with their queries. Figure 1 below provides an extract of the gamified chatbot design. The chosen products for the study were suitcases because of the necessity to use a neutral product with no cultural interferences, to avoid biased results (Fig. 2).

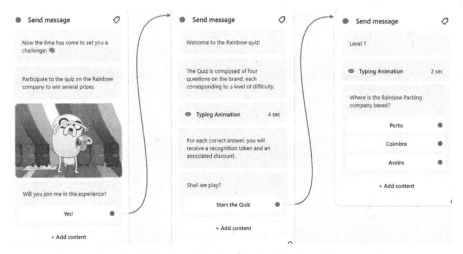

Fig. 2. Extract from the gamified chatbot design

3.2   Main Study: Measurement Development and Sample

The questionnaire was developed with Google Forms and shared online through social networks with participants invited to share, in turn, the survey with their contacts. The data collection took place throughout December 2020. The sample included a population of young Portuguese consumers possessing a Facebook Messenger account (that was required to enable the interaction with the chatbot.

The first part of the survey involved demographic questions, such as age, gender, and profession, while other questions were related to prior chatbot use, online shopping habits, and participants' preference and need for the products. Later, the following constructs of interest were measured: (1) hedonic value, (2) utilitarian value, (3) cognitive engagement, (4) emotional engagement, and (5) behavioural engagement. To measure both hedonic value and utilitarian value (see Table 1 below), we adapted the scales from Babin et al. [3]. The three dimensions of engagement, including the cognitive engagement dimension, emotional engagement dimension, and the behavioural engagement dimension, were assessed to evaluate the brand engagement of consumers. To this end, it was applied Dessart's et al. [14] brand engagement scale. This scale was chosen based on its variety of engagement foci making it a more uniform measure for consumer engagement – and its ability to clarify the dimensionality of engagement. It recognises consumer engagement as a three-dimensional concept and adds more detail to its conceptualization. While the behavioural dimension is related to the level of effort and time spent [33], the cognitive aspect of engagement is about the level of absorption that a user is able to reach, and the emotional dimension relates to the measure of enjoyment and enthusiasm [58].

4   Results

4.1   Demographic Information

The data retrieved from the demographic questions were analysed through SPSS Statistics software version 26.0. The majority of participants were able to reach the final levels. Those participants (38) who could not reach the final levels were discarded from the analysis, which led to a final sample of 165 participants (74 men, 91 women). The majority of participants are between 18 and 23 (66.7%) and 24 and 39 years old (23%). 43.6% of participants possess a Bachelor's degree, 21.25% a Master's degree, and 32.1% a high school diploma. More than half of participants declared to have already experienced an interaction with a chatbot (55.8%) and 57% of participants declared to regularly make online purchases. Almost all participants liked the products showcased by the chatbot (92.1%), while 72.1% of participants reported a need for the products (suitcases).

4.2   PLS Analysis and Measurement Model

To estimate the measurement and structural models, Partial Least Square Structural Equation Modeling (PLS-SEM) [24] through SmartPLS 3.2.8 software [46] was used. Due to a low factor loading, three items were deleted from the subsequent analysis: HV1, BED 5, and EED2, while due to high variance inflation factor (VIF) value, two items were deleted from the hedonic values scale (HV3 and HV7) to avoid collinearity issues that arise when Variance Inflation Factor (VIF) records a value exceeding 5.00 [24]. The final model consisted of 5 constructs and 21 items. All the VIF values and factor loadings for the remaining constructs are reported in Table 1. All indicators have exceeded the threshold established at 0.6. Similarly, the minimum cut-off values, established by Fornell and Larcker [20], at 0.7 for composite reliability, 0.6 for Cronbach's Alfa, and 0.5 for AVE, have been also exceeded. Reliability and convergent validity were respectively assessed by Composite Reliability (CR) and Average Variance Extracted (AVE) and each composite's AVE square-root values were compared with the correlations between the different composites of the model [20]. In all cases the AVE values exceed the corresponding squared inter-composite, correlational values. Discriminant validity was also assessed by HeteroTrait-MonoTrait ratio (HTMT) of correlations, because of its superior performance compared to more traditional methods [27], with values below the threshold 0.90. Standardized loadings were used to assess the indicator reliability. The thresholds for CR, AVE, and lambda are .7, .5, and .6, respectively. For the HTMT criterion, the threshold level of .90 was used [26].

4.3   Structural Model

The hypotheses were tested using 5000 bootstraps resamples. As reported in Table 2, results show that utilitarian value is not related to the cognitive engagement dimension of consumer engagement since the relationship between these variables is not significant ($\gamma = -0.045$, $p = 0.563$), thus not supporting the hypothesis (H1). However, utilitarian value, in line with H2 and H3, is positively related to the behavioural and emotional engagement dimensions (respectively $\gamma = 0.195$, p <0.05 and $\gamma = 0.259$, $p< 0.05$).

Table 1. Loadings, reliability, and validity

Item	Mean (SD)	VIF	Loading	α	Composite Reliability	AVE
Utilitarian value				0.897	0.929	0.766
UV1	5.570 (1.376)	3.24	0.903			
UV2	5.867 (1.333)	1.85	0.798			
UV3	5.673 (1.349)	3.48	0.917			
UV4	5.527 (1.355)	2.71	0.877			
Hedonic value				0.889	0.919	0.694
HV2	5.764 (1.392)	2.30	0.823			
HV4	5.642 (1.339)	2.64	0.863			
HV5	4.818 (1.542)	2.15	0.835			
HV6	5.661 (1.399)	2.60	0.868			
HV8	5.309 (1.579)	1.80	0.774			
Cognitive engagement dimension				0.915	0.940	0.796
CED 1	4.333 (1.756)	2.59	0.866			
CED 2	4.606 (1.661)	3.24	0.901			
CED 3	5.036 (1.456)	3.68	0.924			
CED 4	4.600 (1.617)	2.57	0.878			
Behavioral engagement dimension				0.920	0.943	0.806
BED 1	5.139 (1.375)	2.84	0.886			
BED 2	5.224 (1.363)	2.44	0.853			

(continued)

Table 1. (*continued*)

Item	Mean (SD)	VIF	Loading	α	Composite Reliability	AVE
BED 3	5.200 (1.372)	3.90	0.922			
BED 4	5.145 (1.336)	3.12	0.887			
Emotional engagement dimension				0.910	0.937	0.788
EED 1	5.158 (1.302)	2.64	0.878			
EED 3	5.315 (1.274)	3.04	0.897			
EED 4	5.085 (1.355)	4.07	0.913			
EED 5	5.170 (1.421)	3.68	0.903			

In line with H4, H5 and H6, hedonic value is positively related to the cognitive ($\gamma = 0.764$, $p < 0.001$), behavioural ($\gamma = 0.636$, $p < 0.001$), and emotional ($\gamma = 0.477$, $p < 0.001$) engagement dimensions, thus confirming the three hypotheses. The coefficient of determination value (R^2) for cognitive (0.541), emotional (0.458), and behavioural (0.606) engagement dimensions represent a good value for behavioural research [24]. It was also used the blindfolding procedure to evaluate the relevance of exogenous variables to model performance. [24]. The results of StoneGeisser's blindfolding technique (Q^2) show that the cognitive ($Q^2 = 0.423$), emotional ($Q^2 = 0.349$) and behavioural ($Q^2 = 0.480$) engagement dimensions have satisfactory predictive relevince, since their value is far above 0 [53].

Table 2. Structural model estimates

Hypotheses	Path coefficient	CIs (bias corrected)	t-Value	F2	Supported
H1	-0.045	[−.189, .116]	0.578	0.002	No
H2	0.195	[.048, .348]	2.528	0.054	Yes
H3	0.259	[.087, .431]	2.968	0.070	Yes
H4	0.764	[.616, .888]	11.100	0.714	Yes
H5	0.636	[.471, .770]	8.317	0.577	Yes
H6	0.477	[.289, .640]	5.369	0.236	Yes

5 Discussions, Implications and Future Studies

This study aimed to disentangle the relationships between perceived hedonic and utilitarian values and consumer-brand cognitive, emotional, and behavioral engagement in gamified human-chatbot interactions. A research model grounded on the Means-Ends model by Woodruff and Gardial [62], was developed to test the hypothesised relationships based on Dessart et al. [14] and Hsu and Chen's [34] work.

Similar to other studies, such as the ones from Högberg et al. [30] and Żyminkowska [69], the utilitarian and hedonic values were predictors, and the three dimensions of consumer engagement were considered as criterion (dependent) variables.

Results show that both utilitarian and hedonic values were found to positively affect the emotional dimension of engagement. Reasonably, hedonic value was found to have a higher influence than the utilitarian value ($\beta = 0.259$), probably because of its strong relation to the subjective and emotional level of experience. In fact, as stated by Xi and Hamari [64], when using achievement-related features such as badges, points, and goals, it is easier to achieve emotional engagement because of the sense of winning a prize and thus experiencing an emotional winning state. Similarly, to what emerged with the emotional dimension, both utilitarian and hedonic values were found to be positively related to the behavioural dimension of engagement. According to previous findings, the latter was found to have a higher influence on the behavioural dimension of engagement than the utilitarian value ($\beta = 0.195$). These findings go along with Żyminkowska [69], who found that hedonic value, being an intrinsic characteristic, has a stronger effect than the utilitarian value on behavioural engagement, but are opposite to Yuan, Zhang and Wang [67] who found a higher effect of utilitarian value rather than hedonic value on intention to use artificial assistant, meaning that in a gamified humanchatbot interaction, although the means of the interaction is still task-driven (receiving a discount for a purchase), the role of the intrinsic aspects far outweighs the role of the extrinsic elements.

Interestingly, the current study pinpoints that the utilitarian value does not generate significant effects on the cognitive dimension of brand engagement, as contrary to what was expected, the extrinsic motivation and the cognitive dimension of engagement were not significantly related. Given that cognitively engaged users are supposed to be deeply engrossed in the interaction and to feel present and focused on the brand and its related attributes, and that cognitive engagement holds motivational components [50], the result suggests that only emotional factors (entertainment) and not instrumental factors such as having achieved the goal or the good economic (discount) value help users to feel cognitively engaged.

This study contributes to the marketing literature by providing an exploratory Means-End model to evaluate the values perceived in the interaction with a gamified chatbot and its impact on consumer-brand engagement. The study also advances the gamification literature, which is a fast-emerging topic, mainly applied for educational, health, or civic engagement purposes [49], which makes this investigation on consumer engagement with brands through a gamified chatbot particularly innovative.

The present study also contributes to the emerging literature on consumer engagement, as most studies have not yet considered the multidimensionality of consumer engagement and have not yet explored the relationship between consumer values and consumer engagement in human-chatbot interactions [69]. Unlike previous studies that considered engagement as a unidimensional construct [65], this study analysed engagement as a multidimensional concept including cognitive, emotional, and behavioural dimensions, which allows a more detailed and accurate knowledge of the phenomena compared to a unidimensional approach. Even though businesses are starting to understand the great potential that chatbots present to various activities, there are still no relevant studies on the effect of a gamified experience with a chatbot in an online business setting. In this respect, our study also advances knowledge on the literature concerning human-chatbot interactions. As chatbots have been mainly investigated and applied to support customer service [41], this study takes an innovative approach on the transformation of communication tools, as it recognizes the benefits of using a chatbot and gamified interactions to establish a communication that goes beyond providing mere customer assistance, but rather creates engagement and connection with brands.

The results of this study offer valuable insights for managers. To date, there is still no clear guidance for companies to understand the underlying mechanisms that enable gamified chatbots to effectively boost brand engagement. Thus, we hope to provide insights related to this matter, firstly by providing empirical evidence regarding how gamification could be practically designed to effectively improve brand engagement, and second by identifying the weight of both hedonic and utilitarian values in determining cognitive, emotional, and behavioral engagement. Overall, this study highlights the importance for managers and designers to apply gamification strategies for brand engagement purposes through chatbot interactions. In this perspective, our results open an opportunity for the development of co-branding strategies, capable of adding value and increasing competitiveness through gamified experience. However, not all businesses might fully benefit from using gamification strategies, and by being aware of this, practitioners should find new ways of sustaining consumer-brand engagement [51] and develop different gamified experiences, which ultimately could positively influence brand performance, increase the number of sales, and resistance to competitors offers [33]. With respect to consumer involvement in the products and WOM behavior (behavioral engagement), the entertaining component of the gamified experience has a higher weight compared to utilitarian and instrumental features. Similarly, when it comes to assessing cognitive engagement, intrinsic rather than extrinsic and more utilitaristic motivations prevail, that is, promoting discount alone will not contribute to the development of cognitive engagement unless pure enjoyment and emotional interest are provided. In this light, our results reinforce the shift from the usage of purely extrinsic marketing strategies based on material and monetary rewards, such as discounts, customer loyalty programs and membership systems, to a more hybrid approach of extrinsic and intrinsic motivational strategies.

We conclude the paper by exploring limitations and suggesting some possible avenues for future research. The first limitation of the study lies in the snowball sample, which is a non-probability randomized technique that, although making the sampling more accessible and easier for researchers to select a unit to represent a population, it reduces the possibility of statistical inferences from the sample to the population.

Then, the design of the chatbot consisted of a limited number of achievement-related game features. Using a higher number of game components might increase the gameful experience. The objective of this study includes an exploratory approach: the research was conducted using a cross-sectional design and correlational analysis that may inadequately capture causality. Future studies could apply an experiment with a factorial design to try and test the influence of each gamified feature on perceived values and dimensions of engagement. In addition, future research should delve deeper into examining additional experiential antecedents of consumer-brand engagement. As results showed that the cognitive dimension of engagement has no significant relationship with the utilitarian value, contrary to what happened with the emotional and behavioural dimensions, its interpretation suggests that not all customers might fully benefit from using gamification strategies, especially those who are more task-oriented and with a lower or no need to feel immersed in the gamified interaction. Future research could delve into this research question and find evidence of whether results differ according to the type of consumer (for example in terms of need for affect or need for cognition). We chose a category of products that could be considered of regular use and non-subject to cultural influences, which is a common practice in marketing papers that use experiments as a methodology [43]. Future research could address different kinds of services in new research contexts as there is potential to extend the proposed typology (gamified chatbot interaction) into different markets and firm contexts. Finally, we suggest co-branding strategies involving a real brand and its product and a gaming brand to be explored.

References

1. Araujo, T.: Living up to the chatbot hype: the influence of anthropomorphic design cues and communicative agency framing on conversational agent and company perceptions. Comput. Hum. Behav. **85**, 183–189 (2018)
2. Araujo, T.: Conversational agent research toolkit: an alternative for creating and managing chatbots for experimental research. Comput. Commun. Res **2**(1), 35–51 (2020)
3. Babin, B.J., Darden, W.R., Griffin, M.: Work and/or fun: measuring hedonic and utilitarian shopping value. J. Consum. Res. **20**(4), 644–656 (1994)
4. Babin, B.J., Lee, Y.K., Kim, E.J., Griffin, M.: Modeling consumer satisfaction and word-of-mouth: restaurant patronage in Korea. J. Serv. Mark. **19**(3), 133 (2005)
5. Batra, R., Ahuvia, A., Bagozzi, R.P.: Brand love. J. Mark. **76**(2), 1–16 (2012)
6. Berger, A., Schlager, T., Sprott, D.E., Herrmann, A.: Gamified interactions: whether, when, and how games facilitate self–brand connections. J. Acad. Mark. Sci. **46**(4), 652–673 (2017). https://doi.org/10.1007/s11747-017-0530-0
7. Carpenter, J.M., Moore, M., Fairhurst, A.E.: Consumer shopping value for retail brands. J. Fash. Mark. Manag. **9**(1), 43–53 (2005)
8. Chan, W.Y., To, C.K., Chu, W.C.: Materialistic consumers who seek unique products: how does their need for status and their affective response facilitate the repurchase intention of luxury goods? J. Retail. Consum. Serv. **27**, 1–10 (2015)
9. Cochoy, F., Hagberg, J.: Gamification in the History of Retailing. In Mikolaj M. Dymek P. Zackariasso, (Eds.), The Business of Gamification: A Critical Analysis (Ch. 5). Routledge (2016)
10. Cronin, J.J., Jr., Brady, M.K., Hult, G.T.M.: Assessing the effects of quality, value, and customer satisfaction on consumer behavioral intentions in service environments. J. Retailing **76**(2), 193–218 (2000)
11. Dastan, I., Geçti, F.: Relationships among utilitarian and hedonic values, brand affect and brand trust in the smartphone industry. J. Manage. Res. **6**(2), 124 (2014)

12. De Cicco, R., Iacobucci, S., Aquino, A., Alparone, F.R., Palumbo, R.: Understanding users' acceptance of chatbots: an extended TAM approach. In: Følstad, A., et al. (eds.) Chatbot Research and Design: 5th International Workshop, CONVERSATIONS 2021, Virtual Event, November 23–24, 2021, Revised Selected Papers, pp. 3–22. Springer International Publishing, Cham (2022). https://doi.org/10.1007/978-3-030-94890-0_1

13. De Moor, K., Berte, K., De Marez, L., Joseph, W., Deryckere, T., Martens, L.: User-driven innovation? Challenges of user involvement in future technology analysis. Sci. Publ. Policy **37**(1), 51–61 (2010)

14. Dessart, L., Veloutsou, C., Morgan-Thomas, A.: Capturing consumer engagement: duality, dimensionality and measurement. J. Mark. Manage **32**(5–6), 399–426 (2016)

15. Dorotic, M., Bijmolt, T.H.A., Verhoef, P.C.: Loyalty programmes: current knowledge and research directions. Int. J. Manage. Rev. **14**(3), 217–237 (2012)

16. Eisingerich, A.B., Marchand, A., Fritze, M.P., Dong, L.: Hook vs. hope: how to enhance customer engagement through gamification. Int. J. Res. Mark., **36**(2), 200–215 (2019)

17. Eppmann, R., Bekk, M., Klein, K.: Gameful experience in gamification: construction and validation of a Gameful experience scale [GAMEX]. J. Interact. Mark. **43**, 98–115 (2018)

18. Etemad-Sajadi, R., Ghachem, L.: The impact of hedonic and utilitarian value of online avatars on e-service quality. Comput. Hum. Behav. **52**, 81–86 (2015)

19. Fadhil, A., Villafiorita, A.: An adaptive learning with gamification and conversational UIs: the rise of CiboPoliBot. In: UMAP 2017 - Adjunct Publication of the 25th Conference on User Modeling, Adaptation and Personalization, Bratislava, Slovakia (2017)

20. Fornell, C., Larcker, D.F.: Structural equation models with unobservable variables and measurement error: algebra and statistics. J. Mark. Res. **18**(3), 382–388 (1981)

21. Fredricks, J.A., Blumenfeld, P.C., Paris, A.H.: School engagement: potential of the concept, state of the evidence. Rev. Educ. Res **74**(1), 59–109 (2004)

22. van der Goot, M.J., Pilgrim, T.: Exploring age differences in motivations for and acceptance of chatbot communication in a customer service context. In: Følstad, A., et al. (eds.) Chatbot Research and Design: Third International Workshop, CONVERSATIONS 2019, Amsterdam, The Netherlands, November 19–20, 2019, Revised Selected Papers, pp. 173–186. Springer International Publishing, Cham (2020). https://doi.org/10.1007/978-3-030-39540-7_12

23. Grüsser, S.M., Thalemann, R., Griffiths, M.D.: Excessive computer game playing: evidence for addiction and aggression? Cyberpsychol. Behav. **10**(2), 290–292 (2007)

24. Hair, Joseph F., Sarstedt, M., Ringle, C. M., Gudergan, S. P.: Advanced Issues in Partial Least Squares Structural Equation Modeling. Sage Publications, Thousand Oaks (2017)

25. Hamari, J.: Do badges increase user activity? A field experiment on the effects of gamification. Comput. Hum. Behav. **71**, 469–478 (2017)

26. Henseler, J., Hubona, G., Ray, P.A.: Using PLS path modeling in new technology research: updated guidelines. Ind. Manage. Data Syst. **116**(1), 2 (2016)

27. Henseler, J., Ringle, C.M., Sarstedt, M.: A new criterion for assessing discriminant validity in variance-based structural equation modeling. J. Acad. Mark. Sci. **43**(1), 115–135 (2014). https://doi.org/10.1007/s11747-014-0403-8

28. Hirschman, E.C., Holbrook, M.B.: Hedonic consumption: emerging concepts, methods and propositions. J. Mark. **46**(3), 92–101 (1982)

29. Hofacker, C.F., de Ruyter, K., Lurie, N.H., Manchanda, P., Donaldson, J.: Gamification and mobile marketing effectiveness. J. Interact. Mark. **34**, 25 (2016)

30. Högberg, J., Ramberg, M.O., Gustafsson, A., Wästlund, E.: Creating brand engagement through in-store gamified customer experiences. J. Retail. Consum. Serv. **50**, 122–130 (2019)

31. Holbrook, M.B.: Consumption experience, customer value, and subjective personal introspection: an illustrative photographic essay. J. Bus. Res. **59**(6), 714–725 (2006)

32. Hollebeek, L.D.: Demystifying customer brand engagement: exploring the loyalty nexus. J. Mark. Manage. **27**(7–8), 785–807 (2011). https://doi.org/10.1080/0267257X.2010.500132

33. Hollebeek, L.D., Glynn, M.S., Brodie, R.J.: Consumer brand engagement in social media: conceptualization, scale development and validation. J. Interact. Mark. **28**(2), 149–165 (2014)
34. Hsu, C.L., Chen, M.C.: How gamification marketing activities motivate desirable consumer behaviors: focusing on the role of brand love. Comput. Hum. Behav. **88**, 121–133 (2018)
35. Huang, M.-H., Rust, R.T.: A strategic framework for artificial intelligence in marketing. J. Acad. Mark. Sci. **49**(1), 30–50 (2020). https://doi.org/10.1007/s11747-020-00749-9
36. Huotari, K., Hamari, J.: A definition for gamification: anchoring gamification in the service marketing literature. Electron. Mark. **27**(1), 21–31 (2016). https://doi.org/10.1007/s12525-015-0212-z
37. Kvale, K., Freddi, E., Hodnebrog, S., Sell, O.A., Følstad, A.: Understanding the user experience of customer service chatbots: what can we learn from customer satisfaction surveys? In: Følstad, A., et al. (eds.) Chatbot Research and Design. LNCS, vol. 12604, pp. 205–218. Springer, Cham (2021). https://doi.org/10.1007/978-3-030-68288-0_14
38. Liebrecht, C., Sander, L., van Hooijdonk, C.: Too informal? How a chatbot's communication style affects brand attitude and quality of interaction. In: Følstad, A., et al. (eds.) Chatbot Research and Design. LNCS, vol. 12604, pp. 16–31. Springer, Cham (2021). https://doi.org/10.1007/978-3-030-68288-0_2
39. Miao, F., Holmes, W., Huang, R., Zhang, H.: AI and education: A guidance for policy- makers. UNESCO Publishing (2021)
40. Morschheuser, B., Hamari, J., Werder, K., Abe, J.: How to gamify? A method for designing gamification. In: Proceedings of the 50th Hawaii International Conference on System Sciences, Ha waii, United States, 4–7 January 2017
41. Mozafari, N., Weiger, W.H., Hammerschmidt, M.: Trust me, I'm a bot–repercussions of chatbot disclosure in different service frontline settings. J. Serv. Manage. **33**(2), 221–245 (2022)
42. Nacke, L.E., Deterding, S.: The maturing of gamification research. Comput. Hum. Behav. **71**, 450–454 (2017)
43. Nedungadi, P., Chattopadhyay, A., Muthukrishnan, A.V.: Category structure, brand recall, and choice. Int. J. Res. Mark. **18**(3), 191–202 (2001)
44. Nißen, M., et al.: See you soon again, chatbot? A design taxonomy to characterize user-chatbot relationships with different time horizons. Comput. Hum. Behav. **127**, 107043 (2022)
45. Overby, J.W., Lee, E.J.: The effects of utilitarian and hedonic online shopping value on consumer preference and intentions. J. Bus. Res. **59**(10–11), 1160 (2006)
46. Ringle, C., da Silva, D., Bido, D.: Structural equation modeling with the SmartPLS. Brazilian J. Mark. **13**(2), 56–73 (2015)
47. Ryu, K., Han, H., Jang, S.S.: Relationships among hedonic and utilitarian values, satisfaction and behavioral intentions in the fast-casual restaurant industry. Int. J. Contemp. Hosp. Manage. **22**(3), 416–432 (2010)
48. Schwartz, S.H., Bilsky, W.: Toward a universal psychological structure of human values. Jour. Personal. Soc. Psych. **53**(3), 550–562 (1987)
49. Seaborn, K., Fels, D.I.: Gamification in theory and action: a survey. Int. J. Hum. Comput. **74**, 14–31 (2015)
50. Shin, M., Back, K.J.: Effect of cognitive engagement on the development of brand love in a hotel context. J. Hosp. Tour. Res. **44**(2), 328–350 (2020)
51. Suh, A., Cheung, C.M.K., Ahuja, M., Wagner, C.: Gamification in the workplace: the central role of the aesthetic experience. J. Manage. Inf. Syst. **34**(1), 268–305 (2017)
52. Teo, T.S.H.: Demographic and motivation variables associated with Internet usage activities. Internet Res. Electron. Netw. App. Policy **11**(13), 125–137 (2011)
53. Thakur, R.: The role of self-efficacy and customer satisfaction in driving loyalty to the mobile shopping application. Int. J. Retail. Distrib. **46**(3), 283–303 (2018)

54. Van Doorn, J., et al.: Customer engagement behavior: theoretical foundations and research directions. J. Serv. Res. **13**(3), 253–266 (2010)

55. Venkatesh, V., Brown, S.A.: A longitudinal investigation of personal computers in homes: adoption determinants and emerging challenges. MIS Q. **25**(1), 71–98 (2001)

56. Verhagen, T., Boter, J., Adelaar, T.: The effect of product type on consumer preferences for website content elements: an empirical study. J Comput. Mediat. Commun. **16**(1), 139–170 (2010)

57. Verhagen, T., Swen, E., Feldberg, F., Merikivi, J.: Benefitting from virtual customer environments: an empirical study of customer engagement. Comput. Hum. Behav **48**, 340 (2015)

58. Vivek, S.D., Beatty, S.E., Dalela, V., Morgan, R.M.: A generalized multidimensional scale for measuring customer engagement. J. Mark. Theory Pract. **22**(4), 401–420 (2014)

59. Werbach, K., Hunter, D.: For the Win: How Game Thinking Can Revolutionize Your Business. (1st edn.). Wharton Digital Press, USA (2012)

60. Wirtz, J., et al.: Managing brands and customer engagement in online brand communities. J. Serv. Manage. **24**(3), 223–244 (2013)

61. Wolf, T., Weiger, W.H., Hammerschmidt, M.: Experiences that matter? The motivational experiences and business outcomes of gamified services. J. Bus. Res. **106**, 353–364 (2020)

62. Woodruff, R.B., Gardial, S.: Know Your Customer: New Approaches to Understanding Customer Value and Satisfaction. (1st edn.). Wiley, New York (1996)

63. Woodruff, R.B.: Customer value: the next source for competitive advantage. J. Acad. Mark. Sci. **25**(2), 139–153 (1997)

64. Xi, N., Hamari, J.: Does gamification affect brand engagement and equity? A study in online brand communities. J. Bus. Res. **109**, 449–460 (2020)

65. Xu, F., Buhalis, D., Weber, J.: Serious games and the gamification of tourism. Tour. Manage. **60**, 244–256 (2017)

66. Yang, Y., Asaad, Y., Dwivedi, Y.: Examining the impact of gamification on intention of engagement and brand attitude in the marketing context. Comput. Hum. Behav. **73**, 459 (2017)

67. Yuan, C., Zhang, C., Wang, S.: Social anxiety as a moderator in consumer willingness to accept AI assistants based on utilitarian and hedonic values. J. Retail. Consum. Serv. **65**, 102878 (2022)

68. Zarouali, B., Van den Broeck, E., Walrave, M., Poels, K.: Predicting consumer responses to a chatbot on Facebook. Cyberpsychol. Behav. Soc. Netw. **21**(8), 491–497 (2018)

69. Żyminkowska, K.: Hedonic and utilitarian drivers of customer engagement. Central Euro. Bus. Rev. **7**(4), 15–33 (2018)

Chatbots as Part of Digital Government Service Provision – A User Perspective

Nadia Abbas[1], Asbjørn Følstad[2](✉) ⓘ, and Cato A. Bjørkli[1] ⓘ

[1] Department of Psychology, University of Oslo, Forskningsveien 3A, 0373 Oslo, Norway
[2] SINTEF, Forskningsveien 1, 0373 Oslo, Norway
asf@sintef.no

Abstract. Chatbots are taken up as part of digital government service provision. While the success of chatbots for this purpose depends on these being accepted by their intended users, there is a lack of knowledge concerning user perceptions of such chatbots and the implications of these for intention to use. In response to this, an exploratory qualitative interview study was conducted with 15 users of a chatbot for municipality service provision. The interviews showed the importance of performance expectations, effort expectations, and trust. In particular, while a municipality chatbot supporting service triaging may be perceived as beneficial for their availability and to provide support navigation of municipality services and information, this benefit is compared by users to the benefit of other digital government channels. On the basis of the findings, we present key implications to theory and practice, and suggest avenues for future research.

Keywords: Chatbot · Digital government · Technology acceptance

1 Introduction

Chatbots are increasingly taken up by public sector administrations as a channel to provide information and services to citizens. This uptake of chatbots is part of the transformation to digital government, where public sector service provision is increasingly digitalized. The potential benefits of digital government include increased efficiency and cost-reduction, but also the opportunity to improve information and service provision and, thereby, citizen satisfaction [32]. Within governments, there is strategic push for broad uptake of digital services and particular concern for their human-centricity and availability of services [e.g., 13].

In this context, chatbots are seen as a promising complement to other digital government channels as they may be a low-threshold means for inquiry into government services [23]. This is particularly valuable given the complexity in government service provision, where relevant services span from policymaking, taxation, and law enforcement to social security, education, and healthcare [30]. Chatbots, interaction in the users' everyday language, may serve as a flexible means to help users identify needed information and services across a broad range of government service areas and service providers [27].

A. Følstad et al. (Eds.): CONVERSATIONS 2022, LNCS 13815, pp. 66–82, 2023.
https://doi.org/10.1007/978-3-031-25581-6_5

Successful digital government chatbots depends on substantial citizen uptake. This to ensure quality in content and prediction models and to realize the benefits of the investment. However, there is a lack of knowledge on how citizens perceive chatbots in digital government and, in turn, how these perceptions impact intention to use.

To address this knowledge gap, we present a qualitative exploratory interview study with users of a chatbot for municipality information services. The aim of the study was to investigate users' perceptions of, and intentions to use such a chatbot. The chatbot has been taken up by about 100 municipalities and is involved in about 1M yearly conversations on government information and services. The study was guided by theory on technology acceptance and contributes new knowledge on user perceptions of government chatbots in terms of performance expectations, effort expectations and trust – and how these perceptions impact intentions for future chatbot use.

2 Background

2.1 Digital Government

Digital government is a deep-rooted area of interdisciplinary research and development. The application of information technology to public sector service provision and may concern access to information, provision of transaction services, and facilitation of citizen participation [26]. The evolving of digital government is typically seen as a development towards more increased complexity and contextualization [18].

Gil-Garcia and Flores-Zuniga [15] note that the success of digital government depends on two key factors: How digitalization initiatives are implemented by government agency and how the digital services are taken up by users. Hence, user satisfaction, trust, ease of use, and usefulness are key factors determining digital government success. Likewise, Panagiotopoulos et al. [30] argue for the benefit of considering digital government from the perspective of public value creation, where improved digital government services are seen as better suited to satisfy those who consume them.

The drive towards public benefit of digital government is also seen in government policy documents. For example, the European Commission policy document on digital transformation in Europe, '2030 Digital Compass' [13], foresees human-centric digital public services where 100% of services are available online by 2030. Also, the United Nations E-Government survey 2022 [38] accentuates the importance of digital government to mitigate crises such as the COVID-19 pandemic.

2.2 Chatbots as Part of Digital Government

An increasing number of public sector administrations is taking up chatbots for digital information and service provision where chatbots are employed for a range of purposes such as city information services [40], social services [36], or as a general guide to government services [39].

Chatbots may provide information and support at different levels. Distinguish between service triage, service information gathering and analysis, and service negotiation. On the initial level of service triage, the chatbot provides generic information to anonymous users. On the second level of information gathering and analysis, the chatbot offer assistance on the basis of user profiles, such as public transport information in response to knowledge of the user location. On the top level of service negotiation, the chatbot offers access to transactional services [23, 24].

Androutsopoulo et al. [3] argue that chatbots are appropriate for a broad range of citizen interactions, characterized by ambiguity and complexity. At the same time, van Noordt and Misuraca [40] note that current government chatbots typically provides generic information to citizens reflecting service triage rather than service negotiation. Prospective users of government chatbots have been found to value accuracy, availability, efficiency, and effectiveness [25].

The ongoing covid pandemic has spurred increased interest in chatbots as a channel for information provision to citizens as the public need for support concerning covid-related advice and regulations has far outstripped available resources. Amiri and Karahanna [2] reviewed use cases of chatbots in public health responses, suggesting that chatbots may complement health workers, alleviate capacity constraints, and counter misinformation. Chatbots have also been piloted by government service providers to reduce negative mental health implications of the covid pandemic [44].

While chatbots may hold substantial value to public sector administrations and citizens, chatbot implementation has also led to controversy in cases where the chatbots have not been in line with public service values such as user-orientation, efficiency, adaptability, and trust [24]. Hence, it is critical for public sector administrations to understand both how implemented chatbots are perceived by their users and also the factors which may determine their sustained uptake.

2.3   User Perceptions of Chatbots and Usage Motivation

The study of chatbots in digital government can be informed by the rapidly growing body of knowledge on user perceptions and experiences of chatbots in general. User motivations for chatbot use is highly productivity driven and the pragmatic quality of chatbots seem to be key to how these are perceived by users [6, 14]. At the same time, designing for hedonic quality in chatbots – such as features to strengthen involvement and engagement – may be appreciated by users [17].

A common distinction between chatbots is a distinction between those oriented towards task completion, such as chatbots for information provision, and those oriented towards social interaction, such as companion chatbots and chatbots for social chatter [e.g., 10, 34]. The importance of pragmatic quality clearly is more important to task-oriented chatbots. However, it should be noted that the open character of chatbot interaction – where users are typically allowed to enter requests in free text – allows distinction between task-orientation and social orientation to blur. For example, users have been found to perceive chatbots as a channel more resembling interaction with a human than other channels [19], to respond positively to chatbots with characteristics resembling that of human conversationalists [4, 16], and to engage in collaborative interactions [20]. At the same time, the open character of chatbot interaction may cause users to hold unrealistic expectations of chatbot capabilities [22], which in turn may impact perceptions negatively [43].

In the current literature, user perceptions of chatbots have been studied from perspectives such as usefulness and ease of use [5], social support [7], and trust [31]. Usefulness and ease of use are seen as key aspects to determine chatbot uptake among users, in particular as studies suggests that users may struggle to get the expected benefit from implemented chatbots [1]. Social support may be of particular importance in some use-cases, such as health advice. However, the benefit of chatbots to address users in a supportive or empathic manner has been accentuated also for other domains [42].

Trust in chatbots is considered key to future uptake of chatbots – in particular for more advanced use-cases such as service negotiation. In the customer service domain, key drivers of trust in chatbots have been found to concern factors in the chatbot, such as expertise and responsiveness, factors in the context, such as brand recognition, and factors in the user, such as propensity to trust technology [29].

2.4 Technology Acceptance as Perspective to Understand Intention to Use

Technology acceptance [e.g., 11, 41] is a useful theoretical perspective for understanding users' uptake of chatbots in line with theory of planned behaviour. Here, intention to use is seen as determined by users' perceptions of key technology characteristics such as usefulness and ease of use [11].

Technology acceptance models have been widely used to investigate digital government solutions, typically as adaptations to the initial technology acceptance models adding constructs such as trust [9, 28], enjoyment [35], or access barriers [37]. Technology acceptance has also been shown as a valuable perspective to understand chatbot use [e.g., 12]. However, there is a lack of knowledge on how the different drivers of technology acceptance play out for chatbots in digital government.

To understand user perceptions of chatbots in digital government and the implications of these for chatbot uptake, the second version of the unified theory of technology acceptance and use of technology (UTAUT2) may be a suitable theoretical model. The model explains uptake of technology in a consumer context and therefore has a closer fit to the context of citizens' use of digital government than acceptance models addressing workplace technology [e.g., 11], and also contains a more comprehensive set of factors than technology acceptance models adapted to the public sector domain [e.g., 28, 35, 37]. In UTAUT2 [41], intention to use is determined by the six factors detailed below. In addition, UTAUT2 includes a seventh factor, price value, which is not considered relevant for free-of-charge chatbots in digital government.

(1) *Performance expectancy* and (2) *effort expectancy*, that is, users' perceptions of the usefulness and ease of use to be expected from the technology. These two factors are key in any model of technology acceptance and typically explain substantial variation in usage intention and use.

(3) *Social influence* and (4) *hedonic motivation*, that is, users' perceptions of attitudes and priorities of significant others as well as their perceptions of the engagement and experiential aspects of the technology. Hedonic motivation is particularly relevant for non-work-related technologies.

(5) *Facilitating conditions* and (6) *habit*: Facilitating conditions concerns technology availability or needed infrastructure to benefit from the technology. Habit concerns users' established patterns of use [41].

In line with foundational theory on technology acceptance, it is expected that usage intentions may be determined also by other factors than those included in a generic model [11]. Technology acceptance studies often have included additional factors, such as trust [e.g., 9, 28]. Furthermore, trust has been a topic of substantial interest in chatbot research [e.g., 21, 33]. Given the importance of trust and trustworthiness in digital government, trust is a highly relevant factor to include in technology acceptance studies for this domain. In the context of technology acceptance for government, trust is taken to concern trust in government and trust in the technology, and encompasses the integrity, security, and reliability of the digital government service [28].

3   Research Question

To allow for needed exploration of citizens' intention to use government chatbots, as their determining perceptions of such chatbots, the following research question was formulated:

How do citizens perceive government chatbots and how do these perceptions impact intention to use?

The research question allows for an exploratory investigation of factors included in theory technology acceptance, to understand how these play out in the context of government chatbots. Furthermore, the research question opens for consideration also of additional factors which may emerge as relevant.

4   Method

An exploratory qualitative approach was chosen to adequately address the research question. Specifically, we conducted a series of semi-structured interviews with citizens which had available a chatbot to support them in enquires towards their local municipality. This choice of method was considered adequate given the current limited knowledge concerning user perceptions of government chatbots. The interviews were based on the technology acceptance model UTAUT2 [41] and set up to explore determining factors from this model as well as other potentially relevant factors.

4.1   Participants and Recruitment

The study was conducted in a Norwegian government context, and participants were recruited from three different sized municipalities for which the same type of chatbot was offered. In total, 15 participants were recruited – five from each municipality. Recruitment was conducted through a national panel service provider, Norstat.

Participants were recruited to include both males and females and to reflect a broad range of occupations. Nine males and six females were recruited, with a median age of 44 years (min = 24, max = 66). All had experience from digital interaction with the municipality through email or website visits.

To ensure that all participants had sufficient recent experience with the municipality chatbot, they were requested to use the municipality chatbot at least two times in the week leading up to the interview, for at least three to five minutes each time. Participants were provided a list of possible topics which could represent relevant enquiries to the chatbot and informed that their use of the chatbot would be anonymous.

The research procedure was approved by the Norwegian Centre for Research Data (NSD). Participation in the study only followed informed consent where the participants were informed on the study purpose, their role, the use of study data, and their right to withdraw their consent and discontinue their participation any time.

4.2 The Municipality Chatbot – Kommune-Kari

The study involved a Norwegian chatbot, called Kommune-Kari, which is available to citizens in about 100 municipalities. The chatbot provides information on the municipality and relevant government services, and citizens may use it for enquiries either through the municipality website or through a dedicated smartphone app.

The chatbot provides information on a broad range of topics, ranging from health services and education to municipality infrastructure, planning and regulation. All use of the chatbot is anonymous, and the chatbot provides generic answers to citizens questions – either within the chatbot dialogues or through links to the municipality website or other resources. As such, the chatbot provides *service triage* according to the classification of Makasi et al. [23, 24].

The chatbot is based on an artificial intelligence language model and predicts users' intents on the basis of citizens' messages, that is, the assumed goals which the users' have in mind when entering the question. The breadth of municipality services and information require the chatbot to include 6000 such intents and corresponding actions. Users may also refine chatbot responses through selecting among buttons provided as part of chatbot replies. Due to the commonalities of service provision across municipalities, the chatbot is hosted by a service provider Prokom who provides needed AI training and content updates to the chatbot. The chatbot sees extensive use with about 1 million yearly conversations and is as such a useful context of this study, given its proven success in digital government service provision. The chatbot content is written in a conversational style, intended to be easily digestible by users while keeping up with public sector requirements for precision and quality. The chatbot appearance is a female cartoon avatar and the chatbot name also suggests a female character.

4.3 Interview Process

The interviews were semi-structured, following an interview guide with options for going into depth on relevant themes and reflections by the participants. The interview guide was set up with basis in key factors of UTAUT2: performance expectancy, effort expectancy, social influence, facilitating conditions, hedonic motivation, and habit. In addition, the interviewer asked the participants to detail their experiences with chatbots in general and the municipality chatbot, and also asked them to detail aspects concerning trust in the chatbot. The interview guide was designed so as to allow the participants to reflect freely on each topic and detail how and why each of the theoretical factors were seen as relevant with regard to the municipality chatbot and also prompted for explorations of additional factors or themes.

In preparation to the interviews, five pilot interviews were conducted which allowed for adjustment of the interview guide. The pilot interviews included participants recruited from the authors' personal networks.

The interviews were conducted online over the Zoom video application and lasted between 24 and 60 min. The interviews were audio recorded.

4.4 Analysis

All interview audio recordings were transcribed. The transcripts were then made subject to thematic analysis in line with the guidelines of Braun and Clarke [8], including the steps of (a) familiarizing with data, (b) generating initial codes, (c) searching for themes, (d) reviewing themes, (e) defining and naming themes, and (f) reporting.

The objective of the analysis was to establish data-driven themes associated with the theoretical constructs of UTAUT2; that is, to understand why and how the theoretical drivers were seen as relevant for intention to use the chatbot, as well as to identify any other relevant drivers or themes.

The thematic analysis was conducted by the first author and conducted in the analysis software nVivo. To strengthen quality in the analysis process, the analysis was made subject to critical reflection during analysis meetings involving one or both the co-authors at each step of the analysis process. Here, the authors collaboratively examined the analysis at its current state, e.g., for possible alternative interpretations of data or clarification of themes.

5   Results

In the following, we provide an overview of the key themes from the analysis. The themes are structured under the main factors of the applied technology acceptance mode and provides an overview of key findings from the interviews concerning the factors and how these may impact intention to use. The main factors are structured according to prevalence in the analysis, in the following order: Performance expectancy, effort expectancy, trust, hedonic motivation, habit, social influence, and facilitating conditions.

While the analysis is a qualitative exploration, it may be of relevance to the reader to know the proportions of the participants reporting on the different themes. We use the following phrases to provide information on such proportions of the participants: nearly all (13–15), most (8–12),,some (4–7), a few (1–3).

5.1 The Participants' Chatbot Experience and Intention to Use

All participants reported on prior experience with chatbots, and some also had experience with the municipality chatbot prior to their participation in the study. Most participants described their prior experiences with chatbots in general as being unsatisfactorily, where chatbots were reported not to be able to provide sufficient support. Most, however, also reported on the studied municipality chatbot to exceed their expectations. The participants noted that this was due to the chatbot being able to provide useful help on general questions. Most participants also noted that they intended to use the chatbot for future requests or as a means of navigating municipality service provision.

5.2 Performance Expectancy

The participants expectations on the chatbot performance, was closely associated with its ability to provide sufficiently nuanced and detailed support. The participant reports also show that usefulness expectations were key to their assessments of their own intention to use the chatbot in the future. The performance expectancies in the chatbot were discussed with regards to the foreseen purpose of chatbot use and the type of support needed. The participants also reflected on the possible usefulness of the chatbot from the perspective of the municipality.

Performance Expectancy Depends on Purpose of Use. Most participants reported to see the chatbot was a useful tool for navigating content in the municipality website. That is, by using the chatbot, information and services which otherwise could be difficult to access due to the complexity in public sector service provision was easily identified through the chatbot. This benefit of the chatbot as a tool for navigation seemed a consequence of participants acknowledging the challenge of navigating municipality information and services. As noted by one of the participants:

> "You can ask about relatively difficult things that are rarely asked about, but which [the chatbot] perhaps will be able to find faster if I cannot find it myself." (p2)

However, some participants noted such navigational use of the chatbot as redundant as it may be possible to find needed information also by other means such as browsing the municipality website or using general search engines such as Google. As noted in this example quote:

> "I feel that the things I ask [the chatbot] are the same links which I had been able to identify myself" (p9).

Performance Expectancy Depends on Type of Support Needed. Most participants reported that their view on chatbot performance depended on the complexity and personal character of requests. Most noted that the chatbot could only respond to general questions and not provide, e.g., answers adapted to their personal situation. In consequence, some participants specifically noted positive performance expectations for general requests with a specific answer:

> "It is useful when it comes to simple things. Useful in the form of concrete things which are not nuanced" (p13)

However, most participants reported low performance expectations for personal, subjective or complex questions. For such questions, the chatbot could be seen as an unneeded intermediary, as illustrated by this quote:

"When I write 'when do you pick up paper garbage at my address' [the chatbot] could have responded 'this is Thursdays of such and such week', instead of 'here is the garbage pickup calendar'" (p2)

Taking the Municipality Perspective. During the interviews, some participants also alluded to the potential usefulness chatbots may have seen from the perspective of the municipality. For example, participants noted that the chatbot may reduce the number of calls to the municipality and may also provide insight into what kind of information is needed. At the same time, some made note of the possible trade-off inherent in the uptake of chatbots, and that automating service provision could ultimately reduce human contact with the municipality. As exemplified in the following:

"It may distance you from the municipality. [...] It may be a statical, dead thing you interact with instead of a municipality representative. But so be it, as those in the municipality likely have better things to do than answer questions which a bot might answer" (p3).

5.3 Effort Expectancy

The promise of available and efficient information provision was seen as a key driver for intention to use the chatbot. We detail the participants reflections on this relative to the importance of efficient interactions and, also, its 24/7 availability.

The Importance of Efficient Interactions. Given that the chatbot was seen as particularly useful to facilitate navigation and get answers to simple questions, efficient interactions were reported as key to the participants usage intentions.

Most participants noted the initiating of chatbot interaction to be fast and easy, as it was directly available from any municipality webpage. Some, however, noted that the threshold for initiating use would be further lowered by making the chatbot initiation even more prominent, e.g., by moving the initiation icon from the bottom right corner of the screen to the top or to centre stage.

"If [the chatbot] is only available as the small icon in the corner, I would rather use Google, in contrast to [the chatbot] being available on top" (p4)

The efficiency of the actual interactions was discussed by most participants, and was reported to depend on a range of aspects such as the chatbot's ability to handle typos and dialect terms. The participants also noted it as important for them to understand how to pose questions to be most likely to get a relevant response, such as to refrain from very long messages. A few participants mentioned that it can be challenging to know exactly which words to use, while others noted it as a strength that the chatbot is tolerant in understanding different ways of phrasing a request. Efficiency in use was by most seen as one of the main drivers for future use, as in the following example:

"[Ease of use] means a lot. That it is precise, simple, and that you get the needed answers. It does not take many experiences of not getting an answer before 'no, I will just move on and to this the old way'". (p13)

A few participants also noted that simple closing or dismissal, as provided in the chatbot, was important to efficient use. In particular as this lowers the threshold for trying to use the chatbots for simple questions and requests.

24/7 Availability. For some participants, the availability of a chatbot was important to perceptions of effort expectancy. For example, as a substitute to get simple clarifications – in particular outside office hours. As exemplified in this quote:

> *"Concretely, if I had questions outside office hours, I would use it. Then it is useful."* (p1).

5.4 Trust

Trust in the chatbot was reported by the participants as important to their future use of the chatbot. This trust was in part associated with their trust in the municipality and in part due to aspects of the chatbot such as performance and efficiency.

Trust in the Chatbot Dependent on Trust in the Municipality. Most participants reported that their trust in the chatbot is closely dependent on their trust in the municipality as a responsible actor. Hence, they expected the chatbot to be professional and reliable. As noted by one of the participants:

> *"This is public information from the municipality, so I assume that it is correct"* (p5).

Trust Dependent on Performance and Efficiency. When reflecting on aspects of the chatbot of importance to trust, a few participants noted the importance of chatbot performance and efficiency. That is, trust in the chatbot – apart from its association with the municipality as a trusted actor – was seen as depending on the chatbot delivering value on these two aspects. In particular, participants appreciated means to help them confirm performance and efficiency. As noted in this example quote:

> *"I liked the closed loop communication with [the chatbot saying] 'did you mean this or that?'. This provides a confirmation that my question is understood."* (p15)

Privacy of Lesser Perceived Relevance in a Chatbot for Anonymous Use. While privacy often is seen as important for trust in digital technology, the character of the chatbot as provider of navigation aid and support with simple, general questions, implied that the participants did not see any major privacy issues. Hence, privacy was not considered of substantial relevance for this chatbot.

5.5 Hedonic Motivation

Hedonic motivation concerns the chatbot's ability to engage or provide experiences of emotional character. This factor was seen as of lesser importance to the participants' intention to use the chatbot. However, some aspects were nevertheless reported which may strengthen the hedonic quality of the chatbot use, including hedonic implications of pragmatic aspects of chatbot use, as well as implications of the conversational style and use of human likeness in the chatbot.

Hedonic Implications of Performance and Efficiency. Some participants noted that the pragmatic aspects of the chatbot could also serve to strengthen their sense of engagement from the interaction. For example, it was noted that the chatbot feature for refining answers – where users are provided buttons with alternatives paths to the further interaction – may give insight into municipality relevant content and services which might be unknown to them and, thereby, be seen as stimulating or engaging. Likewise, some participants noted that their sense of having an efficient interaction with the chatbot could also be perceived as a form of engagement, from their appreciation of easily address different topics and rapidly get to needed information. Also, the some noted that the chatbot seeking confirmation as part of its responses, to ensure a fit to users' intents, was seen as nurturing a sense of engagement.

> *"If I go through the municipality, I need to go through different links and spend time looking. With [the chatbot], I can just search 'garbage-collection' and get it served. It is so much easier. It will be fun. It is fun."* (p7)

Some participants noted that the hedonic implications of performance and efficiency also implied that lack of performance and efficiency would be harmful to engagement, potentially leading to frustration.

Hedonic Implications of Conversational Style and Human Likeness. Some participants reflected on the conversational style and visual appearance of the chatbot. For some, an informal style and humanlike avatar image and name was see as contributing positively to the chatbot interaction being engaging. However, others were critical of these same features. The participant reports, hence, suggests marked differences between participants in how conversational style and chatbot appearance is perceived.

5.6   Habit

For a government chatbot to become an effective channel of information and support, it is important that citizens form a habit to use it. The participants reported on life situation, awareness, and chatbot quality to determine habit of use.

Awareness and Chatbot Quality Determine Habit Formation. Forming a habit to use the chatbot depends on awareness of its existence as well as its perceived performance and required effort. These aspects of habit formation were noted as particularly important as chatbots are a relatively novel technology, and all users may not be aware of what the chatbot can be used for, and also that the value of chatbot use depends on it being efficient and effective to use. As noted by one of the participants:

> *"If it is faster for me to find the needed information without using [the chatbot], I will not use it. It needs to have a time-saving function."* (p2)

Life Situation Determines Habit Formation. Some participants noted that life situation will be important for actual habit to form. In some life situations, such as for young adults, the need to get in touch with the municipality may be low – which directly will impact habit. However, following major life changes, needs may change. In these situations, it will be important to be aware of the chatbot to form habit.

5.7 Social Influence and Facilitating Conditions

The participants also reflected on social influence and facilitating conditions as potential drivers of use for the municipality chatbot. None of these were seen as highly important to future use, but the participants nevertheless provided interesting reflections on both.

Social influence was reflected on as a potential driver of future use, provided that important others or professional marketers were to recommend the chatbot for municipality use. None of the participants had experienced such social influence, but some noted the possible impact of social influence provided they had not themselves already used the chatbot. A few participants also noted that increased visibility of the chatbot in the municipality webpage would be a more efficient way to have citizens use the chatbot than social influence.

Facilitating conditions was seen as of lesser importance to the participants intention to use. They discussed the intention to use the chatbot as depending on available other channels. Some reported to likely use the chatbot as a faster means of gathering information available also on the municipality website, whereas others would use the chatbot as a last resort. Likely, the ease of accessing the chatbot and availability of technical infrastructure may have made this factor of lesser relevance to the partners. A few, however, expressed that their intention to use is strengthened by the chatbot being available as a smartphone app – further accentuating the importance of availability and efficiency in interaction for future use.

6 Discussion

6.1 Citizen Perceptions of Government Chatbots and Implications for Intention to Use

The study findings provide a rich source of insight into user perceptions of government chatbots, as well as how such perceptions may impact intention to use. Key among the factors were performance expectancy and effort expectancy. This finding is fully in line with existing theory of technology acceptance [e.g., 11, 41], and also in line with the findings of a recent vignette study of government chatbot usage scenarios [25].

In the current context of digital government where chatbots are an alternative channel to information and support – paralleled with information provided on government websites – the benefit of a government chatbot is not that it is a necessary point of access, but that it is a potential aid to make access easier and more efficient. Furthermore, as the habit-forming potential of a government chatbot may be limited, as government service use may be dependent on, for example, life situation, citizens may have low threshold for not using the chatbot if it does not clearly provide the expected performance to the least possible effort.

The findings indicate that users may see substantial benefit in government chatbots used for purposes of navigating available information and services, as well as for simple requests. Chatbots for this purpose corresponds to what Makasi et al. [23, 24] refers to as service triaging, where the chatbot has a retrieval-based model where user requests are mapped to predefined responses without access to user profiles. Such chatbots may serve as a point of departure for conversational digital government, and perceived benefits for this purpose is promising for future more advanced chatbot solutions.

The findings also show the potential benefit of chatbots as a channel for efficient provision of information and services in digital government. Efficiency in use is important for government services, as such services may be seen as having a utilitarian character. At the same time, the request for efficient interactions represents a substantial challenge to government chatbots for service triaging as it will continuously be compared to other available channels for information or support. Hence, it will be important for government chatbots not just to provide information and support in an effective manner, but also in a manner more efficient that other channels.

In addition to performance and effort expectancies, trust was identified as an important determinant of future intention to use. As previously observed [9, 28], trust in digital government may depend both on trust in the technology and trust in the government institution using the technology. This was found also for the use of government chatbots in our study where participants explicitly associated their trust in the chatbot with the municipality as a known and trusted actor. Likewise, trust in the chatbot was also reported to depend on its performance and efficiency in use. This complements current applications of trust as part of technology acceptance models [9, 28], as we found trust in the technology to be dependent on other drivers of technology adaption rather than orthogonal to these other drivers.

Hedonic value, habit, social support, and facilitating conditions were interestingly found to be of lesser importance to the participants intention to use the municipality chatbot than performance expectations, effort expectations, and trust. This to some extent is counter to our initial assumption that UTAUT2, with its comprehensive set of drivers for technology acceptance, would be a best possible starting point for understanding intention to use government chatbots. The original technology acceptance model [11], tailored to workplace technology use and only including constructs corresponding to performance expectancy and effort expectancy, clearly would have been too restricted given the importance also of trust found in our study. At the same time, UTAUT2, tailored to explain technology acceptance in a consumer context, may possibly include constructs of lesser relevance for the government context. It, hence, seems as if existing attempts to extend the original technology acceptance model toward public sector by including trust as a separate factor [e.g., 9, 28] may be as relevant to explain government chatbots as the later, more comprehensive UTAUT2 model.

6.2 Implications

The study findings entail important implications for theory and practice. We see the following as particularly relevant for theory building:

- Intention to use chatbots as part of digital government may be particularly determined by user expectations of performance and effort, as well as trust in the technology and the relevant government body. Hence, future adaptations of technology acceptance models may benefit from taking these three constructs as a starting point for future theory building.

- Performance and effort expectancies with the chatbot were typically made with reference to the chatbot as part of the larger digital service system including also the municipality website and personnel resources. Theorizing on user perceptions and intentions to use chatbots in digital government need to incorporate a service system perspective to fully capture the impact of this context.

The following are considered particularly relevant implications for practice:

- Chatbots for service triage [23, 24] is found to provide value to citizens. However, in line with the participants' pointing out of limitations to performance expectancy, it will be important to consider how government chatbots can advance also to personalized service negotiation to increase their public value.
- Intention to use a government chatbot for service triage is highly dependent on the chatbot being seen as more efficient than other channels for the same purpose. Hence, service providers need to make sure that that chatbot not only provides relevant answers but that it does so with least possible user effort.

6.3   Limitations and Future Research

The study is an exploratory qualitative study to gain initial knowledge on user perceptions of chatbots in digital government and how these may impact intention to use. As such, the study entails some limitations which suggests possible directions for future research.

The study was conducted in a specific context with only one chatbot; a chatbot for Norwegian municipalities. This characteristic of the study was beneficial to allow for in-depth insight, but also represent a limitation as it does not cover chatbots in an international context nor chatbots from different providers at different levels of sophistication. Future research is needed to gather insight into potential implications of such variation.

The study was conducted at a single point in time, not following chatbot users over a longer timeframe. Furthermore, the users were requested to use the chatbot as part of the recruitment procedure to ensure sufficient recent experience. This limits the study findings as we cannot make claims of how user perceptions and intentions to use may vary over time, or whether there may be differences between planned and spontaneous use. We anticipate future longitudinal studies following users over longer periods of time to understand how their government chatbot use evolve.

Finally, the study was based on the participants self-reports only. While this allowed for participants self-reflection on their perceptions and intentions to use, it did not enable contrasting of participant reflections with their actual behaviour. It will be highly interesting to see future research combining users' self-reports and logs from user chatbot interactions to better understand the correspondence between user perceptions and actual use.

In spite of these limitations, we find the study to represent a useful first step towards understanding user perceptions and intentions to use government chatbots. Hopefully, our study findings motivate needed future research in this engaging field of research.

Acknowledgements. The study was supported in part by the Research Council of Norway grant no. 270940, in part by the EC H2020 grant no. 101004594, ETAPAS.

References

1. Adam, M., Wessel, M., Benlian, A.: AI-based chatbots in customer service and their effects on user compliance. Electron. Mark. **31**(2), 427–445 (2020). https://doi.org/10.1007/s12525-020-00414-7
2. Amiri, P., Karahanna, E.: Chatbot use cases in the Covid-19 public health response. J. Am. Med. Inform. Assoc. **29**(5), 1000–1010 (2022)
3. Androutsopoulou, A., Karacapilidis, N., Loukis, E., Charalabidis, Y.: Transforming the communication between citizens and government through AI-guided chatbots. Gov. Inf. Q. **36**(2), 358–367 (2019)
4. Araujo, T.: Living up to the chatbot hype: the influence of anthropomorphic design cues and communicative agency framing on conversational agent and company perceptions. Comput. Hum. Behav. **85**, 183–189 (2018)
5. Ashfaq, M., Yun, J., Yu, S., Loureiro, S.M.C.: I, Chatbot: modeling the determinants of users' satisfaction and continuance intention of AI-powered service agents. Telematics Inform. **54**, 101473 (2020)
6. Brandtzaeg, PBae, Følstad, A.: Why people use chatbots. In: Kompatsiaris, I., Cave, J., Satsiou, A., Carle, G., Passani, A., Kontopoulos, E., Diplaris, S., McMillan, D. (eds.) INSCI 2017. LNCS, vol. 10673, pp. 377–392. Springer, Cham (2017). https://doi.org/10.1007/978-3-319-70284-1_30
7. Brandtzæg, P.B., Skjuve, M., Kristoffer Dysthe, K.K., Følstad, A.: When the social becomes non-human: young people's perception of social support in chatbots. In: Proceedings of the 2021 CHI Conference on Human Factors in Computing Systems, paper no. 257. ACM, New York (2021)
8. Braun, V., Clarke, V.: Using thematic analysis in psychology. Qual. Res. Psychol. **3**(2), 77–101 (2006)
9. Carter, L., Bélanger, F.: The utilization of e-government services: citizen trust, innovation and acceptance factors. Inf. Syst. J. **15**(1), 5–25 (2005)
10. Chen, H., Liu, X., Yin, D., Tang, J.: A survey on dialogue systems: recent advances and new frontiers. ACM SIGKDD Explor. Newsl. **19**(2), 25–35 (2017)
11. Davis, F.D.: Perceived usefulness, perceived ease of use, and user acceptance of information technology. MIS Q. 319–340 (1989)
12. De Cicco, R., Iacobucci, S., Aquino, A., Romana Alparone, F., Palumbo, R.: Understanding users' acceptance of chatbots: an extended TAM approach. In: Følstad, A., et al. (eds.) CONVERSATIONS 2021. LNCS, vol. 13171, pp. 3–22. Springer, Cham (2022). https://doi.org/10.1007/978-3-030-94890-0_1
13. European Commission: 2030 Digital Compass: the European Way for the Digital Decade. Communication from the Commission (2021). https://ec.europa.eu/info/strategy/priorities-2019-2024/europe-fit-digital-age/europes-digital-decade-digital-targets-2030_en
14. Følstad, A., Brandtzaeg, P.B.: Users' experiences with chatbots: findings from a questionnaire study. Qual. User Exp. **5**(1), 1–14 (2020). https://doi.org/10.1007/s41233-020-00033-2
15. Gil-Garcia, J.R., FloresZúñiga, M.Á.: Towards a comprehensive understanding of digital government success: integrating implementation and adoption factors. Gov. Inf. Q. **37**(4), 101518 (2020)
16. Go, E., Sundar, S.S.: Humanizing chatbots: the effects of visual, identity and conversational cues on humanness perceptions. Comput. Hum. Behav. **97**, 304–316 (2019)
17. Haugeland, I.K.F., Følstad, A., Taylor, C., Bjørkli, C.A.: Understanding the user experience of customer service chatbots: an experimental study of chatbot interaction design. Int. J. Hum. Comput. Stud. **161**, 102788 (2022)

18. Janowski, T.: Digital government evolution: from transformation to contextualization. Gov. Inf. Q. **32**(3), 221–236 (2015)
19. Laban, G.: Perceptions of anthropomorphism in a chatbot dialogue: the role of animacy and intelligence. In: Proceedings of the 9th International Conference on Human-Agent Interaction, pp. 305–310. ACM, New York (2021)
20. Laban, G., Araujo, T.: Working together with conversational agents: the relationship of perceived cooperation with service performance evaluations. In: Følstad, A., et al. (eds.) CONVERSATIONS 2019. LNCS, vol. 11970, pp. 215–228. Springer, Cham (2020). https://doi.org/10.1007/978-3-030-39540-7_15
21. Lee, M., Frank, L., IJsselsteijn, W.: Brokerbot: a cryptocurrency chatbot in the social-technical gap of trust. Comput. Supported Cooper. Work (CSCW) **30**, 79–117 (2021)
22. Luger, E., Sellen, A.: "Like having a really bad PA" the gulf between user expectation and experience of conversational agents. In: Proceedings of CHI 2016, pp. 5286–5297. ACM, New York (2016)
23. Makasi, T., Nili, A., Desouza, K.C., Tate, M.: A typology of chatbots in public service delivery. IEEE Softw. **39**(3), 58–66 (2021)
24. Makasi, T., Nili, A., Desouza, K., Tate, M.: Chatbot-mediated public service delivery: a public service value-based framework. First Monday **25**(12) (2020)
25. Makasi, T., Nili, A., Desouza, K., Tate, M.: Public service values and chatbots in the public sector: reconciling designer efforts and user expectations. In: Proceedings of the 55th Hawaii International Conference on System Sciences, pp. 2334–2343. University of Hawai'i, Manoa (2022)
26. Marchionini, G., Samet, H., Brandt, L.: Digital government. Commun. ACM **46**(1), 25–27 (2003)
27. Mygland, M.J., Schibbye, M., Pappas, I.O., Vassilakopoulou, P.: Affordances in human-chatbot interaction: a review of the literature. In: Dennehy, D., Griva, A., Pouloudi, N., Dwivedi, Y.K., Pappas, I., Mäntymäki, M. (eds.) I3E 2021. LNCS, vol. 12896, pp. 3–17. Springer, Cham (2021). https://doi.org/10.1007/978-3-030-85447-8_1
28. Nemeslaki, A., Aranyossy, M., Sasvári, P.: Could on-line voting boost desire to vote?–Technology acceptance perceptions of young Hungarian citizens. Gov. Inf. Q. **33**(4), 705–714 (2016)
29. Nordheim, C.B., Følstad, A., Bjørkli, C.A.: An initial model of trust in chatbots for customer service—findings from a questionnaire study. Interact. Comput. **31**(3), 317–335 (2019)
30. Panagiotopoulos, P., Klievink, B., Cordella, A.: Public value creation in digital government. Gov. Inf. Q. **36**(4), 101421 (2019)
31. Przegalinska, A., Ciechanowski, L., Stroz, A., Gloor, P., Mazurek, G.: In bot we trust: a new methodology of chatbot performance measures. Bus. Horiz. **62**(6), 785–797 (2019)
32. Robertson, S.P., Vatrapu, R.K.: Digital government. Ann. Rev. Inf. Sci. Technol. **44**(1), 317–364 (2010)
33. Seitz, L., Bekmeier-Feuerhahn, S., Gohil, K.: Can we trust a chatbot like a physician? A qualitative study on understanding the emergence of trust toward diagnostic chatbots. Int. J. Hum. Comput. Stud. **165**, 102848 (2022)
34. Shevat, A.: Designing Bots: Creating Conversational Experiences. O'Reilly Media, Sebastopol (2017)
35. Shyu, S.H.P., Huang, J.H.: Elucidating usage of e-government learning: a perspective of the extended technology acceptance model. Gov. Inf. Q. **28**(4), 491–502 (2011)
36. Simonsen, L., Steinstø, T., Verne, G., Bratteteig, T.: "I'm disabled and married to a foreign single mother". Public service chatbot's advice on citizens' complex lives. In: Hofmann, S., et al. (eds.) ePart 2020. LNCS, vol. 12220, pp. 133–146. Springer, Cham (2020). https://doi.org/10.1007/978-3-030-58141-1_11

37. Sipior, J.C., Ward, B.T., Connolly, R.: The digital divide and t-government in the United States: using the technology acceptance model to understand usage. Eur. J. Inf. Syst. **20**(3), 308–328 (2011)

38. United Nations: E-Government Survey 2022. The Future of Digital Government. UN Report. https://publicadministration.un.org/en/Research/UN-e-Government-Surveys

39. Valverde, M.S.D.R., Vasconcelos, A.F.F.C.: Chatbot in the online provision of government services. In: CAPSI 2019 Proceedings (2019). https://aisel.aisnet.org/capsi2019/41

40. van Noordt, C., Misuraca, G.: New wine in old bottles: chatbots in government. In: Panagiotopoulos, P., et al. (eds.) ePart 2019. LNCS, vol. 11686, pp. 49–59. Springer, Cham (2019). https://doi.org/10.1007/978-3-030-27397-2_5

41. Venkatesh, V., Thong, J.Y., Xu, X.: Consumer acceptance and use of information technology: extending the unified theory of acceptance and use of technology. MIS Q. 157–178 (2012)

42. Xu, A., Liu, Z., Guo, Y., Sinha, V., Akkiraju, R.: A new chatbot for customer service on social media. In: Proceedings of the 2017 CHI Conference on Human Factors in Computing Systems, pp. 3506–3510. ACM, New York (2017)

43. Zamora, J.: I'm sorry, Dave, I'm afraid I can't do that: chatbot perception and expectations. In: Proceedings of the 5th International Conference on Human Agent Interaction, pp. 253–260. ACM, New York (2017)

44. Zhu, Y., Janssen, M., Wang, R., Liu, Y.: It is me, chatbot: working to address the COVID-19 outbreak-related mental health issues in China. User experience, satisfaction, and influencing factors. Int. J. Hum.–Comput. Interact. **38**(12), 1182–1194 (2022)

Understanding the Intention to Use Mental Health Chatbots Among LGBTQIA+ Individuals: Testing and Extending the UTAUT

Tanja Henkel(✉) , Annemiek J. Linn , and Margot J. van der Goot

Amsterdam School of Communication Research (ASCoR), Nieuwe Achtergracht 166, 1018 WV Amsterdam, The Netherlands
t.henkel@uva.nl

Abstract. This empirical study aims to test and extend the unified theory of acceptance and use of technology (UTAUT) in the context of mental health chatbot usage among LGBTQIA+ individuals. The proposed model uses UTAUT variables (performance expectancy, effort expectancy and social influence) as well as chatbot-related variables (willingness to self-disclose, perceived loss of privacy, and trust) to predict the intention to use a mental health chatbot. The online survey (N = 305) indicates that performance expectancy, social influence, and willingness to self-disclose positively predict chatbot usage intention, whereas effort expectancy negatively influences this intention. Moreover, previous experience with healthcare chatbots moderated the relationship between social influence and intention, age moderated the relationship between willingness to self-disclose and intention, and gender identity moderated the relationship between perceived loss of privacy and intention. Overall, the extended UTAUT proved to be useful in explaining technology acceptance of mental health chatbots among the LGBTQIA+ community.

Keywords: Technology acceptance · Mental health chatbots · UTAUT · LGBTQIA+ community

1 Introduction

Mental health chatbots —empathic agents using natural language processing (NLP) to detect and reframe cognitive patterns of users [23]— offer great potential for individuals who suffer from mental health issues but lack access to treatments or are ashamed of their problems [1]. This is because chatbots are always available, easily accessible, cost-effective, offer a non-judgmental space and show both infinite patience as well as immediate feedback [15]. First studies testing applications such as Wysa [64] or Woebot [63] show promising results regarding the effectiveness of mental health chatbots in reducing feelings of stress [38], anxiety [21] and depression [20].

A widely used model to predict people's intention to use technology is the unified theory of acceptance and use of technology (UTAUT) [60, 61]. This model combines several variables derived from the technology acceptance model [17] and the theory of planned behavior [2] and has been used and adopted in numerous contexts [11, 45, 56, 62, 66]. There are at least two current-day trends that the UTAUT needs to be adapted to. First, the traditional UTAUT cannot fully explain the intention to use mental health chatbots as it neglects crucial chatbot-specific aspects like privacy, trust, and individuals' willingness to self-disclose to a chatbot. Second, research explaining technology acceptance has traditionally included gender as a dichotomous variable, whereas we now live in a society where boundaries are increasingly blurred between male, female, non-binary, transgender, and genderfluid identities [8, 9, 12, 13]. Thus, models should take these differential gender categories into account.

The LGBTQIA+ (Lesbian, Gay, Bi, Trans, Queer or Questioning, Intersex, Asexual and other sexual orientations (+)) community could particularly benefit from mental health chatbots. Research has repeatedly shown that this group runs a higher risk of developing a mental illness compared to heterosexual individuals [18, 50, 54, 65] since they still face bullying, harassment and violence [50]. At the same time, LGBTQIA+ individuals often lack the necessary social support and psychological assistance to understand their feelings and inclinations or are ashamed to seek help themselves [50]. Consequently, LGBTQIA+ users distinguish themselves in terms of technology use, because they have a heightened need for a safe, non-judgemental (online) space. Especially when they do not receive enough support from their family or friends, they more often use technologies and online platforms to search for like-minded individuals and other types of support. Also, they generally have a stronger urge for anonymity and therefore potentially a higher willingness to disclose to a chatbot [41]. Hence, this paper aims to answer the overarching research question to what extent the (extended) UTAUT can predict the behavioral intention to use a mental health chatbot among LGBTQIA+ individuals. To be able to test our hypotheses, as well as to answer the more explorative research questions, we chose a survey design. In doing so this study will provide a new perspective on the inclusion of chatbot-specific variables and gender identities into traditional communication models such as the UTAUT.

2   Theoretical Background

2.1   The UTAUT

The UTAUT was initially proposed by Venkatesh and colleagues [60]. In developing this model, the authors combined concepts from eight user acceptance models, among others the technology acceptance model [14, 17], the theory of reasoned action [19] and the innovation diffusion theory [49]. This way, Venkatesh et al. [60] created a unified and theory-based model that predicts user acceptance. According to the original UTAUT, three core variables predict the behavioral intention (BI) to use a certain technology: Performance Expectancy (PE; i.e., how useful one thinks the technology will be), Effort Expectancy (EE; i.e., how easy one expects the technology to be) and Social Influence (SI; whether one believes that one's social environment thinks one should use the technology). Moreover, in the UTAUT, these three relationships are moderated by age, previous experience with the technology (not for PE), gender [59] and voluntariness of use [60]. In the current study, the updated variable for gender is included in the extended model, and voluntariness of use is omitted because in the current study it is a constant (i.e., our research focuses on the voluntary usage of mental health chatbots [7]). Thus, the UTAUT hypotheses are:

H1: PE positively influences BI to use a mental health chatbot among the LGBTQIA+ community and this relationship is moderated by (a) age.

H2: EE positively influences BI to use a mental health chatbot among the LGBTQIA+ community and this relationship is moderated by (a) age and (b) previous experience.

H3: SI positively influences BI to use a mental health chatbot among the LGBTQIA+ community and this relationship is moderated by (a) age and (b) previous experience.

2.2 Extending the Model: Willingness to Self-disclose, Perceived Loss of Privacy, Trust and Gender Identity

Willingness to Self-Disclose. We define WSD as the willingness of LGBTQIA+ individuals to entrust personal information to a mental health chatbot [15]. It has been suggested that mental health chatbots can be highly beneficial for self-disclosure because they provide an anonymous space without stigmatizing the user [3]. This is in line with studies that indicate high WSD to an empathic chatbot [10, 25, 32, 58]. Lucas and colleagues found that participants showed less fear of self-disclosure, more intense expressions of emotions, and overall, a higher WSD with a computer system as opposed to a human operator [37]. On the other hand, the lack of human empathy might decrease people's willingness to disclose personal information [15]. In any case, it is logical to assume that the higher the WSD, the higher the intention to use a mental health chatbot.

Moderations. We expect the effect of WSD on Behavioral Intention (BI) to be stronger for younger compared to older LGBTQIA+ individuals because younger people are often more familiar with modern technology and therefore more likely to entrust personal information to a mental health chatbot [51]. To our knowledge, previous research did not yet explore the moderating role of previous experience and gender identity in the relation between WSD and BI. Therefore, the present study answers the following research questions and tests one hypothesis.

H4: WSD positively influences BI to use a mental health chatbot among the LGBTQIA+ community.

H4a: The relationship between WSD and BI is moderated by age, such that the effect is stronger for younger LGBTQIA+ individuals than for older LGBTQIA+ individuals.

RQ1: To what extent does previous experience with chatbots moderate the relationship between WSD and BI?

RQ2: To what extent does gender identity moderate the relationship between WSD and BI?

Perceived Loss of Privacy. Perceived loss of privacy (LOP) is defined as the extent to which individuals think smart healthcare services such as mental health chatbots violate their privacy [36, 57]. In mobile health applications, where people disclose sensitive data, privacy is an important aspect to consider. One study did not find LOP to be a significant direct predictor of BI [36]. However, other studies did find a negative, direct effect of LOP on the acceptance of chatbot applications [35, 44].

Moderations. An explanation of these mixed findings can be found in people's level of experience with technology. Privacy concerns decrease with more Internet experience [5] which is in line with the findings of Bergström, who found that with most Internet situations, experienced people were less concerned [6]. Regarding the moderating effect of age, previous research has been inconclusive. Some studies found no differences due to research measurements [26, 55] or only small significant differences with younger people being more concerned about privacy [6]. Guo and colleagues found that the effect of privacy concerns on BI is stronger for younger users, whereas older users were not affected [24]. In contrast, Shehaan proposed different user typologies, with older consumers being more alarmed in contrast to younger users [53]. Accordingly, we test the following hypotheses and aim to answer the following research questions:

H5: LOP negatively influences BI.

H5a: The relationship between LOP and BI is moderated by experience, such that the effect is stronger for less experienced (compared to more experienced) LGBTQIA+ individuals.

RQ3: To what extent does age moderate the relationship between LOP and BI?

RQ4: To what extent does gender identity moderate the relationship between LOP and BI?

Trust. Trust in a chatbot is defined as the degree to which LGBTQIA+ individuals perceive mental health chatbots as dependable, reliable, and trustworthy in improving one's mental health [36]. Trust is a crucial factor for establishing strong bonds with someone and has been shown to be equally important when it comes to human-computer interactions [15, 34]. Several studies indicate that trust is an antecedent for BI [36, 48].

Moderations. Schroeder and Schroeder investigated factors that influence trust in chatbots and found that individuals who are more experienced with chatbots and who are younger are more likely to trust a chatbot [51]. Simultaneously, transgender individuals often seek social support online [41]. Considering this unmet need and high online presence, transgender individuals may perceive mental health chatbots more positively, which in turn might increase their trust to use such a chatbot. To our knowledge, no study has yet examined how gender identity moderates the relation between trust and BI. Therefore, we expect and propose the following:

H6: Trust positively influences BI.

H6a: The relationship between Trust and BI is moderated by age, such that the effect is stronger for younger (compared to older) LGBTQIA+ individuals.

H6b: The relationship between Trust and BI is moderated by experience, such that the effect is stronger for more experienced (compared to less experienced) LGBTQIA+ individuals.

RQ5: To what extent does gender identity moderate the relationship between trust and BI?

The proposed extension of the UTAUT to the context of mental health chatbot acceptance among the LGBTQIA+ community is depicted in Fig. 1.

3 Method

3.1 Sampling

Ethical approval was granted by the university's Ethics Review Board (project ID: 2021-PC-14159). The questionnaire was created in English to reach LGBTQIA+ individuals of different nationalities. We used purposive convenience sampling by sharing the survey on the first author's social media as well as posting a recruitment text in relevant LGBTQ+ Facebook groups and Reddit threads. Also, flyers with the survey QR code were spread at a Dutch university. Eligible participants were individuals older than 16 years who (potentially) identify as LGBTQIA+. Participation was completely voluntary and anonymous. Respondents were not compensated. Because of the length of the questionnaire (~10 min), the dropout rate was quite high (32,18%). In total, 354 valid responses were gathered. However, four respondents did not give consent, sixteen participants did not consider themselves as part of the LGBTQIA+ community, and four respondents were aged below 16. These respondents, together with those who did not pass the attention check (n = 28), were excluded from the data set. Additionally, we omitted one case whose answers indicated zero variance (straight liner). This leaves a final sample of N = 305 participants.

3.2 Pretest

The questionnaire was pre-tested with eight LGBTQIA+ individuals. Pre-testers indicated difficulties with imagining what a mental health chatbot would look like. We therefore included a screen recording of an existing mental health chatbot application (Wysa). In the 1 min 42 s video, respondents saw an interaction with Wysa, during which the chatbot explains the importance of mental resilience and sends motivational GIFs (graphics interchange format – a series of pictures that can be static or dynamic [22]) and empathetic messages. Furthermore, participants saw which answer options are provided for the user (pre-selected or typing freely) and how a conversation with a mental health chatbot works in general.

3.3 Procedure

Data were collected between 9th–17th December 2021. Participants who clicked on the survey link or scanned the QR code were exposed to the information letter in the survey tool Qualtrics. Afterwards, participants gave informed consent. If participants did not give consent, they were automatically led to the end of the survey. All participants who agreed to the research terms were asked whether they consider themselves part of the LGBTQIA+ community. This question served to the exclusion of heterosexual and cisgender individuals. Next, respondents indicated their gender identity, age, level of education, mental health, and previous experience with chatbots. Respondents saw a short description and examples of chatbots, and were asked how often they have used these different types of chatbots in the past. Subsequently, we described the concept of a mental health chatbot and showed the video. After that, participants were exposed to the items concerning PE, EE, SI, BI, LOP, trust and WSD.

3.4 Measurements

Appendix 1 provides an overview of the original items and adjusted items. PE, EE, SI and BI were adapted from Venkatesh and colleagues' validated and widely tested scales [60]. Participants' WSD to a chatbot was adapted from Croes and Antheunis [15]. The scales for perceived LOP and trust were adapted from Liu and Tao [36]. All latent constructs were measured on a 7-point Likert scale ranging from 1 (Strongly Disagree) to 7 (Strongly Agree). Appendix 2 shows (very) high Cronbach's α values as well as M and SD of the main variables.

Age was measured with an open text entry and recoded into three groups (1 SD below average, average, and 1 SD above average).

Previous experience with chatbots was measured with the question: "How often have you used one of these chatbots in the past?" For customer service chatbots, healthcare chatbots, social messaging chatbots and other chatbots, respondents indicated their previous experience on a 5-point Likert scale ranging from "Never" to "A lot of times (>20 times)".

Gender identity was measured with the question: "Which of the following most likely describes you?" Participants could choose between "Female", "Male", "Non-binary", "Transgender", "Intersex", "Queer or Questioning", "I prefer not to say" and a text field for individual specification.

Level of education was measured with the question "What is the highest degree or level of education you have completed?", ranging from "No schooling completed" to "Doctoral or equivalent level".

Respondents also had to indicate whether they coped with mental health issues and, if so, whether they received professional help. Lastly, one attention check item ("Please click on 'Agree'") was included between the items addressing BI to check whether respondents paid attention throughout the questionnaire.

3.5 Analysis

Data analyses were carried out in SPSS. To describe the sample, a frequency analysis was conducted. By creating a scatterplot and histogram of the residuals, the assumptions of linearity and homoscedasticity were checked. Afterward, all predictors and moderators were mean-centered. This simplifies the interpretation of interaction effects: all coefficients account for respondents who score average on the predictor variables. Subsequently, interaction variables were created to test moderation effects. All hypotheses, the moderating role of previous experience on the relationship between WSD and BI, and the moderating role of age in the relationship between LOP and BI were tested with regression analyses. First, the traditional UTAUT variables were included as independent variables (PE, EE, SE). Second, age and experience were added as interaction variables. Third, we included the new variables WSD, LOP, trust, and the interaction variables (WSD, LOP, trust, and gender identity). This enabled a comparison between the initial UTAUT and the extended model. To answer the RQs with gender identity, dummy variables for gender identity were created (i.e., female, male, trans, non-binary) with female participants as the reference group. Next, a linear regression model was conducted, in which only PE, EE, SI, WSD, LOP, trust, the dummy variables for males, trans and non-binary individuals, and lastly the interaction variables for the respective predictor*gender identity effects were included.

4 Results

4.1 Sample Characteristics

Appendices 3 and 4 show the sample characteristics. Ages ranged from 16 to 59 years ($M = 24.69$; $SD = 7.28$). For gender identity, the largest category was female (43,60%, $n = 133$). 10,80% specified their gender identity in a separate text field. There, common answers were "Agender", "Genderfluid" and "Questioning". When it comes to previous experience with chatbots, respondents had the most experience (= used a chatbot very often, often or sometimes) with customer service chatbots (39,70%) and social messaging chatbots (22,60%), followed by healthcare chatbots (7,60%). Furthermore, most participants coped with mental health issues without receiving professional help (39,70%). Remarkably, only 12,80% stated to not cope with mental health issues at all. Regarding respondents' level of education, the largest category was "completed upper secondary level" (34,80%).

4.2 Model Fit and Hypothesis Testing

Main Effects. The extended regression model with BI to use a mental health chatbot as dependent variable, with PE, EE, SI, WSD, LOP and Trust as independent variables and with age and previous experience as moderators was significant, $F(31, 304) = 20.17$, $p < .001$, and explained 69,60% of variance in BI to use a mental health chatbot. It also demonstrated a slightly better fit than the initial UTAUT, where only PE, EE and SI were considered as predictors, $F(16, 304) = 35.91$, $p < .001$, $R^2 = 66.60\%$ (see Appendix 5). The extended regression model can therefore be used to predict the BI to use a mental health chatbot among the LGBTQIA+ population.

Only the effects for PE, EE, SI and WSD were significant. PE showed a significant, strong association with BI ($b = 0.67$, $t = 11.70$, $p < .001$, 95% CI [0.56, 0.79]). This indicates that people who believe that a mental health chatbot will help them increase their mental wellbeing, have a higher intention to use a mental health chatbot. Similarly, SI, $b = 0.18$, $t = 3.29$, $p = .001$, 95% CI [0.07, 0.28] showed a significant, weak association with BI. Hence, people who are more influenced by their social environment have a higher intention of using one. WSD showed a significant, weak association with BI ($b = 0.21$, $t = 3.69$, $p < .001$, 95% CI [0.10, 0.32]). We therefore found support for H1, H3 and H4.

Surprisingly, EE showed a weak, negative relationship (b = -0.14, t = -2.40, p = .017, 95% CI [0.08, 0.29]), which is opposed to what we expected. This indicates that, the more people perceive a mental health chatbot as easy to use, the lower is their intention to use such a chatbot. We therefore reject H2. Further, the results show that LOP ($b = 0.03$, $t = 0.91$, $p = .362$, 95% CI [-0.04, 0.11]) and Trust ($b = -0.03$, $t = -0.42$, $p = .672$, 95% CI [-0.14, 0.09]) are no significant predictors of chatbot usage. Thus, H5 and H6 were rejected.

Moderating Effects. In terms of interaction effects, we found only three weak, significant interaction effects. Firstly, the effect of SI on BI is moderated by previous experience with healthcare chatbots ($b = -0.16$, $t = -2.14$, $p = .033$, 95% CI [-0.31, -0.01]). This means that the effect of SI on BI becomes weaker the more experience LGBTQIA+ individuals have with healthcare chatbots. However, this is only the case for previous experience with healthcare chatbots. Previous experience with customer service or messaging chatbots were no significant moderators. Thus, we found partial support for H3b.

Secondly, the effect of WSD on BI seems to be very weakly moderated by age ($b = -0.02$, $t = -2.43$, $p = .016$, 95% CI [-0.04, -0.004]). As hypothesized, the effect is stronger for younger compared to older LGBTQIA+ individuals. H4a was therefore supported.

Thirdly, the relationship between LOP and BI was significantly and weakly moderated by gender identity, where the effect seems to be stronger for male individuals ($b = 0.19$, $t = 2.09$, $p = .037$, 95% CI [0.01, 0.36]) than for females (RQ4).

All other interactions turned out to be insignificant, which means H1a, H2a, H2b, H3a, H5a, H6a and H6b are rejected. In addition, previous experience with a chatbot is not a significant moderator for the relationship between WSD and BI (RQ2), and we did not find support for any other moderating effects of gender identity (RQ3, RQ4, RQ5). Figure 1 shows the significant relationships in the extended model.

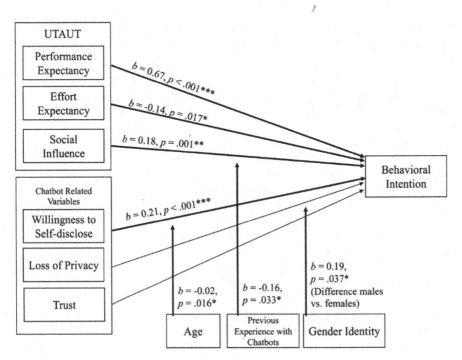

Fig. 1. Significant relationships in the extended model

5 Discussion

This study aimed to take a critical perspective on the UTAUT by exploring whether it can be tested and extended in the context of mental health chatbot usage intention among LGBTQIA+ individuals. Through integrating the chatbot-specific variables willingness to self-disclose (WSD), perceived loss of privacy (LOP), and trust, and by considering gender identity, we were able to demonstrate that the extended UTAUT provides a better understanding of mental health chatbot usage intention among LGBTQIA+ individuals than the original model. Our findings do not only contribute to more inclusive technology acceptance models and the generalizability of the UTAUT, but also give valuable insights into which aspects influence the intention to use a mental health chatbot among LGBTQIA+ individuals.

In the current survey, performance expectancy (PE), Social Influence (SI) and WSD significantly predicted behavorial intention (BI) to use a mental health chatbot. Unsurprisingly, PE has shown to be the strongest positive predictor. PE has repeatedly been an important predictor for technology acceptance in previous research [3, 56, 60]. Hence, the belief that a mental health chatbot would improve their mental health seems to be a crucial driver for the BI to use a mental health chatbot among LGBTQIA+ individuals and should be highlighted in future chatbot interventions. Additionally, in line with prior research, the more a LGBTQIA+ individual believes that their social environment thinks they should use a mental health chatbot (SI), the higher is their BI [56, 62]. This effect seems to be stronger for less experienced people, which means that particularly when individuals have little experience, their social environment can have a significant impact on their BI to use a mental health chatbot. It is worth noting that the effect of SI on BI was very weak and, considering the strong community feeling of LGBTQIA+ individuals, we expected this effect to be stronger. Especially since a study by Fish and colleagues demonstrated that emotional and mental health topics were the most popular themes discussed in a chat-based Internet community support programme [18], thus LGBTQIA+ individuals are generally willing to discuss mental health problems with their peers. It might be that the usage of mental health chatbots is not as widespread as online communities [41] and that therefore SI is less important for the BI to use mental health chatbots. Overall, for future interventions, developers should emphasize the potential benefits mental health chatbots have to improve mental health issues among LGBTQIA+ individuals. In addition, social influence and community aspects should be taken into account, and people's willingness to self-disclose should also be considered as a crucial determinant for mental health chatbot usage intention.

We did not expect the negative relationship between effort expectancy (EE) and BI. The easier the usage of a mental health chatbot seems, the lower is LGBTQIA+ individuals' intention to use it. This negative direction is contradicting existing literature. Some studies found a significant relationship [3, 29, 61, 62] and others did not find a significant association due to common use of the technology under study [56]. However, all studies demonstrated a positive relation instead of a negative one. One explanation for the current findings can be that our results show a high mean EE, which suggests that many participants perceived a mental health chatbot as easy to use anyway. Another possible explanation could be that one of the contextual variables were suppressing the effect of EE since it only became significant when the other variables were added.

Surprisingly, two chatbot-related variables -perceived loss of privacy and trust- were no significant predictors of chatbot usage intention. Especially the results regarding trust do not align with prior research. For Liu and Tao, for instance, trust was the strongest predictor for BI to use a smart healthcare system [36]. Other studies have established trust as a crucial antecedent for chatbot acceptance [43, 44]. A plausible explanation could be that LOP and trust did not directly affect BI to use a mental health chatbot, but indirectly via WSD. Schroeder and Schroeder found that trust positively influences WSD to a chatbot [51]. Similarly, lower privacy concerns seem to increase trust in chatbots [24]. Since WSD directly influenced BI, future studies may consider LOP as antecedent of trust, and trust as predictor of WSD rather than direct predictors of BI.

Moreover, this paper emphasized the importance of including gender identity into the UTAUT. Interestingly, the study did not find support for substantial differences among gender identities. Apparently, LGBTQIA+ regardless of their gender identity, perceive mental health chatbots equally, even though transgender and non-binary individuals show a higher online behavior compared to female or male individuals [41]. Only the effect of LOP on BI was stronger for males than females. This is interesting, as prior research on online behavior revealed that women are more concerned about their privacy [27, 53]. But then again, gender differences measured with non-LGBTQIA+ samples may deviate from our sample. The present findings would suggest that future mental health interventions for LGBTQIA+ individuals do not need to consider different factors for respective gender identities —except stressing privacy protection more among male individuals—, but this seems overly simplistic. The blurring boundaries between gender identities that prevail in our current-day society do ask for an increased attention to this in chatbot research, especially when the technology relates to mental health.

In line with previous research, this study shows that age is a factor to keep taking into account. While the relationship between WSD and BI remains equal for older LGBTQIA+ individuals, younger individuals have a higher intention to use a mental health chatbot when their WSD is also high. However, our sample was quite young (Ø 24 years) and the amount of participants age > 40 years was rather limited. Thus, future research needs to pay more explicit attention to the age factor.

5.1 Limitations and Future Research

One major issue regarding the survey was that participants did not interact with a mental health chatbot themselves. Unfortunately, it was not feasible to develop a properly functioning mental health chatbot in the available time frame, and using existing chatbots like Wysa would have created privacy issues by involving third parties. At the same time, 92% of the participants had never or rarely used a mental health chatbot before, and thus must have had a hard time imagining such an interaction, which could have led to imprecise answers. This problem was already raised during the pre-test, which is why we included a screen recording of a mental health chatbot conversation. Yet, we had no control over whether participants actually watched this video.

Secondly, actual usage of mental health chatbots was not included as a dependent variable. A follow-up study could let participants test a mental health chatbot and, at the end of the study, provide a link to the chatbot application free for them to use. Measuring the click rate may reveal insights into the actual usage of the chatbot and lead to more precise results.

Lastly, as this research topic has not been researched in depth so far, researchers should consider applying a qualitative research design to gain an in-depth understanding of LGBTQIA+ individuals' thoughts on mental health chatbots. Interestingly, especially on reddit, the recruitment text for this study caused elaborate discussions about whether individuals would use such chatbot or not (Tables 1, 2, 3, 4 and 5).

Appendix 1

Table 1. Operationalization of predictors and behavioral intention

Variable	Items as used in previous literature [15, 36, 60]	Adjusted items used in the current study
Performance expectancy [60]	PE1: I would find the system useful in my job PE2: Using the system increases my productivity PE3: Using the system enables me to accomplish tasks more quickly PE4: If I use the system, I will increase my chances of getting a raise	PE1: I would find such a mental health chatbot useful in my daily life PE2: Using such a mental health chatbot would improve my mental health PE3: Using such a mental health chatbot would help me to improve my mental health more quickly PE4: Using such a mental health chatbot improves my mental well-being
Effort expectancy [60]	EE1: Learning to operate the system is easy for me EE2: My interaction with the system would be clear and understandable EE3: I would find the system easy to use EE4: It would be easy for me to become skilful at using the system	EE1: Learning how to use such a mental health chatbot is easy for me EE2: My interaction with such a mental health chatbot would be clear and understandable EE3: I would find such a mental health chatbot easy to use EE4: It would be easy for me to become skilful at using such a mental health chatbot
Social influence [60]	SI1: People who are important to me think that I should use the system SI2: People who influence my behavior think that I should use the system SI3: In general, the organization has supported the use of the system SI4: The senior management of this business has been helpful in the use of the system	SI1: People who are important to me think that I should use such a mental health chatbot SI2: People who influence my behavior think that I should use such a mental health chatbot SI3: In general, my social environment would support the use of such a mental health chatbot

(*continued*)

Table 1. (*continued*)

Variable	Items as used in previous literature [15, 36, 60]	Adjusted items used in the current study
Willingness to self-disclose [15]	WSD1: During the conversation I was able to share personal information about myself WSD2: During the conversation I felt comfortable sharing personal information WSD3: During the conversation it was easy to share personal information WSD4: During the conversation I felt that I could be open	WSD1: I feel I could share personal information about myself with such a mental health chatbot WSD2: I feel I would be comfortable sharing personal information with such a mental health chatbot WSD3: I feel it would be easy to share personal information with such a mental health chatbot WSD4: I feel that I could be open during a conversation with such a mental health chatbot WSD5: How likely are you to confide in an anonymous chatbot for mental health issues?
Perceived loss of privacy [36]	LOP1: I am concerned that smart healthcare services will collect too much personal information from me LOP2: I am concerned that smart healthcare services will use my personal information for other purposes without my authorization LOP3: I am concerned that smart healthcare services will share my personal information with other entities without my authorization	LOP1: I am concerned that such a mental health chatbot will collect too much personal information from me LOP2: I am concerned that such a mental health chatbot will use my personal information for other purposes without my authorization LOP3: I am concerned that such a mental health chatbot will share my personal information with other entities without my authorization
Trust [36]	TRU1: Smart healthcare services are dependable TRU2: Smart healthcare services are reliable TRU3: Overall, I can trust smart healthcare services	TRU1: Such a mental health chatbot is dependable TRU2: Such a mental health chatbot is reliable TRU3: Overall, I can trust such a mental health chatbot
Behavioral intention [60]	BI1: I intent to use the system in the next <n> months BI2: I predict I would use the system in the next <n> months BI3: I plan to use the system in the next <n> months	BI1: I intend to use such a mental health chatbot in the future BI2: I will try to use such a mental health chatbot in my daily life BI3: I plan to use such a mental health chatbot frequently

Appendix 2

Table 2. Eigenvalues, explained variance, Cronbach's α, means and standard deviation of main variables

Variable	Eigenvalue	% of Variance	Cronbach's α	Mean	SD
Performance expectancy	3.43	85.65%	.94	4.12	1.43
Effort expectancy	2.69	67.34%	.83	5.23	1.11
Social influence	2.22	73.98%	.81	3.44	1.23
Willingness to self-disclose	3.94	78.82%	.93	4.10	1.62
Loss of privacy	2.78	92.60%	.96	4.81	1.70
Trust	2.25	74.88%	.83	4.16	1.31
Behavioral intention	2.73	91.13%	.95	3.37	1.55

Note. Factor analysis with direct oblimin rotation was used; M and SD refer to the mean variables

Appendix 3

Table 3. Characteristics of the sample (N = 305)

Characteristics	N (%)
Age	
16–23	157 (51,5%)
24–30	89 (29,2%)
31–35	37 (12,2%)
36–40	10 (3,3%)
>40	12 (3,8%)
Gender Identity	
Male	67 (22,0%)
Female	133 (43,6%)
Non-Binary	54 (17,7%)
Transgender	13 (4,3%)
Intersex	0 (0%)
Other	33 (10,8%)
Level of Education	
No schooling completed	3 (1,0%)
Lower secondary level	31 (10,2%)

(continued)

Table 3. (*continued*)

Characteristics	N (%)
Upper secondary level	106 (34,8%)
Vocational training	13 (4,3%)
Bachelor's or equivalent	96 (31,5%)
Master's or equivalent	36 (11,8%)
Doctoral or equivalent	6 (2,0%)
Other	9 (3,0%)
Mental Health Issues	
Yes, receive professional help	94 (30,8%)
Yes, do not receive professional help	121 (39,7%)
No	39 (12,8%)
I am not sure	51 (16,7%)

Appendix 4

Table 4. Frequency distribution for previous experience with chatbots (N = 305)

Type of Chatbot	Never	Rarely	Sometimes	Often	Very often
Customer service chatbots	82 (26,9%)	102 (33,4%)	97 (31,8%)	17 (5,6%)	7 (2,3%)
Healthcare chatbots	224 (73,4%)	58 (19,0%)	15 (4,9%)	6 (2,0%)	2 (0,7%)
Social messaging chatbots	152 (49,8%)	84 (27,5%)	46 (15,1%)	12 (3,9%)	11 (3,6%)

Appendix 5

Table 5. Comparison of regression models to predict BI of mental health chatbot usage

	Behavioral intention to use mental health chatbots	
	UTAUT model	Extended model
Constant	3.36***	3.35***
Performance expectancy	0.75***	0.67***
Effort expectancy	−0.08	−0.14*
Social influence	0.25***	0.18**
Willingness to self-disclose		0.19**
Perceived loss of privacy		0.04
Trust		−0.01
R^2	0.67	0.70
F	35.91***	20.17***

Note. * $p < .05$, ** $p < .01$, *** $p < .001$

References

1. Abd-alrazaq, A.A., Alajlani, M., Alalwan, A.A., Bewick, B.M., Gardner, P., Househ, M.: An overview of the features of chatbots in mental health: a scoping review. Int. J. Med. Informatics **132**, 103978 (2019)
2. Ajzen, I.: The theory of planned behavior. Organ. Behav. Hum. Decis. Process. **50**(2), 179–211 (1991)
3. Almahri, F.A.J., Bell, D., Merhi, M.: Understanding student acceptance and use of chatbots in the United Kingdom universities: a structural equation modelling approach. In: 2020 6th International Conference on Information Management (ICIM) (2020)
4. Barak, A., Gluck-Ofri, O.: Degree and reciprocity of self-disclosure in online forums. Cyberpsychol. Behav. **10**(3), 407–417 (2007)
5. Bellman, S., Johnson, E.J., Kobrin, S.J., Lohse, G.L.: International differences in information privacy concerns: a global survey of consumers. Inf. Soc. **20**(5), 313–324 (2004)
6. Bergström, A.: Online privacy concerns: a broad approach to understanding the concerns of different groups for different uses. Comput. Hum. Behav. **53**, 419–426 (2015)
7. Brandtzaeg, P.B., Følstad, A.: Why people use chatbots. In: Kompatsiaris, I., et al. (eds.) INSCI 2017. LNCS, vol. 10673, pp. 377–392. Springer, Cham (2017). https://doi.org/10.1007/978-3-319-70284-1_30
8. Carpenter, M.: The human rights of intersex people: addressing harmful practices and rhetoric of change. Reprod. Health Matters **24**(47), 74–84 (2016)
9. Carpenter, C.S., Eppink, S.T., Gonzales, G.: Transgender status, gender identity, and socioeconomic outcomes in the United States. ILR Rev. **73**(3), 573–599 (2020)
10. Chaix, B., et al.: When chatbots meet patients: One-year prospective study of conversations between patients with breast cancer and a chatbot. JMIR Cancer **5**(1), e12856 (2019)

11. Chang, I.C., Hwang, H.G., Hung, W.F., Li, Y.C.: Physicians' acceptance of pharmacokinetics-based clinical decision support systems. Expert Syst. Appl. **33**(2), 296–303 (2007)
12. Chazin, D., Klugman, S.: Clinical considerations in working with clients in the coming out process. Pragmat. Case Stud. Psychother. **10**(2), 132–146 (2014)
13. Cheung, A.S., et al.: Non-binary and binary gender identity in Australian trans and gender diverse individuals. Arch. Sex. Behav. **49**(7), 2673–2681 (2020)
14. Chocarro, R., Cortiñas, M., Marcos-Matás, G.: Teachers' attitudes towards chatbots in education: a technology acceptance model approach considering the effect of social language, bot proactiveness, and users' characteristics. Educ. Stud. 1–19 (2021)
15. Croes, E.A.J., Antheunis, M.L.: 36 questions to loving a chatbot: Are people willing to self-disclose to a chatbot? In: Chatbot Research and Design, pp. 81–95 (2021)
16. D'Alfonso, S.: AI in mental health. Curr. Opin. Psychol. **36**, 112–117 (2020)
17. Davis, F.D.: Perceived usefulness, perceived ease of use, and user acceptance of information technology. MIS Q. **13**(3), 319–339 (1989)
18. Fish, J.N., et al.: Q chat space: assessing the feasibility and acceptability of an Internet-based support program for LGBTQ youth. Prevention Sci. **23**, 130–141 (2021)
19. Fishbein, M., Ajzen, I.: Belief, Attitude, Intention and Behavior: An Introduction to Theory and Research. Addison-Wesley, Reading (1975)
20. Fitzpatrick, K.K., Darcy, A., Vierhile, M.: Delivering cognitive behavior therapy to young adults with symptoms of depression and anxiety using a fully automated conversational agent (Woebot): a randomized controlled trial. JMIR Mental Health **4**(2), e19 (2017)
21. Fulmer, R., Joerin, A., Gentile, B., Lakerink, L., Rauws, M.: Using psychological artificial intelligence (Tess) to relieve symptoms of depression and anxiety: randomized controlled trial. JMIR Mental Health **5**(4), e64 (2018)
22. *GIF\Definition, Meaning, & Facts*. Encyclopedia Britannica (n.d.). https://www.britannica.com/technology/GIF
23. Goklani, B.: Chatbots in healthcare: top benefits, risks and challenges you need to know. Mindinventory, 15 September 2021. https://www.mindinventory.com/blog/chatbots-in-health care/
24. Guo, X., Zhang, X., Sun, Y.: The privacy–personalization paradox in mHealth services acceptance of different age groups. Electron. Commer. Res. Appl. **16**, 55–65 (2016)
25. Ho, A., Hancock, J., Miner, A.S.: Psychological, relational, and emotional effects of self-disclosure after conversations with a chatbot. J. Commun. **68**(4), 712–733 (2018)
26. Hoofnagle, C.J., King, J., Li, S., Turow, J.: How different are young adults from older adults when it comes to information privacy attitudes and policies? (SSRN Scholarly Paper No. ID 1589864). Social Science Research Network, Rochester, NY (2010)
27. Hoy, M.G., Milne, G.: Gender differences in privacy-related measures for young adult facebook users. J. Interact. Advert. **10**(2), 28–45 (2010)
28. Inkster, B., Sarđa, S., Subramanian, V.: An empathy-driven, conversational artificial intelligence agent (Wysa) for digital mental well-being: real-world data evaluation mixed-methods study. JMIR mHealth and uHealth **6**(11), e12106 (2018)
29. Isaias, P., Reis, F., Coutinho, C., Lencastre, J.A.: Empathic technologies for distance/mobile learning. Interact. Technol. Smart Educ. **14**(2), 159–180 (2017)
30. Jackson, S.D.: "Connection is the antidote": psychological distress, emotional processing, and virtual community building among LGBTQ students after the Orlando shooting. Psychol. Sex. Orientat. Gend. Divers. **4**(2), 160–168 (2017)
31. Kretzschmar, K., Tyroll, H., Pavarini, G., Manzini, A., Singh, I.: Can your phone be your therapist? Young people's ethical perspectives on the use of fully automated conversational agents (chatbots) in mental health support. Biomed. Informatics Insights **11**, 1–9 (2019)

32. Lee, Y.C., Yamashita, N., Huang, Y.: Designing a chatbot as a mediator for promoting deep self-disclosure to a real mental health professional. Proc. ACM Human-Comput. Interact. **4**(CSCW1), 1–27 (2020)
33. Lee, Y.C., Yamashita, N., Huang, Y., Fu, W.: "I Hear You, I Feel You": encouraging deep self-disclosure through a chatbot. In: Proceedings of the 2020 CHI Conference on Human Factors in Computing Systems (2020)
34. Lee, J.D., See, K.A.: Trust in automation: Designing for appropriate reliance. Hum. Factors **46**(1), 50–80 (2004)
35. Lipschitz, J., et al.: Adoption of mobile apps for depression and anxiety: cross-sectional survey study on patient interest and barriers to engagement. JMIR Mental Health **6**(1), e11334 (2019)
36. Liu, K., Tao, D.: The roles of trust, personalization, loss of privacy, and anthropomorphism in public acceptance of smart healthcare services. Comput. Hum. Behav. **127**, 107026 (2022)
37. Lucas, G.M., Gratch, J., King, A., Morency, L.P.: It's only a computer: virtual humans increase willingness to disclose. Comput. Hum. Behav. **37**, 94–100 (2014)
38. Ly, K.H., Ly, A.M., Andersson, G.: A fully automated conversational agent for promoting mental well-being: a pilot RCT using mixed methods. Internet Interv. **10**, 39–46 (2017)
39. Magsamen-Conrad, K., Upadhyaya, S., Joa, C.Y., Dowd, J.: Bridging the divide: using UTAUT to predict multigenerational tablet adoption practices. Comput. Hum. Behav. **50**, 186–196 (2015)
40. Mandal, D., McQueen, R.J.: Extending UTAUT to explain social media adoption by microbusinesses. Int. J. Managing Inf. Technol. (IJMIT) **4**(4), 1–11 (2012)
41. McInroy, L.B., Craig, S.L., Leung, V.W.Y.: Platforms and patterns for practice: LGBTQ+ youths' use of information and communication technologies. Child Adolesc. Soc. Work J. **36**(5), 507–520 (2018)
42. Melián-González, S., Gutiérrez-Taño, D., Bulchand-Gidumal, J.: Predicting the intentions to use chatbots for travel and tourism. Curr. Issue Tour. **24**(2), 192–210 (2019)
43. Mostafa, R.B., Kasamani, T.: Antecedents and consequences of chatbot initial trust. Eur. J. Mark. **56**, 1748–1771 (2021)
44. Nadarzynski, T., Miles, O., Cowie, A., Ridge, D.: Acceptability of artificial intelligence (AI)-led chatbot services in healthcare: a mixed-methods study. Digital Health **5**, 2055207619871808 (2019)
45. Neufeld, D.J., Dong, L., Higgins, C.: Charismatic leadership and user acceptance of information technology. Eur. J. Inf. Syst. **16**(4), 494–510 (2007)
46. Pennebaker, J.W.: Emotion, disclosure, and health: an overview. In: Emotion, Disclosure, & Health, pp. 3–10 (1995)
47. Powell, J.: Trust me, I'm a chatbot: how artificial intelligence in health care fails the Turing test. J. Med. Internet Res. **21**(10), e16222 (2019)
48. Prakash, A.V., Das, S.: Intelligent conversational agents in mental healthcare services: a thematic analysis of user perceptions. Pacific Asia J. Assoc. Inf. Syst. **12**(2), 1–34 (2020)
49. Rogers, E. Diffusion of Innovations. Free Press, New York (1995)
50. Russell, S.T., Fish, J.N.: Mental health in lesbian, gay, bisexual, and transgender (LGBT) youth. Annu. Rev. Clin. Psychol. **12**(1), 465–487 (2016)
51. Schroeder, J., Schroeder, M.: Trusting in machines: how mode of interaction affects willingness to share personal information with machines. In: Proceedings of the 51st Hawaii International Conference on System Sciences, Hawaii (2018)
52. Schueller, S.M., Neary, M., O'Loughlin, K., Adkins, E.C.: Discovery of and interest in health apps among those with mental health needs: survey and focus group study. J. Med. Internet Res. **20**(6), e10141 (2018)
53. Sheehan, K.B.: Toward a typology of Internet users and online privacy concerns. Inf. Soc. **18**(1), 21–32 (2002)

54. Steele, L.S., et al.: LGBT identity, untreated depression, and unmet need for mental health services by sexual minority women and trans-identified people. J. Women's Health **26**(2), 116–127 (2017)
55. Taddicken, M.: The 'privacy paradox' in the social web: the impact of privacy concerns, individual characteristics, and the perceived social relevance on different forms of self-disclosure. J. Comput.-Mediat. Commun. **19**(2), 248–273 (2013)
56. Tarhini, A., El-Masri, M., Ali, M., Serrano, A.: Extending the UTAUT model to understand the customers' acceptance and use of internet banking in Lebanon. Inf. Technol. People **29**(4), 830–849 (2016)
57. Toch, E., Wang, Y., Cranor, L.F.: Personalization and privacy: a survey of privacy risks and remedies in personalization-based systems. User Model. User-Adap. Inter. **22**(1–2), 203–220 (2012)
58. van Wezel, M.M.C., Croes, E.A.J., Antheunis, M.L.: "I'm here for you": can social chatbots truly support their users? A literature review. In: Følstad, A. et al. (eds.) Chatbot Research and Design: Fourth International Workshop, CONVERSATIONS 2020, pp. 96–113 (2021)
59. Venkatesh, V., Morris, M.G., Ackerman, P.L.: A longitudinal field investigation of gender differences in individual technology adoption decision-making processes. Organ. Behav. Hum. Decis. Process. **83**(1), 33–60 (2000)
60. Venkatesh, V., Morris, M.G., Davis, G.B., Davis, F.D.: User acceptance of information technology: toward a unified view. MIS Q. **27**(3), 425–478 (2003)
61. Venkatesh, V., Sykes, T.A., Zhang, X.: "Just what the doctor ordered": a revised UTAUT for EMR system adoption and use by doctors. In: 2011 44th Hawaii International Conference on System Sciences (2011)
62. Venkatesh, V., Thong, J.Y.L., Xu, X.: Consumer acceptance and use of information technology: extending the unified theory of acceptance and use of technology. MIS Q. **36**(1), 157–178 (2012)
63. Woebot Health. Relational agent for mental health, 12 January 2022. https://woebothealth.com/. Accessed 31 Jan 2022
64. Mental health support, for everyone. Wysa (2021). https://wysa.io/. Retrieved 27 Jan 2022
65. Yarns, B.C., Abrams, J.M., Meeks, T.W., Sewell, D.D.: The mental health of older LGBT adults. Curr. Psychiatry Rep. **18**(6), 1–11 (2016)
66. Yi, M.Y., Jackson, J.D., Park, J.S., Probst, J.C.: Understanding information technology acceptance by individual professionals: toward an integrative view. Inf. Manage. **43**(3), 350–363 (2006)

Chatbot Design and Applications

Enhancing Conversational Troubleshooting with Multi-modality: Design and Implementation

Giulio Antonio Abbo$^{(\boxtimes)}$ (ID), Pietro Crovari (ID), and Franca Garzotto (ID)

Department of Electronics, Information, and Bioengineering, Politecnico di Milano, Milan, Italy
giulioantonio.abbo@polimi.it

Abstract. Conversational troubleshooting is an increasingly popular technology that consists in utilising dialogue agents to support users of a system through a conversation-based question-answering process, typically through a chatbot. Despite their widespread use, current troubleshooting technologies lack a thorough integration with the applications on which they are overlaid, as they rely only on text to help the users. In this paper, we present TINI, an open-source conversational troubleshooting tool that is multi-modal and multilingual, relies on simple configuration files, and is ready to be deployed in web applications. Users can ask questions to the conversational agent explaining the issue faced; the system analyses it together with the interaction's context to locate the root problem. Finally, it proposes a solution which engages the user multi-modally: with text in the chat and hints in the graphical interface. A table-based configuration improves system maintainability and enables dialogue designers and field experts to work on the conversation without any coding experience required.

Keywords: Multi-modal · Conversational agent · Troubleshooting

1 Introduction

Assisting users of software systems when they encounter a problem has always been of paramount importance [30]. The diagnostic procedure of individuating the probable causes of an issue and finding an action that could solve it is commonly referred to as *troubleshooting* [18].

In the field of user assistance, troubleshooting has usually taken the form of help desks [8]. At a help desk – physical or virtual – customers of a service can ask for information and guidance. Thanks to this procedure, users do not have to read instruction manuals or lists of frequently asked questions; instead, they are helped by a *system expert* [3].

In recent years conversational agents have been employed to automate troubleshooting services [5,22] thanks to their availability and low costs associated compared to their human counterparts. These characteristics make

A. Følstad et al. (Eds.): CONVERSATIONS 2022, LNCS 13815, pp. 103–117, 2023.
https://doi.org/10.1007/978-3-031-25581-6_7

chatbot-based assistance optimal for websites, particularly e-commerce applications [20,31], where 24/7 assistance is considered a key asset for a competitive offer [32].

Today, a wide range of tools for building chatbots is available to automate troubleshooting procedures [14], but they share a fundamental weakness: the definition of the conversation and of the solvable problems are tightly coupled, allowing only a chat-based interaction [5]. Although intuitive in the configuration phase, this choice brings three main unwanted drawbacks.

First, current technologies are not context-aware: they are not designed to complement the information extracted from the conversation with contextual data gathered from the interaction on the graphical interface [21,25]. Consequently, to have good support, users must describe the details of the problem faced and the context in which the problem is encountered, with increased interaction effort.

Second, chat-based conversational troubleshooting can support users only through textual responses, with the added effort for the users of translating the suggestions received into actions on the interface [10,39]. A multi-modal response would allow the troubleshooting system to give actionable solutions to users, for example, by highlighting the relevant element on the interface, further improving the quality of the response [9,11,27,35].

Finally, since the conversation data is mixed with the conversational agent's configuration, it is impossible to edit them separately. A conversation designer or a domain expert can not modify the user experience without minimal programming skills. In the same way, programmers who want to modify the functionalities of the troubleshooting application must have a good understanding of the application domain since they will inevitably intervene in the conversation structure.

To overcome these issues, we propose TINI, a conversational kit for troubleshooting that is natively context-aware and multi-modal. Its table-based configuration allows conversation designers and programmers to work independently on the experience configuration. TINI is an open-source plugin ready to be integrated into a new or existing web application. When TINI is embedded into a website, users can describe the issue faced in a dedicated chat panel in the application interface. TINI analyses users' messages together with the interaction's context to get to the root of the problem and proposes a coherent solution multi-modally, describing it in the chat and highlighting the relevant elements on the graphical interface.

In this paper, we improve and extend the work on MCTK published in a poster paper [1]. Having seen the solution's potential, and thanks to the many comments gathered, we have completely redesigned the system architecture making it a single plug-and-play component – which is lighter, faster, and easier to configure – and introduced multilingual support. On top of that, we formalise the problem with a mathematical formulation and describe a complete case study to clarify its usage.

2   Related Work

2.1   Dialogue Management in Conversational Agents

Conversational agents are generally structured around a *Dialogue Manager* [33], that handles users' intents and dialogue context to control the agent's subsequent actions, modelling the state of the dialogue, the goals, and the policies [29]. Dialogue management can be performed by following two main kinds of techniques [17]: *handcrafted* and *probabilistic*.

In handcrafted dialogue managers, developers must specify the rules to react to each user's intent. These approaches are realised mainly through slot-filling techniques [15] – where the system collects information from the user's messages and asks back for the missing data – or employing finite-state machines [28,41] – where the dialogue status is represented as states in a finite-state automaton [43]. Handcrafted dialogue managers offer developers complete control over the interaction without having to encode all the possible interactions by hand.

The probabilistic strategies for dialogue management consist in training an algorithm from large data sets of samples [42]. These dialogue managers require a large base of conversation examples to be trained, but, based on the samples provided, they can respond to unforeseen user messages that were not considered at design time. Some solutions adopt a mixed approach. For example learning from a corpus with an external knowledge base or ontology [2,26].

In general, many of these solutions are strongly dependent on the conversation that the user will have [4], and make difficult the separation of the conversation from the application context. This is obvious when learning from a corpus, where the samples inevitably mix contents and conversation flow, but this is also true for state machine approaches, because the conversation steps are modelled in a graph and are inextricable from the process on which the conversation is based. Consequently, the behaviour of the software is forcibly linked with the dialogue, making it difficult to support additional features, such as multiple interaction modes and multiple languages.

These approaches are largely uni-modal: the user can interact using only the conversation, be it in written or spoken form, and they require other external components to achieve a multi-modal interaction [24]. Yet, it is proven that multi-modality plays a significant role in the interaction with conversational agents [27]; as reported by Oviatt et al. [35], people tend to prefer to interact multi-modally as the task complexity increases. Multi-modal solutions are being developed to be applied in many fields from theatre [6] to the automotive system [23,36], in most cases with a custom solution. However, multi-modality in chatbots for user assistance in troubleshooting remains largely unexplored.

2.2   Conversational Troubleshooting

Guided troubleshooting is the process of aiding users in a specific field, assisting in the solution of certain problems; usually, the user asks a question, which is then validated to find the root cause and execute a fixing procedure [18].

Creating programs that autonomously guide users in the troubleshooting process requires extracting the intent and specific information from the question, finding an appropriate response, and performing the required actions. There are many approaches to solving this problem [38], and – as in the case of dialogue managers – they can be divided into two groups: those that require manual rules configuration and those that learn from data.

The rule-based approaches, such as taxonomic case-based reasoning [16] or complex slot-filling techniques [44], permit more customisation of behaviour and policies compared to automated learning, for instance, with the integration of external services to improve performance. However, large sets of rules are difficult to manage, and the scope of these troubleshooting frameworks is usually very narrow: they are typically custom solutions for a specific application in a single domain [37]. Subramaniam et al. [37] try to overcome this limitation with a multi-bot system to cover multiple application domains at the cost of a more complex configuration.

The automated approach avoids manually setting up a complex knowledge base by employing automated learning techniques [40]. The problem however is that domain-specific training data sets are difficult to produce, and the quality and consistency of the agent's answers can vary considerably [13].

3   Preliminary Analysis

TINI is a framework to provide users with multi-modal conversational troubleshooting on web applications. Embedding it into a new or existing website allows users to receive suggestions on how to solve the issues they encounter.

3.1   Design Principles

Before proceeding with the description of the system, we present the principles we applied to the design – namely multi-modality, separation of concerns, and extensibility – illustrating the rationale guiding their consideration and how they are pursued in TINI.

Multi-modality. A system is multi-modal if it supports more than one means of interaction: text, graphics, gestures, and more [34]. Multiple research studies prove that the response to multi-modal stimuli is better compared to uni-modal [27,35]. In addition, since the primal interaction ground for a web application is the graphical interface, we want to intervene and guide the user in that environment as much as possible, instead of asking the user to switch to a completely separate conversational one [7].

A thorough integration between multiple modalities also supports the interpretation of users' requests. Indeed, the same way a human field expert asks for details about the state of the system to answer a question, an automated solution should leverage the context of the request to have a better understanding of it. Additional information such as past user's actions on the graphical interface could help provide a solution tailored for each specific instance.

Contrarily to most used chatbot frameworks, TINI will natively support multi-modality. Indeed, the configuration will be based on a Configuration Table that combines the context – here defined as what is currently shown on the screen – with the problem-solution pairs, and allows including in the response the interface elements relevant to the solution, together with the answer. In this way, different views might produce different suggestions tailored to what is happening on the screen.

Separation of Concerns. In software engineering, separation of concerns is the practice of separating the main algorithm from the parts that pertain to specific tasks [19]. We can extend this concept beyond software modules and apply it to the professional figures involved in the different aspects of a system.

We want to empower the conversation designer and the domain expert to customise the behaviour of TINI independently of the developer. To achieve so, we locate the domain-specific data in a single place, on which these experts can directly operate, modifying the conversation as desired. In addition, the structure containing this data must be accessible to those with little programming knowledge.

By operating on the Configuration Table – using any CSV reader – domain experts can insert new problem types, modify the wording of non-effective utterances, or modifying the solution for an existing issue.

Extensibility. An extensible solution allows adding new behaviours and modifying the existing ones with minimal intervention in its internal structure. Indeed, if the filed-specific data is embedded within the application, as the knowledge base grows, introducing changes will require interventions in multiple sites, reevaluation of all the existing rules to understand whether each of them is affected by the changes, and the extension of the features quickly becomes unfeasible.

The table-based configuration fulfils this requirement: all the field-specific knowledge and the data related are detached from the code that implements the logic.

3.2   Usage Scenario

To explain how the proposed system works, we exemplify its usage in a concrete example. Andy is a user of a web application developed by Barb. Barb's app is a simple online image editor with many tools and controls organised in panels. In her system, Barb uses TINI to add a troubleshooting agent to support her users. When Andy needs help, he can click on a button added by TINI to start chatting with the conversational agent.

Andy visits the web app and loads the image he wants to edit, then proceeds to use the available tools to crop and rotate the image. At this point, Andy would like to reduce the image's brightness but does not know how. He clicks on

Fig. 1. A photo editing application, enhanced with the TINI tool. On the right, the chat panel displays the conversation with the chatbot; on the left, the available tools are displayed in a panel, with those relevant to the solution highlighted in red. The developer can customise every aspect of the interface.

the TINI button and writes in the chat: "How do I make the image darker?"; the system elaborates the message with the available information about the active modules and answers: "You can use the highlighted tool to control the brightness of the image". At the same time, the system highlights in the interface the relevant tool and the panel in which it can be found, as shown in Fig. 1. Andy reads the answer, finds the correct tool, and can continue editing the image.

3.3 Problem Formalisation

From a high-level abstraction standpoint, the proposed system has to take as input the question provided by the user and information about the context, consult a knowledge base, and provide an answer indicating the relevant elements that must be notified to the user.

Modules and Parameters Definition. In order to represent the context, we can consider the options available to the user and group them into *modules*. The modules can be active or not, depending on whether they are available to the user. For example, in a photo editing application, the modules could be various tools, such as the brush, crop, or stamp tool. In addition, each module can have one or more *parameters*, representing the settings of its module. In the image editor, these could be the size and transparency levels of the brush tool and the proportions of the area in the crop tool. The system will then receive the information about which modules are active, as inactive modules are not available to the user and cannot be used to solve the issue the user is facing.

Mathematical Formulation. In mathematical terms, the problem can be formalised as follows. Let M be the set of all the modules in the system and P the set of parameters; we suppose that each parameter is associated with one and only one module. Let q be the question of the user. Given A, a set of active modules, $A \subseteq M$, we describe the system as the relation $\sigma(A, q) = \langle \overline{M}, \overline{P}, \mathbf{r} \rangle$ that, given in input the question and the active modules, returns the sets of highlighted modules $\overline{M} \subseteq A$ and parameters $\overline{P} \subseteq P$, and the response $\mathbf{r}$ explaining the actions to perform. A description of the execution will be given in Sect. 4.3.

4 System's Overview

The central component of TINI is the *Configuration Table*, a data structure representing connections between problems and solutions in a specific field of application whose aspect is presented in Sect. 4.1. We can describe the action of TINI in four steps, as shown in Fig. 2. The system receives an issue from the interface, described by the user in the chat, for example: "How do I make the image darker?" with the active modules on the screen; in the example, these are the active tools. The sentence is used to identify the problem faced, through intent extraction. This is used in the Configuration Table to retrieve the list of possible solutions for the active modules. These solutions are finally communicated to the users through a sentence in the chat that guides them through the resolution, and some visual hints, such as the tools to use and their parameters to edit, that suggest to users where to operate on the interface.

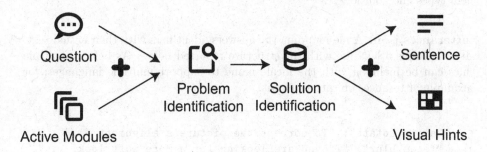

Fig. 2. Sequence of operations performed by the system.

4.1 Configuration

Before presenting in detail the system's structure, we propose an overview of the data models and configuration files. TINI can be configured using three files: the *training*, the *configuration table*, and the *utterances* files.

training.json. This file provides examples of user sentences for each type of problem; it is used to train an NLU engine to extract the intent – representing the problem type – from the users' questions. The format follows the specifications of NLP.js[1] as displayed below. Multiple languages can be supported by providing multiple files with the language locale name: for example, training-en, training-it.

```
{
    "name": "training",
    "locale": "en-US",
    "data": [
        {
            "intent": "alignment",
            "utterances": [
                "The image is tilted",
                "The picture is not aligned",
                ...
            ]
        },
        ...
    ]
}
```

configuration-table.csv. This table, as reported in Table 1, contains the connections between problem types, modules, parameters, and answers. This structure balances maintainability, relevant when reading and updating the table, with extensibility, which is important when expanding the table with new problem types and solutions.

utterances.json. A file mapping the answers' identifiers with their actual text. It is a simple JSON file with the structure reported below. As before, multiple files can be included with the locale name to support multiple languages: for example, utterances-en, utterances-it.

```
{
"align.rotate": "To correct the picture's alignment ...",
"focus.blur": "If you are looking for a more soft look, ...",
"focus.sharp": "To increase the sharpness of the image ...",
...
}
```

The proposed system has the necessary extensibility requisites. Adding a module or a parameter is as easy as adding a row to the table, adding a new

---

[1] www.github.com/axa-group/nlp.js.

Table 1. Structure of the Configuration Table. Each row corresponds to a module parameter, and every column is a problem TINI wants to address. The presence of an utterance identifier in a cell means that the corresponding parameter is a possible solution to the problem in the column. The conversation designer can directly operate on this table to add problems and utterances and create new connections between problems and parameters.

Module	Parameter	Composition	Style	Focus
Crop	Tool	comp.crop		
Filter	Grayscale		style.generic	
Filter	Sepia		style.generic	
Filter	Vintage		style.generic	
Filter	Blur			focus.blur
Filter	Sharpen			focus.sharp
Filter	Pixelate		style.generic	focus.pixel

problem type can be done by adding a column. Adding or changing a connection between problem types and parameters is done by modifying an utterance identifier in the corresponding cell, and the use of identifiers, instead of putting the utterances themselves in the cell, allows reusing the same utterance multiple times without duplication and support multiple languages; these operations do not require interventions on the code, only on the data structure and on the NLU configuration, fulfilling the separation of concerns.

These three files are provided during the initialisation of the frontend component. In this phase, the developer can also customise the interface's appearance and provide the active modules, as described in Sect. 4.4.

4.2   Architecture

The system is structured in five modules, as presented in Fig. 3. It consists of and can be used as a self-contained Vue.js[2] library, which is available as open-source.

Interface Component. This component is available to the developer and can be embedded in the web application. It displays a circular overlay button on the bottom right of the screen. The button allows toggling the visibility of a chat panel, which handles the communication with the conversational agent. When the user sends a message, the interface will forward it to the *Core* component, and when it receives a response, it will display it in the chat; in addition, it will update the information on which modules and parameters should be highlighted in the application. The component is implemented in Vue.js; when used, it accepts several configuration parameters, including the configuration files' URLs and the list of active modules, and fires an event when the highlighted elements change.

---

[2] www.vuejs.org.

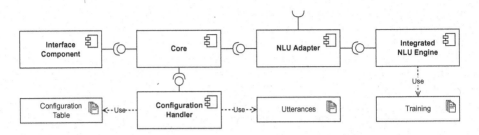

Fig. 3. The components of the system and the configuration files.

Core. The *Core* implements the logic of the system. It is initialised with information about which modules are currently active. When it receives the user's question, it uses the *NLU Adapter* and the *Configuration Handler* to obtain the response, consisting of an answer and a list of elements to highlight in the interface. The details about the algorithm are reported in Sect. 4.3. The response is returned to the *Interface Component*. This part is implemented in JavaScript and is independent of the interface: in the future, other interfaces can be added, extending the library to other frontend frameworks.

NLU Adapter and Integrated NLU Engine. The *NLU Adapter* is in charge of extracting the intent, which represents the problem encountered by the user, from the user's question. To achieve this, it employs an *Integrated NLU Engine*, which is a NLP.js instance, a JavaScript library implementing machine learning models for natural language understanding. We chose NLP.js because it can run in the browser and natively supports 41 languages, 104 with the BERT [12] extension. When the web app is loaded in the client browser, it is trained with the examples in the *Training* file and is ready to identify the intent from the user sentences. In addition, the *NLU Addapter* detects the language of the user's question.

Alternatively, the adapter can be configured with an external, pre-trained NLU service: in this second case, the *Training* configuration file can be omitted.

Configuration Handler. Finally, the *Configuration Handler* retrieves and parses the *utterances* and *configuration table* documents and provides their contents to the *Core* component. The documents can be provided through a URL or as strings directly.

4.3 Runtime Behaviour

The behaviour of the *Core* component can be portrayed using the mathematical notation introduced in the previous section. Given the users' question q, the NLU Adapter extracts the intent, representing the problem type t. For example, from the sentence "How do I make the image darker?" the NLU Adapter would extract the intent representing the problem type *image.dark*. The system can extract only one intent from the given question q. For this reason, if the conversation designers want to accept composite questions (e.g. "I want to cut and make the image bigger") they have to create specific intents.

Let A be the set of active modules as before. The algorithm scans the Configuration Table – where the rows contain the parameters p_i (with the corresponding module m_i), the columns contain the problem types t_j, and the corresponding cell is denoted with u_{ij}, representing an utterance identifier – and finds all the $\langle m_i, p_i, u_{ij} \rangle$ that satisfy $t_j = t$ and $m_i \in A$; in other words, it finds all the parameters of the active modules connected with the problem and the corresponding sentences. The language of the input (e.g., English) is recognised in the user sentence and used to retrieve the actual utterances constituting the answer from the *utterances* document. These are then concatenated to produce a single final response **r**.

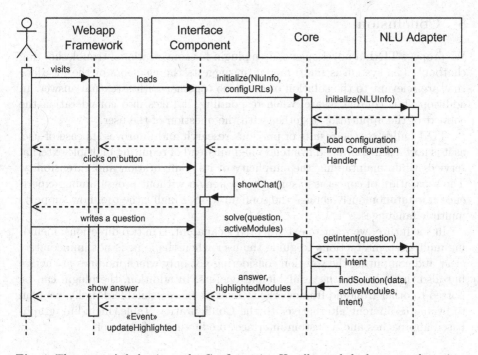

Fig. 4. The system's behaviour; the Configuration Handler and the language detection are not shown for simplicity.

In practice, the sequence of interactions of the user with the system can be modelled as in Fig. 4, which represents its behaviour from the moment the application is initialised. During the initial phase, the *Integrated NLU Engine* – if used – is quickly trained. The user can interact with the system and ask a question. The system interprets the question, keeps track of the active modules, and produces a response. When the operation is completed, an event is fired to inform the application that it is necessary to update the highlighted elements.

4.4   Deployment

To use TINI, it is sufficient to import the package, which is publicly available, into a new or existing Vue application. When adding the provided component to the application, the developer will be able to specify the configuration files' URLs, provide a list of active modules – to be kept updated during the execution – and use the provided props to customise the behaviour of the system. Specific CSS classes can be used to refine the graphical appearance. To use the multimodal response, the developer will listen to a specific event that provides the list of modules relevant to the answer: this can be used to update some CSS classes of other components to highlight them.

5   Conclusion

We propose TINI, a novel open-source plugin for conversational troubleshooting chatbots. The system is multi-modal: it suggests the elements of the interface that are relevant to the solution of the issue together with a textual answer. In addition, it is context aware: when responding, it takes into consideration the context of the application together with the question of the user.

TINI builds on the results of previous research and improves its ease of use, as it is now a self-contained frontend plugin instead of requiring multiple external services while maintaining the simplicity of its configuration and extensibility. The separation of concerns ensures that a person without programming experience can autonomously change the configuration. Finally, the tool now supports multiple languages.

In the future, we want to extend TINI's capabilities in two directions: including multi-step interactions to guide the user when the issue is not immediately clear and computing the solution considering not only which modules are active but also the values of the available parameters. In addition, the plugin can be ported to other frontend frameworks to make it more available. Finally, we plan to evaluate different alternatives to the Configuration Table, including graph-based approaches and a custom interface to edit the configuration.

References

1. Abbo, G.A., Crovari, P., Pidò, S., Pinoli, P., Garzotto, F.: MCTK: a multi-modal conversational troubleshooting kit for supporting users in web applications. In: Proceedings of the 2022 International Conference on Advanced Visual Interfaces, AVI 2022, pp. 1–3. Association for Computing Machinery, New York (2022)
2. Agarwal, S., Dusek, O., Konstas, I., Rieser, V.: A knowledge-grounded multimodal search-based conversational agent. arXiv:1810.11954 (2018)

3. Al-Hawari, F., Barham, H.: A machine learning based help desk system for IT service management. J. King Saud Univ. Comput. Inf. Sci. **33**(6), 702–718 (2021)
4. Baez, M., Daniel, F., Casati, F.: Conversational web interaction: proposal of a dialog-based natural language interaction paradigm for the web. In: Følstad, A., et al. (eds.) CONVERSATIONS 2019. LNCS, vol. 11970, pp. 94–110. Springer, Cham (2020). https://doi.org/10.1007/978-3-030-39540-7_7
5. Bavaresco, R., et al.: Conversational agents in business: a systematic literature review and future research directions. Comput. Sci. Rev. **36**, 100239 (2020)
6. Bhushan, R., et al.: ODO: design of multimodal chatbot for an experiential media system. Multimodal Technol. Interact. **4**(4), 68 (2020)
7. Boshrabadi, A.M., Biria, R.: The efficacy of multimodal vs. print-based texts for teaching reading comprehension skills to Iranian high school third graders. Int. J. Lang. Learn. Appl. Linguist. World **5**, 17 (2014)
8. Corea, C., Delfmann, P., Nagel, S.: Towards Intelligent Chatbots for Customer Care - Practice-Based Requirements for a Research Agenda (2020)
9. Crovari, P., Pidó, S., Garzotto, F., Ceri, S.: Show, don't tell. reflections on the design of multi-modal conversational interfaces. In: Følstad, A., et al. (eds.) CONVERSATIONS 2020. LNCS, vol. 12604, pp. 64–77. Springer, Cham (2021). https://doi.org/10.1007/978-3-030-68288-0_5
10. Crovari, P., et al.: GeCoAgent: a conversational agent for empowering genomic data extraction and analysis. ACM Trans. Comput. Healthc. **3**(1), 1–29 (2021)
11. De Cicco, R., Iacobucci, S., Aquino, A., Romana Alparone, F., Palumbo, R.: Understanding users' acceptance of chatbots: an extended TAM approach. In: Følstad, A., et al. (eds.) Chatbot Research and Design. LNCS, pp. 3–22. Springer, Cham (2022). https://doi.org/10.1007/978-3-030-94890-0_1
12. Devlin, J., Chang, M.W., Lee, K., Toutanova, K.: BERT: Pre-training of Deep Bidirectional Transformers for Language Understanding (2019)
13. Følstad, A., Nordheim, C.B., Bjørkli, C.A.: What makes users trust a chatbot for customer service? An exploratory interview study. In: Bodrunova, S.S. (ed.) INSCI 2018. LNCS, vol. 11193, pp. 194–208. Springer, Cham (2018). https://doi.org/10.1007/978-3-030-01437-7_16
14. Følstad, A., Taylor, C.: Conversational repair in chatbots for customer service: the effect of expressing uncertainty and suggesting alternatives. In: Følstad, A., et al. (eds.) CONVERSATIONS 2019. LNCS, vol. 11970, pp. 201–214. Springer, Cham (2020). https://doi.org/10.1007/978-3-030-39540-7_14
15. Goddeau, D., Meng, H., Polifroni, J., Seneff, S., Busayapongchai, S.: A form-based dialogue manager for spoken language applications. In: Proceeding of Fourth International Conference on Spoken Language Processing, ICSLP 1996, vol. 2, pp. 701–704 (1996)
16. Gupta, K.M.: Taxonomic conversational case-based reasoning. In: Aha, D.W., Watson, I. (eds.) ICCBR 2001. LNCS (LNAI), vol. 2080, pp. 219–233. Springer, Heidelberg (2001). https://doi.org/10.1007/3-540-44593-5_16
17. Harms, J.G., Kucherbaev, P., Bozzon, A., Houben, G.J.: Approaches for dialog management in conversational agents. IEEE Internet Comput. **23**(2), 13–22 (2019)
18. Heckerman, D., Breese, J.S., Rommelse, K.: Decision-theoretic troubleshooting. Commun. ACM **38**(3), 49–57 (1995)
19. Hürsch, W.L., Lopes, C.V.: Separation of concerns. Technical report (1995)
20. Janssen, A., Rodríguez Cardona, D., Breitner, M.H.: More than FAQ! chatbot taxonomy for business-to-business customer services. In: Følstad, A., et al. (eds.) CONVERSATIONS 2020. LNCS, vol. 12604, pp. 175–189. Springer, Cham (2021). https://doi.org/10.1007/978-3-030-68288-0_12

21. John, R.J.L., Potti, N., Patel, J.M.: Ava: from data to insights through conversation. In: CIDR, p. 10 (2017)
22. Kvale, K., Freddi, E., Hodnebrog, S., Sell, O.A., Følstad, A.: Understanding the user experience of customer service chatbots: what can we learn from customer satisfaction surveys? In: Følstad, A., et al. (eds.) CONVERSATIONS 2020. LNCS, vol. 12604, pp. 205–218. Springer, Cham (2021). https://doi.org/10.1007/978-3-030-68288-0_14
23. Lemon, O., Georgila, K., Henderson, J., Stuttle, M.: An ISU dialogue system exhibiting reinforcement learning of dialogue policies: generic slot-filling in the TALK in-car system. Demonstrations 4 (2006)
24. Liao, L., Ma, Y., He, X., Hong, R., Chua, T.S.: Knowledge-aware multimodal dialogue systems. In: Proceedings of the 26th ACM International Conference on Multimedia, MM 2018, pp. 801–809. Association for Computing Machinery, New York (2018)
25. Liu, W., Li, X., Huang, D.: A survey on context awareness. In: 2011 International Conference on Computer Science and Service System (CSSS), pp. 144–147 (2011)
26. Madotto, A., Wu, C.S., Fung, P.: Mem2Seq: effectively incorporating knowledge bases into end-to-end task-oriented dialog systems. arXiv:1804.08217 (2018)
27. Massaro, D.W.: A framework for evaluating multimodal integration by humans and a role for embodied conversational agents. In: Proceedings of the 6th International Conference on Multimodal Interfaces - ICMI 2004, State College, PA, USA, p. 24. ACM Press (2004)
28. Mathur, V., Singh, A.: The rapidly changing landscape of conversational agents. arXiv:1803.08419 (2018)
29. McTear, M., Callejas, Z., Griol, D.: The Conversational Interface. Springer, Cham (2016). https://doi.org/10.1007/978-3-319-32967-3
30. Morana, S., Pfeiffer, J., Adam, M.T.P.: User assistance for intelligent systems. Bus. Inf. Syst. Eng. **62**(3), 189–192 (2020)
31. Moriuchi, E., Landers, V.M., Colton, D., Hair, N.: Engagement with chatbots versus augmented reality interactive technology in e-commerce. J. Strateg. Mark. **29**(5), 375–389 (2021)
32. Nursetyo, A., Setiadi, D.R.I.M., Subhiyakto, E.R.: Smart chatbot system for E-commerce assitance based on AIML. In: 2018 International Seminar on Research of Information Technology and Intelligent Systems (ISRITI), pp. 641–645 (2018)
33. O'Shea, J., Bandar, Z., Crockett, K.: Systems engineering and conversational agents. In: Kacprzyk, J., Tolk, A., Jain, L.C., Jain, L.C. (eds.) Intelligence-Based Systems Engineering, vol. 10, pp. 201–232. Springer, Heidelberg (2011). https://doi.org/10.1007/978-3-642-17931-0_8
34. Oviatt, S.: Multimodal interfaces. In: The Human-Computer Interaction Handbook, 2nd edn. CRC Press, Boca Raton (2007)
35. Oviatt, S., Coulston, R., Lunsford, R.: When do we interact multimodally? Cognitive load and multimodal communication patterns. In: Proceedings of the 6th International Conference on Multimodal Interfaces, p. 8 (2004)
36. Pieraccini, R., et al.: Multimodal conversational systems for automobiles. Commun. ACM **47**(1), 47–49 (2004)
37. Subramaniam, S., Aggarwal, P., Dasgupta, G.B., Paradkar, A.: COBOTS - a cognitive multi-bot conversational framework for technical support. In: Proceedings of the 17th International Conference on Autonomous Agents and MultiAgent Systems, AAMAS 2018, Richland, SC, pp. 597–604. International Foundation for Autonomous Agents and Multiagent Systems (2018)

38. Thorne, C.: Chatbots for troubleshooting: a survey. Lang. Linguist. Compass **11**(10), e12253 (2017)
39. Turk, M.: Multimodal interaction: a review. Pattern Recogn. Lett. **36**, 189–195 (2014)
40. Vinyals, O., Le, Q.: A Neural Conversational Model (2015)
41. Wilks, Y., Catizone, R., Worgan, S., Turunen, M.: Some background on dialogue management and conversational speech for dialogue systems. Comput. Speech Lang. **25**(2), 128–139 (2011)
42. Williams, J.D., Asadi, K., Zweig, G.: Hybrid code networks: practical and efficient end-to-end dialog control with supervised and reinforcement learning (2017)
43. Zeigler, B., Bazor, B.: Dialog design for a speech-interactive automation system. In: Proceedings of 2nd IEEE Workshop on Interactive Voice Technology for Telecommunications Applications, pp. 113–116 (1994)
44. Zhao, G., et al.: MOLI: smart conversation agent for mobile customer service. Information **10**(2), 63 (2019)

A Framework and Content Analysis of Social Cues in the Introductions of Customer Service Chatbots

Charlotte van Hooijdonk[1]([✉]) [iD], Gabriëlla Martijn[1] [iD], and Christine Liebrecht[2] [iD]

[1] Utrecht University, Trans 10, 3512 JK Utrecht, The Netherlands
{C.M.J.vanHooijdonk,G.N.Martijn}@uu.nl
[2] Tilburg University, PO Box 90153, 5000 LE Tilburg, The Netherlands
C.C.Liebrecht@tilburguniversity.edu

Abstract. Organizations are increasingly implementing chatbots to address customers' inquiries, but customers still have unsatisfactory encounters with them. In order to successfully deploy customer service chatbots, it is important for organizations and designers to understand how to introduce them to customers. Arguably, how a chatbot introduces itself as well as its services might influence customers' perceptions about the chatbot. Therefore, a framework was developed to annotate the social cues in chatbot introductions. In order to validate our framework, we conducted a content analysis of introductions of customer service chatbots ($n = 88$). The results showed that the framework turned out to be a reliable identification instrument. Moreover, the most prevalent social cue in chatbot introductions was a humanlike avatar, whereas communication cues, indicating the chatbot's functionalities, hardly occurred. The paper ends with implications for the design of chatbot introductions and possibilities for future research.

Keywords: Self-introduction · Customer service chatbots · Social cues · Anthropomorphism · Content analysis

1 Introduction

Organizations are increasingly implementing online conversational agents, such as chatbots, for customer service purposes to increase productivity while simultaneously reducing costs [16]. Chatbots are systems which are designed to communicate with customers using natural language, i.e., through text or speech [16]. Nowadays chatbots address about 80% of customers' inquiries [20]. The chatbot market revenue is currently 106.6 million and is expected to increase to 454.8 million in 2027 [39].

Although the number of customer service chatbots increases, customers have unsatisfactory encounters with them. For example, customers perceive chatbots to lack empathy and chatbot conversations as impersonal [8, 31]. Also, chatbots are not always able to provide adequate responses to customers' requests due to poor intent recognition [12, 14, 23]. These unsatisfactory encounters indicate a gap between customers' expectations and the chatbot's performance [30], which leads to resistance against chatbots.

A. Følstad et al. (Eds.): CONVERSATIONS 2022, LNCS 13815, pp. 118–133, 2023.
https://doi.org/10.1007/978-3-031-25581-6_8

In order to successfully deploy customer service chatbots, it is important for organizations and designers to understand how to introduce them to customers [1]. The look and feel as well as the initial chatbot messages may influence customers' perceptions about the chatbot and the organization. For example, Kull et al. [22] show brand engagement increases when the initial messages emphasize the chatbot's helpfulness.

Previous research identified several cues in the chatbot's introduction and how they influence users' perceptions, but a well-defined classification of potential chatbot introduction cues that allows more valid comparisons across studies, is lacking. It is therefore valuable to obtain an overview of cues of chatbot introductions. Such a framework is useful for chatbot designers who develop customer service chatbots, and for researchers who aim to systematically investigate how different cues in chatbot introductions affect customers' perceptions of the chatbot and the affiliated organization. Furthermore, little is known about how organizations tailor these introductions to selectively reveal information about the chatbot. Our study extends the role of chatbot introductions and proposes a framework of social cues based on previous research. By means of a content analysis, we subsequently examined which social cues occur in the introductions of customer service chatbots. In summary, the following research questions have been investigated:

RQ 1: To what extent can social cues in the introductions of customer service chatbots be identified reliably?
RQ 2: To what extent do the social cues identified in our framework occur in the introductions of customer service chatbots?

2 Theoretical Framework

2.1 Managing Customers' Expectations of Customer Service Chatbots with Chatbot Introductions

Organizations increasingly use chatbots to handle customers' service inquiries. Chatbots are implemented on websites, apps, and social media channels, and as such they provide a new form of human-computer interaction [11]: customers can request the information they need through a dialogue screen and receive information in natural language in return [41]. Customers primarily engage with customer service chatbots for efficiency reasons, i.e., they want to receive the requested information in a fast and convenient way [3, 13, 42].

However, chatbots generally fail to meet customers' expectations [4, 19, 30]. For example, they sometimes do not understand customers' requests correctly, their responses only partly address customers' requests, and they tend to communicate in an impersonal manner [8, 13, 23]. One way to manage customers' expectations is in the first stage of customers' communication journey with the chatbot, i.e., the chatbot introduction. Figure 1 shows an example of a chatbot introduction: the first screen of a chatbot of a meal kit delivery service. This introduction consists of three parts: 1) a header with an avatar depicting a chef's hat, 2) three welcome messages in which the chatbot discloses its artificial identity, and 3) customers' response options consisting of buttons and a text field.

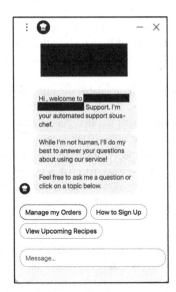

Fig. 1. Chatbot introduction of an (anonymized) meal kit delivery service.

When customers engage in a conversation with a customer service chatbot, they have three conversation goals [30, 37]. The first goal concerns the task customers want to perform with the chatbot. For example, the response buttons in the chatbot introduction in Fig. 1 indicate customers can view upcoming recipes. The second goal concerns how customers can have a smooth conversation with the chatbot. For example, the introduction shows customers can communicate with the chatbot by clicking on the response buttons or by typing their query in the text field (see Fig. 1). The third goal refers to the relationship between the customer and the chatbot. Customers prefer personal interaction and a 'human touch' in service encounters, even when they converse with a chatbot [24, 36]. This can be achieved by using anthropomorphic cues, such as an avatar and a conversational communication style [1, 17, 26]. The chatbot in Fig. 1 introduces itself as a 'support sous-chef' and uses personal pronouns (e.g., 'I', 'my', 'me'). Thus, customers' expectations about reaching their goals with the chatbot can be managed by the cues present in the introduction.

2.2   Social Cues in Chatbot Introductions

The Computers Are Social Actors (CASA) paradigm demonstrates that people mindlessly apply social scripts from human-human interaction when they use computers [33, 34]. Recently, extensions to the paradigm have been suggested to account for technological advances and the changes in how people interact with technologies [15, 28]. Lombard and Xu [28] propose the Media are Social Actors (MASA) paradigm which explains the effects of social cues and psychological mechanisms (i.e., mindlessness and anthropomorphism) of social responses. Social cues can be defined as "biologically and physically determined features salient to observers because of their potential as channels of useful information" [10: 2]. Examples of social cues are a humanlike avatar or informal language use. When a medium itself presents social cues, users are likely to perceive it as a social entity instead as a medium [27]. Therefore, if a chatbot contains social cues, such as a humanlike avatar, users will perceive its social entity and respond to it similarly as in human-to-human interaction [27, 28].

The effects of social cues in chatbots have been investigated in several experimental studies [1, 6, 17]. In these experiments, the manipulated social cues occur in multiple stages of the users' communication journey with the chatbot. For example, Go and Sundar [17: 308] created two versions of a chatbot that, amongst other variables, differed in the disclosure in the introduction (i.e., humanlike: 'Hi! I'm Alex, a sales associate' vs. machinelike: 'Hi! I'm Alex, an automated chatbot'). They also manipulated message interactivity: the chatbot was less (i.e., simple back-and-forth exchange) or more (i.e., contingent message exchange) responsive to participants' messages. An interaction effect was found between the introduction and message interactivity: participants evaluated the chatbot positively when it was introduced as human and delivered a highly interactive conversation than when it delivered a less interactive conversation.

Although experimental studies provide insights into the effects of one particular social cue in chatbot introductions, multiple social cues are present in the introductions of existing customer service chatbots as Fig. 1 demonstrates. Social cues do not occur in isolation and should be considered together as the combination of cues can strengthen or weaken their effects [9]. For example, the chatbot introduction in Fig. 1 contains visual and verbal identity cues (i.e., the avatar is a chef's hat, and the words 'automated sous-chef', and 'I'm not human' are used) which marks the chatbot's artificial identity. Thus, it is important to identify the social cues in chatbot introductions from existing literature. Building on a previous classification of social cues for chatbots [9] and research on social cues in chatbot introductions, we developed a framework (see Table 1) in which the identified cues were classified into four main categories: identity cues, competence cues, conversational cues, and communication cues.

Identity Cues. Is the interlocutor that pops up on the customer's screen a human service employee or a chatbot? There are several cues that can either mark or mask the chatbot's artificial identity. The first way is through a disclosure (e.g., 'I am a chatbot', 'I am a virtual assistant'). De Cicco et al. [7] investigated the effects of a disclosure in chatbot introductions. They found that the presence of a disclosure in a chatbot introduction led to less social presence, trust, and attitude towards the brand compared to the absence of a disclosure. Similar results were found by Luo et al. [31] who conducted a field study in which the chatbot did or did not disclose its artificial identity. Results showed a disclosure at the beginning of the conversation reduced purchase rates and customers perceived the chatbot as less knowledgeable and emphatic.

Other cues can also mask or mark the chatbot's artificial identity. One design aspect of customer service chatbots that received much attention in research and practice is anthropomorphism [2, 5, 13, 16]. This refers to humanizing chatbots by adding social cues, such as a name and an avatar. Several scholars conducted experimental studies in which oftentimes so-called humanlike chatbots are compared with machinelike chatbots. The operationalization of the humanlike chatbots differed across studies. Araujo [1], for example, used communication style and a name to differentiate between the humanlike and machinelike chatbot. Participants interacted with either a humanlike chatbot named

Emma that used informal language, or a machinelike chatbot named ChatBotX that used formal language. In contrast, Go and Sundar [17: 308] manipulated the disclosure and the avatar in the chatbot introduction. They created four versions of a chatbot introduction which ranged from machinelike (i.e., disclosure: 'Hi! I'm Alex, an automated chatbot', avatar: dialog bubble figure) to humanlike (i.e., disclosure: 'Hi! I'm Alex, a sales associate', avatar: a profile picture of an actual person). An expectancy violation effect was found: the attitudinal and behavioral outcomes were lower when the chatbot was introduced with a humanlike avatar and machinelike disclosure compared to an introduction with a machinelike avatar and machinelike disclosure [17].

Competence Cues. One way to increase customers' trust in customer service chatbots is by stressing the chatbot's competence [35]. For example, Mozafari et al. [32] investigated the effects of communicating expertise combined with a disclosure in the chatbot's introduction on participants' trust. Results showed merely disclosing negatively affected trust, whereas combining the disclosure with a statement about the chatbot's expertise (e.g., 'Due to my high efficiency I am able to find the best offer for you') or weaknesses (e.g., 'Please note that I'm only in use for a year now and am still learning') positively affected trust [32: 2919]. Another study investigated the effects of communicating the chatbot's expertise using metaphors [21]. A wizard-of-oz study was conducted in which participants received a prompt in which the expertise of the chatbot was explained with a metaphor (e.g., 'The bot you are about to interact with is modeled after a shrewd travel executive') [21: 9]. Next, participants engaged in a conversation with an agent. Findings showed that metaphors that communicated the chatbot's low competence (e.g., 'young student') were evaluated higher than metaphors that communicated the chatbot's high competence (e.g., 'trained professional'). Kull et al. [22: 844] compared chatbot's welcome messages in which its competence (e.g., 'Years of experience in the travel industry enable me to answer any travel question') or warmth (e.g., 'I will take care of you and try answering any travel questions you might have') was stressed. Participants' brand engagement increased when the chatbot initiated the conversation with a warm welcome message.

Conversational Cues. How can the chatbot display conversational habits? Three verbal cues have been identified which influence the chatbot's conversational etiquette. As chatbots mimic human-to-human communication [29], customers expect that chatbots express a word of welcome, such as 'hi' [5, 16, 19]. Another common social cue when meeting someone for the first time is a self-introduction (e.g., 'My name is…'). Moreover, chatbots should adhere to turn-taking protocols [5]. After the chatbot has introduced itself, it has to give the turn to the customer (e.g., 'How can I help you?').

Communication Cues. How can the chatbot communicate which functionalities and which message types it can handle? Several cues have been identified which might improve the chatbot's communicability [5, 40]. Several scholars argue that the chatbot's purpose should be clarified in the introductory messages (i.e., what is the chatbot supposed to do?) in order to manage users' expectations about the chatbot's capabilities [5, 16, 19]. Besides, an explanation should be provided on how to communicate effectively with the chatbot, for example by typing keywords or clicking on response buttons [19].

Table 1. Framework of social cues in chatbot introductions

Identity cues	Competence cues	Conversational cues	Communication cues
Disclosure	Statement stressing expertise	Greeting	Explanation purpose
Avatar type	Statement stressing weakness	Self-introduction	Explanation interaction
Name type		Turn-taking	

In order to validate our framework, we conducted a content analysis of introductions of customer service chatbots. This analysis allowed us to investigate whether our framework is reliable to analyze social cues in chatbot introductions. Moreover, we obtained insights into which social cues organizations use in chatbot introductions and whether they correspond with the cues in our framework.

3   Method

3.1   Sample of Chatbot Introductions

The introductions of customer service chatbots of various organizations in the Netherlands were manually searched in 2021. The search was narrowed to Dutch organizations to ensure a valid comparison between industries without confounding factors, such as variations in language and cultures. The sampling strategy consisted of three stages. First, different branches and organizations belonging to these branches were identified. Second, for each brand we noted an organization as well as its competitors. For example, in the financial branch we listed different banks. Third, the organizations' websites were visited and searched for the presence of a customer service chatbot which were usually located at the homepage, contact page, or specific domain pages. Once a customer service chatbot was found, a screenshot was made of the chatbot's first screen. In ten cases the chatbot immediately started with a call to action to the user, whereby the chatbot could be activated through clicking or typing. In all other cases, a screenshot of the chatbot's first screen was made without having any interaction with the bot. In seven cases, the introduction did not contain cues (i.e., disclosure and/or avatar) about the artificial identity of the agent. We interacted with the agent to determine whether it was a chatbot. Data saturation was reached at 88 chatbot introductions which belonged to 78 Dutch organizations: non-profit or governmental organizations ($n = 8$), employment agency ($n = 1$), education ($n = 1$), electronics ($n = 5$), financial ($n = 6$), furniture ($n = 4$), insurance ($n = 14$), logistics and postal service ($n = 3$), retail ($n = 15$), telecom ($n = 6$), travel ($n = 2$), utility ($n = 7$), other ($n = 6$). The sample can be found on OSF (https://osf.io/8wut9/).

3.2   Codebook

All screenshots were analyzed using a codebook to identify the social cues in chatbot introductions. The codebook was structured on the basis of the three parts of a chatbot introduction: 1) the header, 2) the welcome messages, and 3) the customers' response options. The social cues were assigned to (either of) these three parts.

Regarding the header five subcategories were coded. The presence of an avatar was annotated (yes/no), and if so, its appearance (i.e., a brand logo, a robot, a human, an object, or other). The name of the chatbot (yes/no), and if so, the name type (i.e., brand name, robotlike name, human name, other) were also coded. Moreover, whether the chatbot disclosed itself with the label 'chatbot' (yes/no) was annotated. Lastly, the codebook contained an open category for other elements in the header (e.g., communicating expertise). In sum, the header's subcategories involved identity cues.

For the chatbot's welcome messages, nine subcategories were distinguished. First, the number of chatbot messages was coded. Thereafter, the presence of an avatar was coded (yes/no), and if so, its appearance (i.e., a brand logo, a robot, a human, an object, or other). Also, the presence of a greeting (e.g., 'Hello'; yes/no) and a self-introduction (e.g., 'My name is ...'; yes/no) was annotated. Furthermore, it was coded whether the chatbot's competence and/or its purpose was communicated, and if instructions were given to ensure a smooth interaction (all subcategories: yes/no). Lastly, it was coded whether the chatbot gave the turn to the customer at the end of the introduction (e.g., 'How can I help you?'). Thus, in the welcome messages two identity cues, three conversational cues, one competence cue, and two communication cues were identified.

For the response options, coders annotated the type of response options (buttons, open text field, or both). In case the chatbot allowed customers to communicate via buttons, the number of buttons was annotated. In case an open text field was present, it was annotated whether the chatbot indicated the number of characters customers can use to compose a written message (yes/no). Finally, the codebook contained an open field in which the coder could describe other observations regarding the chatbot introduction, such as whether the avatar in the first chatbot messages differed from the avatar in the header. The codebook can be found on OSF (https://osf.io/8wut9/).

3.3 Coding Procedure

Before coding the sample, a training was conducted by showing the chatbot introductions, discussing the codebook and illustrating it with examples. During the discussion two new cues were identified and added to the codebook, and one cue was slightly adjusted. These cues involved:

- Proactive cues. The discussed chatbot introductions often contained information the chatbot proactively provided. Two proactive cues were identified: 1) the presence of a privacy-disclaimer (yes/no), and 2) the presence of information about actions, offers, corona measures, or other topics (yes/no).
- Communication cues. The discussed chatbot introductions often contained messages in which the possibility to be redirected to a human employee (i.e., a handover [23]) was explained. This cue was added as a subcategory of communication cues as it explains what happens if a chatbot is not able to handle a message.
- Competence cue. The discussed chatbot introductions did not contain any statements about the chatbot's expertise, whereas statements about the chatbot's weaknesses did

occur. Therefore, we decided to annotate whether the chatbot's incompetence was communicated.

Next, a training set ($n = 10$) of chatbot introductions was created. The training set was individually coded by six annotators. Subsequently, the codings were compared and discussed, leading to final agreement and minor revisions of the codebook. Thereafter, the sample was divided over the six trained coders. To calculate intercoder reliability, a seventh independent coder double coded a subset of 25 chatbot introductions.

3.4 Data Analysis

To examine the reliability of our framework, intercoder reliability scores (Krippendorff's α) were calculated with SPSS v. 27 using the KALPHA macro [18]. Subsequently, descriptive statistics (frequencies and percentages) were computed to determine to what extent the cues identified in our framework occur in the chatbot introductions. Finally, the sample was analyzed qualitatively to describe how organizations tailor chatbot introduction using different social cues.

4 Results

4.1 Reliability of Social Cues in Chatbot Introduction

Table 2 shows the reliability scores of the double-coded social cues in chatbot introductions. The scores of the cues in the header were acceptable to satisfactory. In two instances the coders disagreed about the chatbot's name type. The name types were related to the brands (e.g., 'Tracy' for a postal service), but could also belong to other subcategories (e.g., humanlike name). Also, the scores of the cues in the welcome messages were satisfactory. However, the subcategory greeting showed insufficient reliability, although the agreement percentage was high indicating category prevalence [38]. Finally, the reliability score of the response options was acceptable (Krippendorff's α: 0.65; agreement percentage: 80.0). An explanation for this relatively low reliability score is that in some cases the buttons were less noticeable as they were integrated in the chatbot's message, whereas in other cases, the text field was less noticeable compared to buttons. The reliability score of the two other response cues were satisfactory to perfect (number of buttons: Krippendorff's α: 0.92; agreement percentage: 90.91; number of characters in text field: Krippendorff's α: 1.00; agreement percentage: 100).

4.2 Usage of Social Cues in Chatbot Introductions

Table 2 shows the social cues identified in the introductions of Dutch customer service chatbots. Our content analysis revealed half of the introductions' headers contained an avatar which was most often humanlike (16: 32.0%). Robotlike avatars and brand-related avatars occurred equally (14: 28.0%) as well as avatars depicting an object or something else (3: 6.0%). Names occurred in 44.3% of the introductions' headers and were mostly humanlike (26: 66.7%). Robotlike names (8: 20.5%) or other names (5: 12.8%) occurred

Table 2. Reliability scores (Krippendorff's α and percentage agreement) usage of social cues (frequencies and percentages)

Category	Intercoder reliability scores		Usage of social cues (n = 88)	
	Krippendorff's α	%	Frequencies	%
Header				
Avatar	1.00	100.00	50	56.8
Avatar type	0.91	93.33	16	32.0
Humanlike			14	28.0
Robotlike			14	28.0
Brand-related				
Object			3	3.4
Other			3	3.4
Name	0.92	96.00	39	44.3
Name type	0.65	80.00	26	66.7
Humanlike			8	20.5
Robotlike			5	12.8
Other				
Disclosure 'chatbot'	0.87	96.00	26	29.5
Welcome messages				
Number of messages	1.00	100.00		
Avatar	0.92	96.00	57	64.8
Avatar type	1.00	100.00		
Greeting	0.47	92.00	73	83.0
Self-introduction	0.89	96.00	56	63.6
Giving turn to customer	0.92	96.00	61	69.3
Statement incompetence	1.00	100.00	6	6.8
Explanation purpose	0.87	96.00	11	12.5
Explanation interaction	0.81	92.00	29	33.0
Explanation handover	1.00	100.00	16	18.2
Proactive information	0.71	92.00	8	9.1
Privacy disclaimer	1.00	100.00	5	5.7

less frequently. Almost three out of ten headers contained the disclosure 'chatbot'. In addition, other disclosure formulations were found as well, such as 'virtual assistant', 'digital assistant', and 'service bot'.

The mean number of welcome messages was 1.77 (*SD* 0.85). An avatar accompanied these messages in almost two-thirds of the cases. Humanlike avatars were most frequent (21: 36.8%), followed by a brand logo (18: 31.6%) and robotlike avatars (14:

24.6%). Avatars depicting an object (1: 1.8%) or something else (3: 5.3%) were least frequent. The welcome messages often contained conversational cues. Greetings (73: 83.0%) were most frequent, followed by giving the turn to the customer (61: 69.3%) and self-introductions (56: 63.6%). Moreover, statements of incompetence, such as 'I am new but do my best to help you' or 'chatbot in training' hardly occurred (6: 6.8%). Also, welcome messages did not often contain communication cues. Explanations about the interaction (e.g., 'Formulate your question briefly and concisely') occurred most often (29: 33.0%), followed by the possibility to be redirected to a human agent (16: 18.2%), and explanations about the chatbot's purpose (11: 12.5%, e.g., 'I can help you with entrepreneurial questions'). Finally, welcome messages hardly contained pro-active information (8: 9.1%) and privacy disclaimers (5: 5.7%).

The response options mostly consisted of text boxes only (38: 43.2%). Buttons as well as the combination of a text box and buttons equally occurred (25: 28.4%). In almost five out of ten text boxes, the number of characters customers could use to compose a message was communicated (12: 19.0%). The mean number of buttons present in chatbot introductions was 3.88 (*SD* 2.50) and varied from 1 to 12 buttons.

4.3 Qualitative Analysis of Social Cues in Chatbot Introductions

The current section discusses five examples of our sample. These examples were selected as they represent atypical and prototypical chatbot introductions.

Fig. 2. Anonymized atypical chatbot introductions of two telecom providers (left and middle) and an insurance company (right).

The chatbot introductions of two telecom providers are shown in Fig. 2. The left screenshot highlights an atypical chatbot introduction with some distinctive features. The header contains a humanlike avatar and a humanlike name ('Sam'). Moreover, a green dot is present which mimics a convention from human computer-mediated communication, i.e., a person is online and available. The first chatbot message contains a greeting ('Hi'), and a self-introduction ('I am Sam, the virtual customer expert of [brand]'). Interestingly, second chatbot message contains mixed signals by describing the chatbot's capabilities on the one hand, but also providing instructions on how to formulate questions on the other hand: 'I know quite a lot already. Describe your question or problem as short as possible, and everything will be alright:-)'. The latter is also stressed by the number of characters in the text field (i.e., 255 characters). Remarkably, the words 'Talk to Sam' are added in the text field to invite the customer in the conversation. The screenshot in the middle also illustrates an atypical introduction as it contains mixed signals regarding the chatbot's identity. The header only contains the brand logo. Furthermore, the customer is greeted in an informal way in the first message ('hey!' and an emoji), which is presented in an irregular typeface and font size. The chatbot's identity is disclosed in the second chatbot message, (i.e., 'the chatbot of [brand]'). Lastly, the chatbot communicates the possibility of a handover in the third message, but with the notion that human employees are available as from the next day 8 o'clock. Below the messages, the words 'virtual assistant' are shown. The last example of an atypical chatbot introduction is from an insurance company (Fig. 2, right). The header contains an avatar (smiley in a square), which resembles the brand logo. The words 'chat with [brand]' do not make it explicit that the customer will chat with a chatbot, nor do the welcome message or response buttons. Furthermore, it is interesting that the chatbot poses an open question to the user ('about which product would you like to chat?'), but the response buttons show the topics the chatbot is trained on.

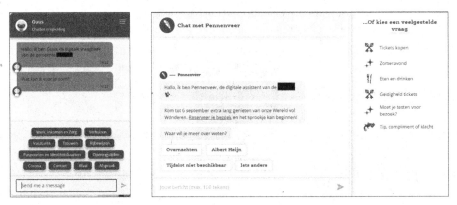

Fig. 3. Anonymized prototypical chatbot introductions of a municipality (left) and theme park (right)

An example of a prototypical chatbot introduction is from a Dutch municipality, which is shown on the left in Fig. 3. The header contains a robotlike avatar, a human-like name ('Guus'), a chatbot disclosure ('chatbot'), and a description of the chatbot's incompetence ('in training'). Remarkably, the avatar next to the chatbot's messages differs from the avatar in the header. Also, after the greeting ('Hello') and self-introduction ('I am Guus'), the chatbot refers to itself with the unusual words 'digital Q&A'. Even though the chatbot's incompetence was communicated in the header, the appearance of eleven response buttons and an open text field suggests the chatbot is capable to answer questions on a wide range of topics. Finally, the screenshot on the right shows the chatbot introduction of a theme park. The header contains both an avatar and a name of an object ('pen quill'). The first welcome message contains a disclosure 'digital assistant'. Interestingly, the second message contains proactive information about the extended opening hours until September 6, with a call to action to make a reservation by clicking on the hyperlink. Different from other introductions is that the chatbot's name and avatar are located above the messages instead of next to them. Response buttons, a text field as well as FAQs, give users ample possibilities to respond.

5 Conclusion and Discussion

The aim of this study was to determine (1) to what extent social cues in customer service chatbot introductions can be analyzed reliably, and (2) to what extent the social cues identified in our framework occur in the introductions of customer service chatbots.

We identified five main categories of social cues that can occur in chatbot introductions, see Table 3. The first main category concerns identity cues through which the chatbot's artificial identity is masked or marked. Three subcategories are identified: a chatbot disclosure, the avatar type, and the name type. The second main category consists of competence cues through which the chatbot's weaknesses are communicated. Moreover, conversational cues are identified which concern the chatbot's conversational etiquette, such as the presence of a greeting, a self-introduction, and explicitly giving the turn to the customer after the chatbot's welcome messages. The fourth main category involves communication cues through which the chatbot indicates its functionalities. Three subcategories are identified: an explanation of the chatbot's purpose, an explanation about how to interact with it, and the possibility of being redirected to a human agent. The last main category entails proactive information, such as the presence of a privacy-disclaimer and information about offers, corona measures, or other topics.

Table 3. Updated framework of social cues in chatbot introductions

Identity cues	Competence cues	Conversational cues	Communication cues	Proactive cues
Disclosure	Statement stressing weakness	Greeting	Explanation purpose	Privacy disclaimer
Avatar type		Self-introduction	Explanation interaction	Proactive information
Name type		Turn-taking	Handover	

In order to validate our framework, we conducted a content analysis of 88 introductions of Dutch customer service chatbots. For each part of the chatbot introduction (i.e., header, welcome messages, and response options), the presence and/or type of social cues was annotated. A subset of the sample was double coded. The results of the intercoder reliability analysis showed that the agreement was sufficient for the identity cues in the chatbot's header (i.e., disclosure, avatar, and name). Also, most scores of the social cues in the welcome messages were satisfactory. Only the reliability of the subcategory 'greeting' was low, due to category prevalence [38]. It was difficult to obtain a sufficient reliability score because in most chatbot introductions a greeting was present. Lastly, the intercoder agreement of the response cues were acceptable to satisfactory. An explanation for the relatively low agreement score for the response options is that in some cases the buttons were less noticeable as they were integrated in the chatbot's message, whereas in other cases, the text field was less noticeable due to the many buttons.

Our framework turned out to be a reliable identification instrument for social cues in chatbot introductions. However, we feel improvements can be made. For example, we noticed that the self-introduction often contained a name as well as a disclosure. Regarding the chatbot's disclosure, only the label 'chatbot' was annotated, but other labels were used as well, such as 'virtual assistant', 'smart assistant' and 'digital agent'. These labels should also be incorporated in the framework as the explicitness of the disclosure influences customers' expectations [7]. Furthermore, the framework can be extended by annotating whether competence cues are present, and if so, whether this cue stresses the chatbot's competence or incompetence, since competence cues could enhance users' perceptions of trust [32]. Lastly, the adoption of informal language could be added to the main category identity cues, since elements like emoji and interjections mimic human-human interactions [25] that could mask the chatbot's identity.

Regarding the usage of social cues in chatbot introductions it was found that the most prevalent social cue in the header of chatbot introductions is a humanlike avatar. Also, a humanlike name was often present in the header. Compared to these anthropomorphic identity cues, the chatbot's disclosure was less frequent in headers. Thus, organizations seem to combine social cues which both mask and mark the artificial identity of the chatbot. Regarding the social cues in welcome messages, our findings show that a humanlike avatar as well as the three conversation cues are frequently used. This could indicate that organizations try to give customers the impression they are communicating with a humanlike interlocutor rather than an artificial entity, and that they aim to welcome customers warmly. In contrast, while competence cues have received quite some attention in previous research [21, 22, 32], we noticed that incompetence cues occurred in chatbot introductions. Taking the findings of Khadpe et al. [21] and Kull et al. [22] into account, it is beneficial for organizations to focus on cues that stimulate expectations of warmth rather than competence.

Given the fact that chatbots are not always able to provide adequate responses to customers' requests due to poor intent recognition [13, 23], it is remarkable that organizations often offer customers the possibility to formulate their questions in a text field without character restrictions. This response option invites customers to formulate their messages in their own words resulting in an increased risk of failed intent recognition and subsequently miscommunication. Only in some cases, the open text field contained a character limit to force customers to send short messages with only keywords. In a similar vein, it is remarkable that communication cues hardly appear in chatbot introductions, while they could steer the customer's expectations and behavior towards the chatbot [5, 16, 19].

The current study's framework is tested on a relatively small sample of chatbot introductions belonging to Dutch organizations. In order to validate its reliability and to enhance the generalizability of our findings, a content analysis should be conducted on a larger sample that also contains customer service chatbots in other countries and languages. Moreover, a follow-up study would allow us to take factors into account that could impact the presence of social cues in chatbot introductions, such as the platform type of the chatbot (i.e., a public website versus WhatsApp), and organization type (profit versus non-profit). Furthermore, it is valuable to investigate how and why conversational designers deliberately adopt social cues in their chatbot designs. Their considerations can be compared with customers' perceptions and expectations of social cues in chatbot introductions. Lastly, the framework allows experimental research in which different chatbot introductions are manipulated and compared in a more systematic way. As multiple social cues are present in chatbot introductions, future research should examine whether certain combinations of social cues have a stronger impact on customers' expectations than other combinations. For example, the chatbot's perceived competence might not only be determined by a statement of its competence, but also an explanation on how customers should interact and which response options they can use. This way, chatbot introductions that steer users' expectations beforehand could bridge the gap between organizations that aim to successfully deploy chatbots in their customer service, and customers who are hesitant to use the chatbot.

Acknowledgements. The authors would like to thank Louise Braat, Boet Bruijniks, Myrthe Jagers, Marco Krijthe, and Sammie Smaak for collecting and coding the sample. This research is part of the NWO-funded project 'Smooth Operators: development and effects of personalized conversational AI', grant no: KIVI.2019.009.

References

1. Araujo, T.: Living up to the chatbot hype: The influence of anthropomorphic design cues and communicative agency framing on conversational agent and company perceptions. Comput. Hum. Behav. **85**, 183–189 (2018)
2. Brackeen, B.: How to Humanize Artificial Intelligence with Emotion (2017). https://medium.com/@BrianBrackeen/how-to-humanize-artificial-intelligence-with-emotion-19f981b1314a. Accessed 21 Sept 2022
3. Brandtzaeg, P.B., Følstad, A.: Why people use chatbots. In: Kompatsiaris, I., Cave, J., Satsiou, A., Carle, G., Passani, A., Kontopoulos, E., Diplaris, S., McMillan, D. (eds.) INSCI 2017. LNCS, vol. 10673, pp. 377–392. Springer, Cham (2017). https://doi.org/10.1007/978-3-319-70284-1_30
4. Brandtzaeg, P.B., Følstad, A.: Chatbots: changing user needs and motivations. Interactions **25**(5), 38–43 (2018). https://doi.org/10.1145/3236669
5. Chaves, A.P., Gerosa, M.A.: How should my chatbot interact? A survey on social characteristics in human–chatbot interaction design. Int. J. Hum.–Comput. Interact. **37**(8), 729–758 (2021)
6. Crolic, C., Thomaz, F., Hadi, R., Stephen, A.T.: Blame the bot: anthropomorphism and anger in customer–chatbot interactions. J. Mark. **86**(1), 132–148 (2022)
7. De Cicco, R., da Costa e Silva, S.C.L., Palumbo, R.: Should a chatbot disclose itself? Implications for an online conversational retailer. In: Følstad, A., Araujo, T., Papadopoulos, S., Law, E.L.-C., Luger, E., Goodwin, M., Brandtzaeg, P.B. (eds.) CONVERSATIONS 2020. LNCS, vol. 12604, pp. 3–15. Springer, Cham (2021). https://doi.org/10.1007/978-3-030-68288-0_1

8. Drift: The 2018 State of Chatbots Report (2018). https://www.drift.com/wp-content/uploads/2018/01/2018-state-of-chatbots-report.pdf. Accessed 20 Sept 2022
9. Feine, J., Gnewuch, U., Morana, S., Maedche, A.: A taxonomy of social cues for conversational agents. Int. J. Hum.-Comput. Stud. **132**, 138–161 (2019)
10. Fiore, S.M., Wiltshire, T.J., Lobato, E.J.C., Jentsch, F.G., Huang, W.H., Axelrod, B.: Toward understanding social cues and signals in human-robot interaction: effects of robot gaze and proxemic behavior. Front. Psychol. **4**, 859 (2013)
11. Følstad, A., Brandtzæg, P.B.: Chatbots and the new world of HCI. Interactions **24**(4), 38–42 (2017)
12. Følstad, A., Nordheim, C.B., Bjørkli, C.A.: What makes users trust a chatbot for customer service? An exploratory interview study. In: Bodrunova, S.S. (ed.) INSCI 2018. LNCS, vol. 11193, pp. 194–208. Springer, Cham (2018). https://doi.org/10.1007/978-3-030-01437-7_16
13. Følstad, A., Skjuve, M.: Chatbots for customer service: user experience and motivation. In: Proceedings of the 1st International Conference on Conversational User Interfaces, pp. 1–9 (2019)
14. Følstad, A., Taylor, C.: Investigating the user experience of customer service chatbot interaction: a framework for qualitative analysis of chatbot dialogues. Qual. User Exp. **6**(1), 1–17 (2021)
15. Gambino, A., Fox, J., Ratan, R.A.: Building a stronger CASA: extending the computers are social actors paradigm. Hum.-Mach. Commun. **1**, 71–85 (2020)
16. Gnewuch, U., Morana, S., Maedche, A.: Towards designing cooperative and social conversational agents for customer service. In ICIS. (2017)
17. Go, E., Sundar, S.S.: Humanizing chatbots: the effects of visual, identity and conversational cues on humanness perceptions. Comput. Hum. Behav. **97**, 304–316 (2019)
18. Hayes, A.F., Krippendorff, K.: Answering the call for a standard reliability measure for coding data. Commun. Methods Meas. **1**(1), 77–89 (2007)
19. Jain, M., Kumar, P., Kota, R., Patel, S.N.: Evaluating and informing the design of chatbots. In: Proceedings of the 2018 on Designing Interactive Systems Conference, pp. 895–906. ACM (2018)
20. Jovic, D.: The Future is Now - 37 Fascinating Chatbot Statistics (2022). https://www.smallbizgenius.net/by-the-numbers/chatbot-statistics. Accessed 20 Sept 2022
21. Khadpe, P., Krishna, R., Fei-Fei, L., Hancock, J.T., Bernstein, M.S.: Conceptual metaphors impact perceptions of human-ai collaboration. In: Proceedings of the ACM on Human-Computer Interaction, vol. 4, no. CSCW2, pp. 1–26 (2020)
22. Kull, A.J., Romero, M., Monahan, L.: How may I help you? Driving brand engagement through the warmth of an initial chatbot message. J. Bus. Res. **135**, 840–850 (2021)
23. Kvale, K., Sell, O.A., Hodnebrog, S., Følstad, A.: Improving conversations: lessons learnt from manual analysis of chatbot dialogues. In: Følstad, A., Araujo, T., Papadopoulos, S., Law, E.L.-C., Granmo, O.-C., Luger, E., Brandtzaeg, P.B. (eds.) CONVERSATIONS 2019. LNCS, vol. 11970, pp. 187–200. Springer, Cham (2020). https://doi.org/10.1007/978-3-030-39540-7_13
24. Laban, G., Araujo, T.: Working together with conversational agents: the relationship of perceived cooperation with service performance evaluations. In: Følstad, A., Araujo, T., Papadopoulos, S., Law, E.L.-C., Granmo, O.-C., Luger, E., Brandtzaeg, P.B. (eds.) CONVERSATIONS 2019. LNCS, vol. 11970, pp. 215–228. Springer, Cham (2020). https://doi.org/10.1007/978-3-030-39540-7_15
25. Liebrecht, C., Tsaousi, C., van Hooijdonk, C.: Linguistic elements of conversational human voice in online brand communication: manipulations and perceptions. J. Bus. Res. **132**, 124–135 (2021)

26. Liebrecht, C., van der Weegen, E.: Menselijke chatbots: een zegen voor online klantcontact?: Het effect van conversational human voice door chatbots op social presence en merkattitude. Tijd. Com. **47**(3) (2019)

27. Lombard, M., Ditton, T.: At the heart of it all: the concept of presence. J. Comput.-Mediat. Commun. **3**(2), JCMC321 (1997)

28. Lombard, M., Xu, K.: Social responses to media technologies in the 21st century: the media are social actors paradigm. Hum.-Mach. Commun. **2**, 29–55 (2021)

29. Luff, P., Gilbert, N.G., Frohlich, D. (eds.): Computers and Conversation. Academic Press, Cambridge (1990)

30. Luger, E., Sellen, A.: "Like having a really bad PA": the gulf between user expectation and experience of conversational agents. In: Proceedings of CHI 2016, pp. 5286–5297. ACM, New York (2016)

31. Luo, X., Tong, S., Fang, Z., Qu, Z.: Frontiers: machines vs. humans: the impact of artificial intelligence chatbot disclosure on customer purchases. Mark. Sci. **38**(6), 937–947 (2019)

32. Mozafari, N., Weiger, W.H., Hammerschmidt, M.: Resolving the chatbot disclosure dilemma: leveraging selective self-presentation to mitigate the negative effect of chatbot disclosure. In: Proceedings of the 54th Hawaii International Conference on System Sciences, p. 2916 (2021)

33. Nass, C., Moon, Y.: Machines and mindlessness: social responses to computers. J. Soc. Issues **56**(1), 81–103 (2000)

34. Nass, C., Steuer, J., Tauber, E.R.: Computers are social actors. In: Proceedings of the SIGCHI Conference on Human Factors in Computing Systems, pp. 72–78 (1994)

35. Nordheim, C.B., Følstad, A., Bjørkli, C.A.: An initial model of trust in chatbots for customer service—findings from a questionnaire study. Interact. Comput. **31**(3), 317–335 (2019)

36. Paluch, S.: Remote Service Technology Perception and Its Impact on Customer-Provider Relationships: An Empirical Exploratory Study in a B-to-B-Setting. Springer, Cham (2011). https://doi.org/10.1007/978-3-8349-6936-1

37. Shechtman, N., Horowitz, L. M.: Media inequality in conversation: how people behave differently when interacting with computers and people. In: Proceedings of the SIGCHI Conference on Human Factors in Computing Systems, pp. 281–288 (2003)

38. Spooren, W., Degand, L.: Coding coherence relations: reliability and validity. Corp. Ling. Ling. Theory **6**(2), 241–266 (2010)

39. Thormundsson, B.: Chatbot market revenue worldwide from 2018 to 2027 (2022). https://www.statista.com/statistics/1007392/worldwide-chatbot-market-size/. Accessed 20 Sept 2022

40. Valério, F.A., Guimarães, T.G., Prates, R.O., Candello, H.: Here's what I can do: chatbots' strategies to convey their features to users. In: Proceedings of the XVI Brazilian Symposium on Human Factors in Computing Systems, pp. 1–10 (2017)

41. van der Goot, M.J., Hafkamp, L., Dankfort, Z.: Customer service chatbots: a qualitative interview study into the communication journey of customers. In: Følstad, A., Araujo, T., Papadopoulos, S., Law, E.L.-C., Luger, E., Goodwin, M., Brandtzaeg, P.B. (eds.) CONVERSATIONS 2020. LNCS, vol. 12604, pp. 190–204. Springer, Cham (2021). https://doi.org/10.1007/978-3-030-68288-0_13

42. van der Goot, M.J., Pilgrim, T.: Exploring age differences in motivations for and acceptance of chatbot communication in a customer service context. In: Følstad, A., Araujo, T., Papadopoulos, S., Law, E.L.-C., Granmo, O.-C., Luger, E., Brandtzaeg, P.B. (eds.) CONVERSATIONS 2019. LNCS, vol. 11970, pp. 173–186. Springer, Cham (2020). https://doi.org/10.1007/978-3-030-39540-7_12

An Affective Multi-modal Conversational Agent for Non Intrusive Data Collection from Patients with Brain Diseases

Chloe Chira[1], Evangelos Mathioudis[1(✉)], Christina Michailidou[2],
Pantelis Agathangelou[1], Georgia Christodoulou[2], Ioannis Katakis[1],
Efstratios Kontopoulos[2], and Konstantinos Avgerinakis[2]

[1] Department of Computer Science, School of Sciences and Engineering,
University of Nicosia, 2417 Nicosia, Cyprus
{chira.c,katakis.i}@unic.ac.cy,
{mathioudis.e,agathangelou.p}@live.unic.ac.cy
[2] CataLink Limited, Nicosia, Cyprus
{cmichailidou,georgiach,e.kontopoulos,koafgeri}@catalink.eu

Abstract. This paper presents Zenon, an affective, multi-modal conversational agent (chatbot) specifically designed for treatment of brain diseases like multiple sclerosis and stroke. Zenon collects information from patients in a non-intrusive way and records user sentiment using two different modalities: text and video. A user-friendly interface is designed to meet users' needs and achieve an efficient conversation flow. What makes Zenon unique is the support of multiple languages, the combination of two information sources for tracking sentiment, and the deployment of a semantic knowledge graph that ensures machine-interpretable information exchange.

Keywords: Conversational agents · Chatbot · Brain diseases · e-Health · Sentiment analysis · Knowledge graph

1 Introduction

Parkinson's Disease, Multiple Sclerosis, and Stroke are three of the most frequent chronic neurological diseases that lead to significant cognitive and motor disability. Neurodegenerative diseases, such as Parkinson's, are following an increasing trend in rates along with the aging of the global population. Additionally, the number of people living with stroke is estimated to increase by 27% between 2017 and 2047 in the European Union [29], mainly due to population aging and improved survival rates.

A Conversational Agent (chatbot) is designed to simulate verbal conversations. Because of their potential to improve patient care by interacting with them via Instant Messaging applications Conversational Agents have become popular in the healthcare domain. Despite their popularity, many Conversational Agents

A. Følstad et al. (Eds.): CONVERSATIONS 2022, LNCS 13815, pp. 134–149, 2023.
https://doi.org/10.1007/978-3-031-25581-6_9

are not able to meet users' expectations, and promoting a positive user experience is a difficult endeavor [13,30].

Zenon is part of the European-funded project, called ALAMEDA[1] and was first introduced in [25]. The aim of ALAMEDA is to provide patients with Parkinson's Disease, Multiple Sclerosis, and Stroke with personalised rehabilitation treatment assessments through the use of Artificial Intelligence and healthcare support systems. Apart from the conversational agent, ALAMEDA utilizes a plethora of technologies like smart mattresses, smart bands, smart insoles, and smart belts. Zenon in this context is responsible to collect information complementary to the other sensors. It handles different tasks such as sentiment analysis on open 'chit-chat' user input, filling medical questionnaires according to a schedule, and gathering data for specific lifestyle attributes proposed by the medical partners.

The main motivation for implementing a Conversational Agent within a project like ALAMEDA are: a) The use of a familiar conversation-like interface to collect information that normally would have to be collected in the hospital or medical office, or to monitor the patient's mood through free-text conversations, b) The ability to use multiple channels of information (text messages and face expressions) to extract knowledge about the patient's mood, c) The fact that can quickly ask questions about their medical status and the most recently recorded measurements. The **contributions** of this paper are the following:

- To the best of our knowledge, Zenon is the first agent specifically designed to assist patients suffering from Parkinson's, MS, and Stroke. Zenon's conversational manager addresses the modeling of complex scheduled health questionnaires as conversations, analyzes the patient's mood through free-text conversations related to psychological or social status, and provides quick query capabilities for patient health status (see Sects. 3.2, 3.5).
- A linguistic model developed for text-based sentiment analysis that supports four languages (*English, Greek, Italian, Romanian*) (see Sect. 3.2), that combines the extraction of local features and the exploitation of global features in a single unit.
- A facial expression sentiment analysis component (see Sect. 3.3). The service monitors the facial expressions of the patient through the camera of the phone and provides estimations of their mood. We extend the capabilities of the state-of-the-art facial emotion recognition CNN models that are designed to provide real-time inference on edge devices. After appropriate architecture design changes and training of the model on our dataset, the model achieved acceptable real-time performance accuracy (75%).
- A sentiment aggregation component that receives input from two modalities (text, video) and annotates where these agree or disagree. This is beneficial for the system to fuse this information by considering the labels of both components and the confidence of each one. Moreover, future research will benefit from the generated dataset of multi-modal sentiment analysis, as currently there are no such datasets available (see Sect. 3.4).

---

[1] https://alamedaproject.eu/.

– A data integration infrastructure based on W3C-compliant semantic technologies that allow the agent to retrieve information from and send information to the ALAMEDA platform (e.g., questionnaire responses, sentiment analysis results) in a uniform, efficient and scalable fashion (see Sect. 3.5).

2   Related Work

We organize related work in two parts: a) Conversational agents that are utilized in health applications, and b) Sentiment analysis in systems that are based on machine learning and assume the availability of relevant training data.

2.1   Conversational Agents for Health

Concerning the conversational agents' role in health, several directions have been identified: treatment and monitoring, health services support, health care education, addressing the various health risk factors that can be modified through lifestyle and diagnosis, and collecting data of various types.

People with asthma can use the Puffbot chatbot [28] to support their treatment. Puffbot integrates a conversational ontology, Natural Language Processing (NLP) to handle conversations with patients. Chatbot EVA [4] also relies on NLP methods to extract entities from users' input and classify users' intents. EVA assists people to manage their diabetes by providing education, and recommendations related to their health issues. HOLMeS [3] is enhanced with NLP, and text mining techniques, to act like a human physician and help patients pick their disease prevention pathway by autonomously handling discussions with patients and chatting. In [26], the authors developed a counseling chatbot enhanced with multi-modal emotional analysis to provide conversational services for mental health. Also, MoSCHA [18], a healthcare mobile assistant, improves patient-doctor communication and assists patients to manage their chronic diseases. The method integrates several wearable and other sensors to gather data for each patient. [24] reports that the use of agent-based dialogue management is rare in the healthcare domain. All in all, there is a significant effort towards utilizing chatbots for health. However, work towards brain diseases, with a focus on collecting information and utilizing sentiment analysis to affect the conversation flow is very limited. This is the gap we aspire to fill with this work.

2.2   Sentiment Analysis from Text and Video

Analysis of user-generated text in medical text and online social media can provide valuable information about public opinion trends and specific aspects of information spaces in the health domain.

In [23] a framework to automatically extract COVID-19-related topics from social media and apply Long Short-Term Memory for sentiment classification on

COVID-19-related comments is described. The team applies NLP methods to discover COVID-19-related issues from public opinions. Additionally, they apply LSTM recurrent neural networks, enhanced with the LDA to analyze COVID-19 comments based on their sentiment. The performance of the presented approach was better than other machine learning algorithms for Sentiment classification. Another work [2], to assist patients to browse and search specific information, scraped anonymous posts from online medical forums related to Lyme disease to extract content-free, content-specific, and meta-level features. These features are fed as input to a multi-class neural network. The approach outperformed other classification algorithms in sentiment classification of posts about Lyme disease from several relevant forums. In [5] the authors present the Multi-input RIMs, a novel extension of the Recurrent independent mechanisms utilizing a modular system to leverage several readily available knowledge sources such as part-of-speech information and gazetteer lists. Experiments conducted on three sentiment analysis tasks and two health-related tweet classification tasks showed improvements without increasing the number of parameters.

Facial expressions and certain muscle movements can prove to be a strong indicator of how a person feels and in combination with other techniques, such as text sentiment analysis, can help us draw safer conclusions about the emotional state of the person. The most recent and commonly exploited technology for the development of facial expression recognition is the training of Convolutional Neural Networks (CNN). For example, in [15] a real-time computer vision system for emotion prediction is presented, which is based on a pre-trained CNN, while in [7] a CNN (ExpNet) is trained to estimate 3D facial expression coefficients which are then used to detect the facial emotions. In [6,14] a combination of Convolutional Neural Network and Recurrent Neural Network (RNN) is exploited for video-based emotion recognition, while in [20] one 2D CNN and one 3D CNN are used for audio and visual emotion recognition respectively and the features of the models are fused in order to reach a final prediction. In the Healthcare domain [19], develops a 3D CNN model for capturing and analysing video frames from the house of the patient and reporting back to the clinicians the detected emotional status of the patient.

In our work, not only we redesign, integrate, train and fine-tune state-of-the-art models for the purposes of the specific chatbot, but we also provide the ability to aggregate the sentiment information from the two modalities (text and video).

3   Zenon Conversational Agent

Requirements Collection. Zenon was designed after careful consideration of patient requirements and thorough discussions with medical experts. For this reason, the research team has developed local community groups in order to list and prioritize the requirements. The local community groups were composed of representatives from the categories impacted most in each use case as well as people involved in their care such as professionals from healthcare domains apart from their specialty care physicians (e.g. physical therapists, psychologists), relatives, and informal caregivers of the patients. Depending on each brain disease studied in this project, different questionnaires were designed to collect such input from the aforementioned groups.

What is challenging in ALAMEDA is the need to adapt to three different brain diseases, in three use cases that take place in three different countries with patients that speak three different languages: a) Stroke in Romania, b) Multiple Sclerosis in Italy, and c) Parkinson's in Greece. One of the main functionalities of Zenon is to help the user submit information related to medical questionnaires that were normally filled in a medical office or in a hospital. The Stroke case questionnaires need to be modeled as a conversation in order to capture the complexity of question-answer-follow-up questions. Additionally, patients with chronic diseases such as Stroke or Parkinson's Disease found using a chatbot interface helpful when asking about their medical status. For the Multiple Sclerosis case, the local community group identified a chatbot interface as appropriate to allow MS patients to report symptoms that signal an increase in the chance of suffering a disease relapse. Lastly, medical partners suggested the option of free-text conversations on the topic of psychological or social status situations of the patients, where the existence of such conversations acts as an additional input modality to assess weekly emotional state.

The functional requirements can be summarized into the following points:

1. Collect patient-reported outcomes on health status, lifestyle and well-being, and psychological factors
2. Enable multi-modal sentiment estimation through analysis of free-text conversations and facial expressions.
3. Enable access to information on patient health status through simple user queries.

Overview. Following these requirements the system was designed according to the architecture that can be seen in Fig. 1.

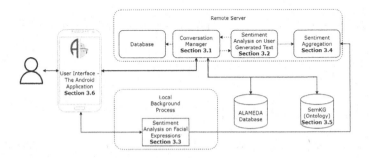

Fig. 1. Zenon overview

The user starts the chatbot and types a message. While interacting with the app, the Sentiment Analysis on Face Expressions runs in the background and makes predictions in real time. The result of this and the original text is sent to the Conversation Agent hosted on the dedicated server for analysis. The Conversation Manager sends every user input directly to the Sentiment Analysis model to extract the sentiment which will influence the conversation flow. After the agent processes the input, the dialogue, and the results are stored in the Semantic Knowledge Graph (SemKG).

3.1 Conversation Manager

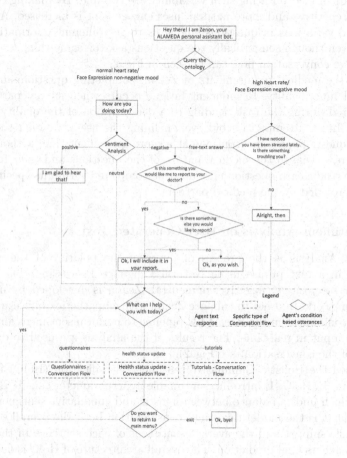

Fig. 2. Main conversation flow

Carefully crafted conversation flows are the foundation of every efficient conversational agent. Zenon's flow was constructed based on design guidelines for task-oriented chatbots for healthcare and other domains [9,17,22].

There are two ways to start the conversation. In the first one, Zenon initiates the discussion when the user clicks on a notification. Zenon's initial message is based on the notification's context. The second way is when the user initiates the discussion. In both cases the chatbot will at some point ask the user about their emotional state and whether there is something they would like to report. Based on the user requirements the agent has to exhibit empathetic traits while engaging in such discussions. This will evoke a more natural user-chatbot relation, increasing engagement and ensuring a better quality of answers. To achieve an empathetic personality we integrated a sentiment analysis model which infers the sentiment of the users' text input in real-time (see Sect. 3.2).

Paraphrases were incorporated for the questions and answers of the agents. The benefits of incorporating such variability are two-fold. By making conversations less repetitive and more natural, user engagement is increased. Additionally, lexical variations in questions enable us to get different information from the user even though semantically the questions ask the same thing.

The core conversation flow can be seen in Fig. 2.

Given the medical requirements of Zenon, completing questionnaires is its most used functionality. Respondent fatigue occurs when survey participants become tired during the task, leading to a deterioration of the quality of their responses. In an attempt to avoid overwhelming the users, we offer the option to stop a questionnaire and continue at a more convenient time without losing their progress. Due to the medical nature of the questions and their frequency within the study, each questionnaire must be completed within its specified time frame as provided by the medical partners.

3.2 Sentiment Analysis on User Generated Text

Sentiment Analysis is the process of inferring the polarity of the emotions expressed in a text phrase using Natural Language Processing. The polarity can either be positive, negative, or neutral. Zenon is developed by using the Rasa[2] framework. In order to enhance Zenon with empathetic abilities we added a custom component in the Rasa NLU pipeline to perform sentiment analysis on the user's input in real-time. The results of the analysis are used to determine the flow of the conversation (see Fig. 2).

We used the Holistic Cumulative sentiment classification (HolC) model as proposed in [1]. HolC [1] introduces a tunable hyperparameter called "Balancing Factor" which finds a balance between holistic and cumulative sentiment classification. That is the model takes into consideration both the overall sentiment of the whole snippet and the average sentiment of each sentence in the text in order to make its final prediction. The overall architecture of HolC is depicted in Fig. 3. The model was trained on opinionated reviews from Amazon's repository[3] from several domains such as Health and Personal Care, Books, etc.

As one of the main requirements of this project was accessibility we extended the original HolC model to be language agnostic and support multiple languages.

---

[2] https://rasa.com/docs/rasa/2.x.

[3] https://jmcauley.ucsd.edu/data/amazon/.

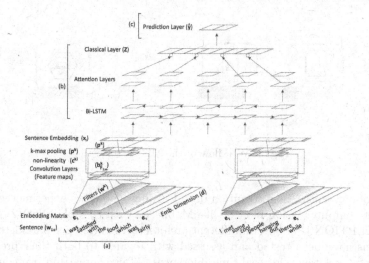

Fig. 3. HolC architecture, taken from [1]

The training datasets were mass-translated using Google translate in the Romanian, Italian and Greek languages. The model was trained using a corpus containing tokens for all these languages. Combining several languages in a single model provides more benefits than having one model per language. Firstly, the predictions are more robust. Moreover, the model is language agnostic i.e. It is able to process and support combinations of these languages or all of them together in a single phrase without losing content or context.

3.3 Sentiment Analysis on Facial Expressions

The goal of this module is to monitor the face of the patient while they interact with the Chatbot. The analysis takes place on a per-frame basis and was facilitated through the design, deployment, and training of a Machine Learning model which takes as input video frames and outputs the emotional state estimation of the user. The overall workflow of the application is depicted in Fig. 4. As in textual sentiment analysis, the results of the Facial Expression Analysis can also affect the flow of the discussion (see Fig. 2).

The first step is the localization of the user's face within the video frame. This is realized through the exploitation of the ML Kit[4] that is able to locate the face of a user and draw a bounding box around it. As a result, the region of interest is cropped and fed to the emotion recognition computer vision model, which outputs the prediction regarding the emotional state of the user. Each frame is classified into one of the following classes: "negative", "positive", or "neutral".

Our module builds and fine-tunes state-of-the-art CNN models that are designed particularly for mobile and embedded vision applications. For the

---

[4] https://developers.google.com/ml-kit.

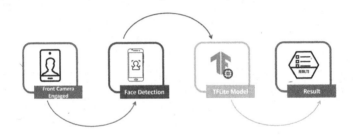

Fig. 4. Workflow of the MEAA service

design of our sentiment recognition deep learning model, we experimented with different computer vision models, like MobileNetV1 [21], MobileNetV2 [27] and miniXCEPTION [15]. Several different architectures and hyper-parameter combinations have been tested and assessed with regards to both their prediction accuracy and latency for real-time inferences. After comparison, we concluded that miniXCEPTION demonstrated the best prediction performance (approximately 75% prediction accuracy under real conditions) and the shortest latency.

For the training of the emotion recognition model, large amounts of imagery data are required. However, since there is a limited amount of freely available face images, the model was trained using Transfer Learning. According to this technique, a pre-trained model can be re-purposed on a new problem. For our training, we use as a starting point the miniXCEPTION network, that has been pre-trained on the ImageNet [12] dataset. Then, the fully-connected layers are removed and new ones are added, while all the convolutional layers remain frozen (i.e. they are set as non-trainable). The model is re-trained, but this time on the emotion recognition dataset.

For our model training, our data has been carefully chosen so that it represents well the population. Specifically, we collected facial images of people with various facial expressions, from different ages, with and without accessories (like glasses), and faces under different lighting conditions. In that way, we managed to improve the generalization ability of our model. The emotion recognition dataset is a combination of data collected from different sources like Kaggle (FER 2013 dataset[5], Jafar Hussain Human emotions dataset[6]) and other open source databases such as Unsplash[7], Pexels[8] and Pixabay[9]. Once the model was trained, it was converted into a TFLite[10] version, which is suitable for running on edge devices respecting the limited resources.

User privacy and transparency concerns have also been considered and addressed. As regards privacy, the analysis is conducted only on the device.

---

[5] https://www.kaggle.com/datasets/msambare/fer2013.
[6] https://www.kaggle.com/jafarhussain786/datasets.
[7] https://unsplash.com/.
[8] https://www.pexels.com/search/face/.
[9] https://pixabay.com/vectors/.
[10] https://www.tensorflow.org/lite.

The extracted video frames are not stored on any external server but instead, they are discarded after the emotion recognition model detects the emotion. As for transparency, the user is aware of the background service and of the video record, since the application pops-up a notification "Camera opened". As long as the application is open, there is a notification at the top of the screen, notifying the user that is being recorded. Moreover, the first time that the application is opened, it asks the user for permission to access the camera.

3.4   Sentiment Aggregation

The two models described above utilize different modalities to infer the sentiment of a user at a given time: One takes advantage of user-typed data and the other the user's facial expressions. The frequency of the data of these models varies significantly. Text is only collected when the user sends a message whereas the video frames are processed throughout the duration of the user's interaction with the applications. Most of the time, facial expressions are not static throughout the experience of an emotion, they are dynamic events that unfold over time. It is rather important to take advantage of both components to increase the ability to capture the users' actual sentiment.

The information integration of the two models is as follows. For each text message, we took the textual sentiment analysis results. The timestamp of the message was used to get the corresponding results from the frames recorded by emotion recognition. In consideration of the dynamic nature of facial expressions, instead of taking into account just the single frame coinciding with that timestamp, we considered the interval containing all frames that were recorded 3s before the message was sent and 3s after. In that timeframe, the average sentiment from the frames is calculated (see Fig. 5). In the end, the output of both components plus their (dis)agreement is recorded.

3.5   The Semantic Knowledge Graph (SemKG)

The sentiment analysis results from the two modalities, along with the accompanying data (dialogue, timestamps), populate an underlying semantic model (i.e., the ALAMEDA ontology) via the SemKG. SemKG is an "umbrella" framework that, besides the populated semantic model, also encompasses the repository for persisting the populated semantic model, as well as a RESTful API for interacting with the information residing in the repository.

The motivation behind SemKG is based on the fact that we wished to establish a scalable semantic infrastructure for handling heterogeneous inputs and interactions from diverse components, and semantic technologies are a perfect fit for this affair [8]. Moreover, the adopted framework adheres to universal open standards recommended by the W3C; specifically, RDF [11] and OWL [16] for knowledge representation, and SPARQL [10] for querying the stored knowledge.

The corresponding workflow is seen in Fig. 6: An HTTP request (GET or POST) is submitted to the appropriate endpoint on the SemKG REST server, which forwards it to the internal query engine that converts requests to SPARQL

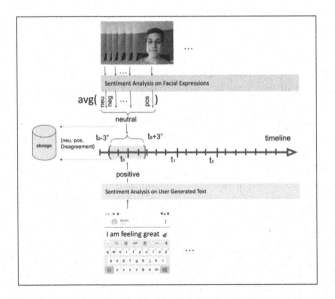

Fig. 5. Sentiment aggregation

queries. The queries are forwarded to the RDF triplestore, i.e., the repository hosting the semantic model. Once a response is received from the triplestore, the query engine handles the conversion of the SPARQL result-set into a JSON response, which, in turn, is channeled back to the requesting entity via the REST server. SemKG's RESTful API serves, thus, as the sole point of interaction for submitting to and retrieving data from the ontology.

Within the particular context of this work, SemKG offers valuable holistic insights related to patients' mood fluctuations, coming from both input sources (text and video), analysed and presented uniformly. Examples include retrieval of the average mood for a given time period, assessment of the max and min mood values during a specific day/week/month, and many more.

3.6   User Interface - The Android Application

As part of ALAMEDA we designed and developed an Android application that serves as the front end of the server-side conversation module described in the

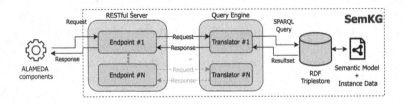

Fig. 6. Workflow of the interaction of SemKG with the rest of the components

previous sections. The chatbot application packs a minimal user interface which resembles common messaging apps, offering a familiar user experience to patients of various backgrounds and age groups. Patients will require less time to learn and adapt to this interface which will shift the focus on the conversation itself hence increasing the usability of the app.

The Chatbot App can handle a variety of input methods. Users can interact with the app by directly typing their answers in the dedicated input box at the bottom of the screen, by voice-typing, or by clicking on buttons where applicable. Examples of the aforementioned input methods are depicted in Fig. 7.

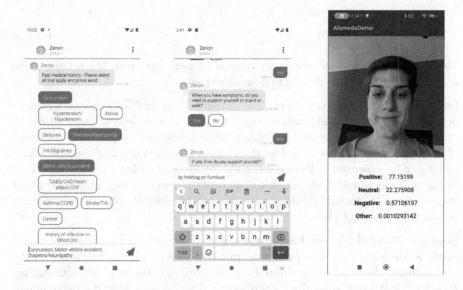

Fig. 7. The Android Application: a) on the left: a question with multiselection from Dizziness and Balance questionnaire, b) in the middle: questions with buttons and a conditional question that accepts free text answers, c) on the right: a demo application for the facial expression analysis (note that this actually runs in the background).

Regarding Face Expression Analysis, one of the aspects that had to be considered was the fact that, if the patients felt that they were being monitored, they wouldn't express their actual feelings. Hence, this module was implemented as a background service and does not provide a visible user interface. It is worth noting that, although the service is not visible, the user is fully aware that the service is running by a dedicated "Toast" notification on the screen.

4 Evaluation, Feedback, and Lessons Learned

Since this is a system of multiple components we present the preliminary evaluation of those components plus the initial feedback we got from our end users.

Table 1. Model parameters of the sentiment analysis model

Embeddings (#dimension)	Vocabulary (#terms)	Sent. Length (#tokens)	Languages (#n)
(300)	(310211)	(150)	(4)

Table 2. Performance scores of the sentiment analysis model

	Precision	Recall	F_1 score
Negative	69.49	72.68	71.05
Neutral	54.57	56.77	55.65
Positive	79.69	73.45	76.44

More thorough user-involving evaluation is taking place with the collaboration of our local community groups and medical partners.

Sentiment Analysis on Text. We evaluated the HolC model performance on the sentiment analysis task on eight joined datasets and set up the model hyperparameters as presented in Table 1. Table 2 provides the performance scores of the sentiment analysis model on the test set (Amazon dataset - see Sect. 3.2). What can be observed is the overall good performance of the model, especially in the positive and negative classes. The neutral class is where many sentiment analysis models struggle [1] due to the limited number of opinionated words in the examples of that class.

Sentiment Analysis on Face Expressions. Regarding the face expressions analysis, the validation was performed initially with a group of ten people, men, and women, whose ages vary from 22 to 60 years old and have different characteristics (i.e. glasses, short/long beards etc.). The model achieved a performance accuracy of 75%. A second validation is expected to happen through the pilots of the ALAMEDA project where the actual patients will interact with the application. Based on the feedback that we will receive, improvements and fine-tuning of the model will take place.

Sentiment Aggregation. In regards to the performance alignment of the two models, an initial validation was performed on a dataset created after a user interacted with the system. The sentiment of each text message was compared with the overall sentiment from the facial analysis (as described in Sect. 3.4). Table 3 shows the percentage of agreement/disagreement among the predictions of the individual models. From the evaluation, we noticed that in some cases the two components complimented each other. In cases where the sentiment analysis struggles to decide between two polarities, for instance between neutral and positive, emotion recognition can be used to infer the patient's mood. Conversely, when emotion recognition struggles, the textual sentiment analysis might be able to provide a more confident result of the overall sentiment. However, given the lack of ground truth in this evaluation and the demanding nature of the task

Table 3. Agreement/Disagreement overview for the two sentiment analysis models.

		Video Output Class		
		Positive	Neutral	Negative
Text Output Class	Positive	23.33 %	13.33 %	0 %
	Neutral	13.33 %	13.33 %	10 %
	Negative	6.66%	10%	10%

(i.e. patients recovering from brain diseases might have trouble expressing their emotions through facial expressions), a more throughout evaluation is required. Once more data is collected through the pilots, throughout analysis of the fused capabilities of the two components for each disease will be performed and the necessary adjustments will be made.

User Feedback. A preliminary version of the Conversational agent was provided to the medical partners and to the local community groups for an initial evaluation. Both groups confirmed the accessibility and user-friendliness of the graphical interface of the mobile application. They also agreed that the chatbot as a tool is very promising for collecting the medical questionnaire data required by the project. From the first evaluations, the medical partners identified additional features that the agent should encompass in order to improve its usability and thus the quality of the collected data. Such features include the ability to type answers of specific forms, for instance dates and numbers, in various formats. To realize these entity recognition capabilities, semantic mapping was incorporated in the agent. Furthermore, extending the agent to support health status updates based on the data collected in the SemKG was discussed. The medical partners agreed on which information would be beneficial to present to the patients through the agent without affecting the study. Based on the agreed information, we extended the agent to include this functionality.

5   Conclusions and Next Steps

In this paper, an overview of a conversational agent designed for the treatment of brain diseases is presented. The elements that make Zenon unique is the variety of conversation flows, two different modalities for sentiment analysis (text, video), multi-lingual support, and an underlying semantic knowledge graph framework. We present an overview of the main intelligent components as well as a preliminary evaluation of each component and the chatbot as a whole. Obviously, a more thorough user evaluation of the integrated system as well as of the individual components is our first priority in our research agenda.

Despite the fact that the system suggested in this work is designed specifically for brain diseases, many of the components (and at some cases their integration) can be utilized in other domains or in other use cases. For example, the functionality of the multi-modal sentiment analysis can be useful in other health domains or in applications where tracking the emotion of the user is important. On top of that, we are currently working on an extension of Rasa that will lead to a development framework that will make the implementation of questionnaires in a conversational agent much easier in terms of implementation, deployment, and maintenance. This naturally will benefit multiple applications.

Acknowledgement. This research received funding from the European Union's Horizon 2020 research and innovation program under grant agreement No GA 101017558 (ALAMEDA).

References

1. Agathangelou, P., Katakis, I.: Balancing between holistic and cumulative sentiment classification. Online Soc. Netw. Media **29**, 100199 (2022)
2. Alnashwan, R., Sorensen, H., O'Riordan, A., Hoare, C.: Multiclass sentiment classification of online health forums using both domain-independent and domain-specific features. In: Proceedings of the Fourth IEEE/ACM International Conference on Big Data Computing, Applications and Technologies, Austin, Texas, USA, pp. 75–83. ACM (2017)
3. Amato, F., Marrone, S., Moscato, V., Piantadosi, G., Picariello, A., Sansone, C.: Chatbots meet ehealth: automatizing healthcare. In: WAIAH@AI*IA (2017)
4. Anastasiadou, M., Alexiadis, A., Polychronidou, E., Votis, K., Tzovaras, D.: A prototype educational virtual assistant for diabetes management. In: 2020 IEEE 20th International Conference on Bioinformatics and Bioengineering (BIBE), Cincinnati, OH, USA, pp. 999–1004. IEEE (2020)
5. Bagherzadeh, P., Bergler, S.: Multi-input recurrent independent mechanisms for leveraging knowledge sources: case studies on sentiment analysis and health text mining. In: Proceedings of Deep Learning Inside Out (DeeLIO): The 2nd Workshop on Knowledge Extraction and Integration for Deep Learning Architectures, pp. 108–118. Association for Computational Linguistics (2021)
6. Cai, Y., Zheng, W., Zhang, T., Li, Q., Cui, Z., Ye, J.: Video based emotion recognition using CNN and BRNN. In: Tan, T., Li, X., Chen, X., Zhou, J., Yang, J., Cheng, H. (eds.) CCPR 2016. CCIS, vol. 663, pp. 679–691. Springer, Singapore (2016). https://doi.org/10.1007/978-981-10-3005-5_56
7. Chang, F.J., Tran, A.T., Hassner, T., Masi, I., Nevatia, R., Medioni, G.: Expnet: landmark-free, deep, 3D facial expressions (2018)
8. Cheatham, M., Pesquita, C.: Semantic data integration. In: Zomaya, A.Y., Sakr, S. (eds.) Handbook of Big Data Technologies, pp. 263–305. Springer, Cham (2017). https://doi.org/10.1007/978-3-319-49340-4_8
9. Clark, L., et al.: What makes a good conversation? Challenges in designing truly conversational agents. In: Proceedings of the 2019 CHI Conference on Human Factors in Computing Systems, pp. 1–12 (2019)
10. World Wide Web Consortium: SPARQL 1.1 overview (2013)
11. World Wide Web Consortium: RDF 1.1 concepts and abstract syntax (2014)
12. Deng, J., Dong, W., Socher, R., Li, L.J., Li, K., Fei-Fei, L.: Imagenet: a large-scale hierarchical image database, pp. 248–255 (2009)
13. Diederich, S., Brendel, A., Morana, S., Kolbe, L.: On the design of and interaction with conversational agents: an organizing and assessing review of human-computer interaction research. J. Assoc. Inf. Syst. **23**(1), 96–138 (2022)

14. Fan, Y., Lu, X., Li, D., Liu, Y.: Video-based emotion recognition using CNN-RNN and C3D hybrid networks. In: Proceedings of the 18th ACM International Conference on Multimodal Interaction, pp. 445–450 (2016)

15. Gogate, U., Parate, A., Sah, S., Narayanan, S.: Real time emotion recognition and gender classification, pp. 138–143 (2020)

16. OWL Working Group: OWL 2 web ontology language document overview: W3C recommendation 27 October 2009 (2009)

17. Guo, Y., Wang, J., Wu, R., Li, Z., Sun, L.: Designing for trust: a set of design principles to increase trust in chatbot. CCF Trans. Pervasive Comput. Interact. 1–8 (2022)

18. Hommersom, A., et al.: MoSHCA - my mobile and smart health care assistant. In: 2013 IEEE 15th International Conference on e-Health Networking, Applications and Services (Healthcom 2013), Lisbon, Portugal, pp. 188–192. IEEE (2013)

19. Hossain, M.S., Muhammad, G.: An audio-visual emotion recognition system using deep learning fusion for a cognitive wireless framework. IEEE Wirel. Commun. **26**(3), 62–68 (2019)

20. Hossain, M.S., Muhammad, G.: Emotion recognition using deep learning approach from audio-visual emotional big data. Inf. Fusion **49**, 69–78 (2019)

21. Howard, A.G., et al.: Mobilenets: efficient convolutional neural networks for mobile vision applications. arXiv (2017)

22. Hu, Y., Qu, Y., Maus, A., Mutlu, B.: Polite or direct? Conversation design of a smart display for older adults based on politeness theory. In: CHI Conference on Human Factors in Computing Systems, pp. 1–15 (2022)

23. Jelodar, H., Wang, Y., Orji, R., Huang, S.: Deep sentiment classification and topic discovery on novel coronavirus or COVID-19 online discussions: NLP using LSTM recurrent neural network approach. IEEE J. Biomed. Health Inform. **24**(10), 2733–2742 (2020)

24. Laranjo, L., et al.: Conversational agents in healthcare: a systematic review. J. Am. Med. Inform. Assoc. **25**(9), 1248–1258 (2018)

25. Maga-Nteve, C., et al.: A semantic technologies toolkit for bridging early diagnosis and treatment in brain diseases: report from the ongoing EU-funded research project ALAMEDA. In: Garoufallou, E., Ovalle-Perandones, M.-A., Vlachidis, A. (eds.) MTSR 2021. CCIS, vol. 1537, pp. 349–354. Springer, Cham (2022). https://doi.org/10.1007/978-3-030-98876-0_30

26. Oh, K.J., Lee, D., Ko, B., Choi, H.J.: A chatbot for psychiatric counseling in mental healthcare service based on emotional dialogue analysis and sentence generation. In: 2017 18th IEEE International Conference on Mobile Data Management (MDM), Daejeon, South Korea, pp. 371–375. IEEE (2017)

27. Sandler, M., Howard, A.G., Zhu, M., Zhmoginov, A., Chen, L.: Mobilenetv 2: inverted residuals and linear bottlenecks. In: CVPR, pp. 4510–4520. Computer Vision Foundation/IEEE Computer Society (2018)

28. Teixeira, M.S., Maran, V., Dragoni, M.: The interplay of a conversational ontology and AI planning for health dialogue management. In: Proceedings of the 36th Annual ACM Symposium on Applied Computing, Virtual Event Republic of Korea, pp. 611–619. ACM (2021)

29. Wafa, H., Wolfe, C., Emmett, E., Roth, G., Johnson, C., Wang, Y.: Burden of stroke in Europe: thirty-year projections of incidence, prevalence, deaths, and disability-adjusted life years. Stroke **51**, 2418–2427 (2020)

30. Walker, T., et al.: Developing an intelligent virtual agent to stratify people with cognitive complaints: a comparison of human-patient and intelligent virtual agent-patient interaction. Dementia **19**, 1173–1188 (2018)

Interactive Journaling with AI: Probing into Words and Language as Interaction Design Materials

Max Angenius[1]([⊠]) and Maliheh Ghajargar[1,2] [iD]

[1] School of Arts and Communication, Malmö University, Malmö, Sweden
max.angenius@gmail.com, maliheh.ghajargar@mau.se
[2] Internet of Things and People Research Center, Malmö University, Malmö, Sweden

Abstract. Conversational Agents (CAs) are making human-computer interaction more collaborative and conversational through using natural language. The HCI and interaction design communities, have been experimenting with and exploring the area of designing conversational interactions. Furthermore, interaction designers may need to acquire new skills for designing, prototyping, and evaluating artifacts that embody AI technologies in general, and CAs in particular. This paper builds upon a previous study on principles of designing interactive journaling experiences with CA and explores the practice of designing such experiences, using words, language, and conversations as design materials. We present a prototype for interactive and reflective journaling interaction with CA and the result of a Wizard of Oz experiment. Our findings suggest that designing interactions with CA challenges designers to use materials with inherently different natures and qualities. Despite this challenge, words appear to have unique characteristics to support designers to externalize and iterate on ideas, e.g., tone and intent. Hence, we suggest considering words, language, and conversations as the primary design materials, and the AI's predictability, adaptivity, and agency as secondary materials, while designing human interactions with Conversational Agents.

Keywords: Reflective journaling · Conversational agents · Human-AI interaction · Design methods · Design materials · User experience · Interaction modality

1 Introduction

The daily practice of journaling and the narration of personal experiences, thoughts, and emotions is a reflective practice that supports individuals and groups in discovering meaning, gaining perspective about others, and developing critical thinking and affective skills, among others [1]. Computer-supported reflective learning is a research area within HCI, where journaling is a tool for learning and reflection [2]. Previous research confirms that interacting with other people, having conversations, and giving and receiving feedback positively impact reflective activities, such as learning or journaling [3, 4].

Conversational interfaces such as Conversational Agents (CA) as a form of Artificial Intelligence (AI) use language as the primary mode of interaction [5] to engage with

A. Følstad et al. (Eds.): CONVERSATIONS 2022, LNCS 13815, pp. 150–170, 2023.
https://doi.org/10.1007/978-3-031-25581-6_10

users in a conversation or collaboration [6]. CA is an emerging AI technology, and the interaction with CAs has been the subject of Interaction Design studies [2, 6, 8–10]. Further, it has been ongoing discussions in HCI and Interaction Design communities on what can be considered design materials and how interaction designers can shape those materials in their practices–such as AI or data as a design material [7, 11, 12]. However, in designing interactions with CAs, similar to those with GPT-3 [13], there is another challenge that we face, and that is how to design for interactions where human language is the primary interaction modality [5] and how to design realistic services that use AI in a way that can be prototyped and evaluated during the development stage [14].

This paper seeks to explore that area through ideating and prototyping a reflective and interactive journaling experience with CA. It aims to answer the research question: How can we design an interactive journaling experience with words, language, and conversations as the primary design material?

In this paper, we will present and discuss the process of prototyping and testing a conversational agent and offer insights on using words as interaction design material.

2 Background

2.1 Journaling and Reflection

Reflection is a process of sense-making that supports discovering and understanding relationships and connections between experiences and actions to develop new perspectives [2, 15, 16]. Reflection is influenced by both internal and individual activity, and external and collective components, e.g., relationships to artifacts, activities, places, and people [15]. Reflective journaling is an activity where a human documents their personal experiences by writing down and connecting thoughts and emotions with the goal of reflection and personal growth [1, 16, 17]. Journaling as a reflection method enables persons to organize, clarify, and connect knowledge in a concrete form, allowing them to process old and new knowledge [4]. Furthermore, the journal writer actively engages in a learning process [1] as they create meaning and context from their experiences [18]. A few examples of different journaling methods are the Double Entry Journal [4], Dialogue Journal, and Personal Journal [3]. The Double Entry Journal and Dialogue Journal methods are collaborative, where two or more people engage with an individual's written reflections, either with peers or a mentor [3, 4]. The Personal Journal, on the other hand, is a solitary method where only the individual journal writer takes part in the writing and reflection processes [3]. While having value as a tool for reflection, individual journaling also risks looping personal reflections and beliefs because they are not challenged or questioned [3]. A more collaborative approach allows for personal growth by enabling the opportunity for feedback from others which amplifies critical self-assessment [3], and learning occurs when knowledge is moved from "an investigative state to a socially constructed one" [4]. Transforming journaling into a dialogue between multiple people instigates ethical considerations, specifically regarding the journal reader's perceived trustworthiness, clarity of expectations, and the feedback's quantity and quality [3]. These ethical considerations must be met for the conversation around the journal content [3]. Another method of journaling that is more craft-based is Bullet Journaling which appeals to journal writers, who appreciate an open-ended and organic way of using materials and having the freedom to express themselves and their information in a personalized manner [19].

In HCI and Interaction Design, journaling has been explored in different areas and applications. For instance, MEMEory is a mobile journaling application that uses memes as a medium for reflecting [17], and Eat4Thought is a food journaling application to identify eating behaviors [20]. Another study used blogging as a computer-mediated journaling tool in a classroom environment to encourage discussions and reflections [18]. Finally, Robota is a CA to support self-learning in a work environment through written and voice interaction [8].

2.2 Human-AI Interaction

AI as a design material supports interaction designers to shape experiences and functionalities of computing artifacts, such as prediction, adaptivity, and agency [11, 14]. Among them, designing with adaptivity is about considering how the system adapts and changes and how it functions over time according to specific and different user needs [14, 21]. An adaptive system like AI needs to store information and remember the user's previous interactions to support the user in making connections between the data collected over time [14].

Human-AI interaction can be designed in different ways where the user and the system can be assigned different levels of the agency [7]. Intermittent human-AI interaction is a turn-taking paradigm of interaction where the user retains all of the agency and initiates interaction, while continuous human-AI interaction is a paradigm where the agency is divided between human and system, where the system listens to an uninterrupted flow of input from the user and responds throughout the interaction [22]. Proactive human-AI interaction is where the system has the most agency and is allowed to initiate and complete tasks independently [22]. Each paradigm of human-AI interaction has different complexity and use cases that designers can explore in their design process [22]. Accordingly, the HCI and design community have developed several design principles for human-AI interaction for different domains, such as Amershi et al. [7]'s Guidelines for Human-AI Interaction, Kulesza et al. [23]'s Principles of Explanatory Debugging to Personalize Interactive Machine Learning, Cronholm & Göbel [24]'s Design Principles for Human-Centred AI and Design Principles for Interactive and Reflective Journaling with Conversational Agent [25].

2.3 Conversation as Interaction Modality

Conversation can be defined as a cascade of behaviors and cues unfolding between two speakers responding to each other [5] and is considered as one of the oldest interfaces [26]. Conversation is collaborative in principle [5] and goal-oriented [26]. Similarly, a dialogue is a back-and-forth conversation between two entities and includes characteristics such as turn-taking, overlap, interruption, cues, and repair [5]. In a design situation, such as human-CA interaction design, where language and conversation are the primary modes of human-computer interaction, words can be considered one of the design materials as they are building blocks for the user experience and a fundamental part of the interaction design as a whole [26].

Human history has had different conversational cultures that evolved over time: oral culture, literate culture, and secondary orality [26]. Oral culture was temporal and context-specific, where the knowledge and meaning existed as long as it was attractive to the individuals who remembered and repeated it; literate culture, thanks to writing, was portable, replicable, and fostered reflection and creating knowledge; secondary orality made possible by technology and made writing immediate, group-minded, collaborative, conversational, and intertextual [26].

In conversational design, the design starts with an interaction or dialogue [26], and words and language are the primary modalities to give input and receive responses; the interaction is back-and-forth and mimics how a human would interact with another human [5]–that is, the system is endowed with humanlike behavior and qualities [9]. A conversational system, such as a Conversational Agent (CA), uses Language Models and collaborates with the user and other artifacts to engage in conversations [6, 27].

Context creates meaning for conversations, and people interact with the context based on what they hear and see and according to any previous experiences during the conversation [5]. It is called longitudinal context when a computing system collects information and builds documents from multiple conversations and sessions over time [5]. Longitudinal context allows the CA to store the data from previous conversations with the user and recall them when required, giving a personality to the CA and it helps it to build an emotional connection with the user [5]. Artifact personality in a conversational interface includes character traits, behaviors, choice of words, and tone of voice and is a core part of the user experience [5]. Personality is also connected to the user's expectations, as a user decides how to interact with the artifact based on how the personality of the artifact is described and perceived [26], during interactions [5, 10, 14].

In a conversational interface, often the information is not presented through a traditional GUI [28]. Hence users need to get familiar with the CA's form of interaction [5]–emphasizing the importance of first impressions and onboarding [5, 9, 26]. Onboarding occurs over multiple sessions and could be designed as a learning process for the system [5]. The stakes are the highest in the initial interaction between the user and the system [5, 26], and the goal of the first conversation is not to explain every potential interaction but rather to encourage the user to engage in the interaction and to learn more about it over time progressively [5]–which is also known as progressive disclosure [26].

3 Methodology

In this work, we used an explorative and qualitative Research through Design approach, which employs a diversity of methods and tools, such as sketching for ideation purposes–against a standardized and controlled process–for its generative purposes [29].

The authors have previously conducted literature and qualitative user studies on interactive journaling experiences with CA [25, 30]. Based on the previous study, we defined and revised a set of design principles for designing interactive and reflective journaling experiences [25, 30]. The results presented an opportunity to explore CAs specifically for an interactive and reflective journaling experience. Additionally, previous research suggests that interaction designers need methodological knowledge and material skills about designing with conversations, words, language [5, 31], and AI [7, 14] and that there is a need for additional research when it comes to using CA technology specifically [6, 7].

In this work, we were interested in prototyping a reflective and interactive journaling experience based on our previously developed design principles (Table 1) [25]. We started the process with a creative exploration of this space. We reviewed existing research on the topic, experimented with different journaling methods, and interviewed experienced journalers. The participants recruited for this study were graduate students in the Interaction Design program at Malmö University, in their twenties and thirties, experienced journalers, and interested in technology. Five out of six participants identified themselves as women, and the one identified themself as a man. Additionally, the participants had different nationalities and different approaches to journaling. Five 30-min semi-structured interviews were conducted and recorded with permission [30].

The results of this exploration were coded using affinity diagramming to find patterns and insights in the data. The design principles were used to frame the design requirements and user needs of the study's design space and for ideation. The ideation process explored different methods used for designing with words and language as design material, including designing the personality, agent behavior and sentiment, and dialogue, to mention a few. The ideation process converged in a final prototype of an interactive journaling experience with a conversational agent, which was tested using the method of Wizard of Oz with three participants, all of whom previously participated in the study (Fig. 1) [30].

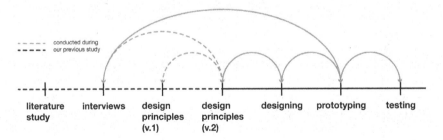

Fig. 1. An overview of the methodological steps and design process.

Table 1. Revised version of design principles for interactive and reflective journaling with conversational agent

Design principles	User needs	Artifact requirements
01. The system acts as a confidant	The journaler needs to have the opportunity to build synergy with the system	The artifact's features and interactions need to be intentionally designed to be a judgment-free and perceived as a patient listener
02. The system expresses a personality	The journaler attributes a personality to the artifacts and builds a close relationship with them. The relationship sets expectations and impacts synergy	The personality of an interactive artifact needs to be carefully crafted to support this relationship, without anthropomorphizing and creating deceitful character

(continued)

Table 1. (*continued*)

Design principles	User needs	Artifact requirements
03. The system supports personal expressions and aesthetics	The journaler needs to be able to express their personal feelings and thoughts and to have the freedom to use various materials and tools	The user should be allowed to express themselves personally, e.g., through writing and speaking to CA. In addition to this, the system features need to support users in different journaling goals, depths of reflection, and modes of interaction
04. The system prompts deeper reflection	The journaler needs encouragement and guidance for deeper reflection. e.g., through prompts or questions	The system needs to support reflection through providing e.g., prompts, questions, or a reflective dialogue–part of the paradigm of intermittent human-AI interaction [22]
05. The system augments human memory	The journaler needs to remember the previous events, thoughts and feelings written about in their journal. That supports user in recognizing patterns, reflections, and personal growth	The system needs to collect data to support memory augmentation, pattern recognition, and continual adaptive use over time, using ethical and explicit data collection: e.g., recognizing written and voice input from the user, categorization of journal entries, applying the paradigm of intermittent human-AI interaction [22]
06. The system updates and adapts	The jounaler's needs, goals and expectations change over time and in different contexts. The journaler needs a flexible journaling experience and practice	The system needs to be able to adapt to the user's needs and context. The system needs to be designed for longitudinal context and be able to collect data from multiple sessions over an extended period of time
07. The system encourages social interactions for reflection	The journaler needs social interaction to externalize thoughts and to seek second opinions and perspectives The user needs to share their experiences and knowledge with others to get alternative perspectives	The system needs to provide a platform for co-writing and sharing journal entries. It needs to provide features such as question and answer, space for comments or drawings on individual journal entries

(*continued*)

Table 1. (*continued*)

Design principles	User needs	Artifact requirements
08. The system participates just enough	The journaler's consider the moment of writing as sacred and as a meditative state that should not be disturbed	The system can act proactively and collect data, but explicit interactions with the user need to be done intermittently, waiting for its turn (when the user finished journaling or needs the system to interact with)
09. The system explains and is transparent	The journaler needs to know about the systems' functionalities, data collection methods, its activities in the background	The system needs to explain what it can and cannot do. This is especially important in forming a better relationship with the user. The system needs to slowly onboard the user using progressive disclosure. During the onboarding process, the previously mentioned principles are relevant to bring up as information
10. The system onboards slowly	The user needs to get to know the system slowly and the first impression of a system is essential in making a more sustainable relationship	
11. The system lets the user manage and control the data and use	The journaler needs to be able to leave the system anytime. They need to have control over data usage and be able to manage it	The system must provide the user with opportunities to stop data collection at any moment and to be able to delete journal entries as they require

4 Designing Conversational Interactions

Following our explorative and qualitative Research through Design approach [29], we started with an ideation and sketching process. Sketching [32] was executed in two rounds; the first round was a regular brainstorming activity with pen and paper to externalize the ideas and resulted in 24 different sketches on the topic of interactive journaling with CA. The themes that emerged were diverse, ranging from the usage of specific technologies or tools to the type of conversation, data to collect, etc. (Fig. 2).

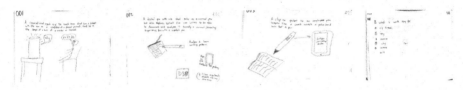

Fig. 2. A selection of sketches

For the second round of ideation, the first author of this paper designed an ideation activity to challenge the comfort zone of divergent thinking [29]. The activity was named

The Interaction Design Wheel(s) of Fortune and included seven wheels based on different frameworks and concepts from our literature review [30] (Appendix B). These were: (1) Interaction Attributes [33], (2) Interaction Perspectives [34], (3) Interaction Gestalt [35], (4) Interaction Perspectives [36], (5) Conversational Cultures [26], (6) Levels of Reflection [37], and (7) Paradigms of Human-AI Interaction [22]. These different concepts were added into a tool for randomizing decisions called Wheel Decide [38], and the goal was to combine unexpected and novel elements from the different wheels to invite designers to ideate around unexpected and creative combinations. Each wheel was spun once, resulting in a list of seven elements for the sketch or idea to appropriate. For example, sketch number 25 used: *fast, tool, continuity, control, secondary orality, dialogic reflection,* and *continuous human-AI interaction.* The method is reminiscent of Cut-up, a Dadaist creativity method, where artists cut up and rearrange material to form new and unexpected creations [39]. This second round resulted in 15 sketches, each with its unique set of elements (Appendix C), which allowed the participants to reflect on and describe different shapes the interaction could take and how the users might experience them.

Some combinations worked better than others (e.g., combination 34, Fig. 3). The interaction attribute *approximate* is described as a more profound analysis and allows room for variation, competence in new ideas, and exploration–which is essential for journaling. For instance, the interaction perspective of *dialogue partner* and *dialogic reflection* are appropriate as we designed an artifact to facilitate a conversation between the user and AI. The *interaction gestalt attribute speed* is related to the speed of the user's action and the system's response. Finally, *intermittent human-AI interaction* is closely related to the nature of conversation as it is based on turn-taking.

Fig. 3. Combinations 34 and 37.

Some other combinations did not work very well (e.g., combination 37, Fig. 3). The incidental interaction attribute is about having a low level of challenge, without room to experience competence or improvement, which are clearly experiences we do not want to design for reflective journaling. The exploration of various sketches and combinations of elements allowed us to explore what elements of interaction were more suitable based on the design principles (Table 1). This creative exploration supported prototyping the CA's personality, conversational prompts, functionality, and how the interaction would play out.

4.1 Prototyping CA'S Personality and Conversations

The design of conversational interfaces often requires a consideration of personality design, prompt design, intent definition, and pathway documentation [5]. We applied Deibel and Evanhoe's framework [5] for designing the CA's personality, which includes six elements: interaction goals, level of personification, power dynamics, character traits, tone, and key behaviors.

For designing a personality for an interactive artifact for journaling, we used the design principles (Table 1) [25, 30]. Designing these six elements of the agent's personality was the foundation for the interactive experience and conversation. For instance, concerning key behaviors included defining specific behavior and prompts for specific situations: in a situation where the CA makes a mistake in responding to a user's question, it asks for clarification of the task requested and an example of a prompt in that situation can be "I am sorry, I didn't understand that. Do you mind clarifying or repeating?" (Appendix A).

With the agent's personality in place, sample scripts and audio mockups (Table 2) were designed for prototyping the conversation. The sample script was written and iterated upon multiple times in a text document, while the audio mockups were created using AI-powered text-to-speech software Descript. Listening to the scripts in a conversation between two AI-generated voices allowed for improvements and iterations of the prototype conversation—iterating, for example, tonality, different vocalizations, and choice of the agent's voice, which are all essential features of the personality [30]. This iterative conversation design process allowed for a more authentic experience during the Wizard of Oz experiment.

4.2 Testing Journaling Experiences with CA

Talkus AI-relius [30] is the research prototype, representing an example of a possible design configuration for an interactive and reflective journaling system with CA following the set of design principles (Table 1) and an exploratory Research through Design approach [29]. The research prototype ("look and feel" [40] or the "experience prototype" [41]) consists of two connected objects: (1) a journaling application on a tablet with a smart pen and (2) a Bluetooth speaker, which simulates a CA speaker through audio mockups (Fig. 4). We used 18 pre-recorded prompts to test the prototype based on the audio mockups and the key behaviors (Appendix A). Additionally, a few extra prompts were added based on the assumption that the person testing the prototype would improvise, challenge the agent's capabilities, or request something unexpected–which was encouraged.

The research prototype embodies our design principles, such as supporting reflection, e.g., requesting a reflective prompt and supporting personal expression and aesthetics by diverse input modalities–written and voice [30]. We tested the prototype through a Wizard of OZ method called *Pay no attention to the man behind the curtain*, where participants are aware of the presence of the person who controls the interactions [14]. Wizard of Oz is a suitable method for testing AI-infused conversational interfaces [5, 14, 26] as it allows designers to simulate the behavior of the interactive artifact by having the designer perform the tasks of the system [26]. Furthermore, it removes the limitations of

Table 2. Selection of sample script.

Speaker	Dialogue
Agent	Hello there, my name is Ethan, and I am your journaling companion. What's your name?
User	Max
Agent	Nice to meet you, Max. Today is the 9th of May 2022. Would you like to journal today?
User	Yes, I would like to journal today
Agent	Ok, great. You can journal in two different ways, the first way is by using the pen to write in the journal, and the second is to speak to me using your voice. Are you ready to start our first journaling session together?
User	Yes
Agent	Alright. One last thing. When you are done, put the pen back on the journal, and I will know that it is time to conclude our journaling session for today
Journaling period, undisturbed	
Agent	I noticed that you have stopped journaling. Are you done for today?
User	I am done
Agent	Great job today, I will save your journal entry in your journal. I hope I will see you tomorrow for our next session of journaling

technological constraints [5, 26], and it makes it possible to test the core interaction of the prototype [26] and the intended behavior and prompts [5], which makes it suitable for this study's goals. Although suitable for this study, the Wizard of Oz method also has limitations.

First, human performance compared to machine performance [14, 42]–the designer simulating the artifact's behavior is limited to the number of triggers and responses they can control [42]. Second, the human simulating the artifact's behavior needs to stay consistent with the interaction protocols–avoiding improvised responses or interactions that are not part of the artifact experience [14].

Three testing sessions were conducted with participants who are avid journal writers. Each testing session lasted 30 min and consisted of three primaries and four optional tasks. The primary tasks were: (1) to journal using both pen and voice; (2) to dig deeper into personal experiences and to personalize the journal entry; and (3) to ask for a reflective prompt from CA. The optional (and encouraged) tasks were: (1) to ask something unrelated or irrelevant; (2) to ask something difficult that the AI supposedly cannot answer; (3) to ask a personal question, and (4) to ask CA what is in their mind. The wizard controlled the prototype, wrote notes during the test, and observed the interactions. The tests were followed up with short semi-structured interviews where we asked participants about their experiences.

Fig. 4. Components for Wizard of Oz test for the look and feel (experience) prototype.

5 Results

In this section we report the results of designing and testing of the interactive journaling experience with CA. We report the findings in two sections by reflecting on the different qualities of journaling experiences with CA that emerged from our study and those that confirm the previous studies, (1) *interactive* and *reflective* journaling with AI and (2) *conversational* and *collaborative* journaling with AI.

5.1 Interactive and Reflective Journaling with AI

There is an intriguing tension in supporting journaling with an interactive artifact. On the one hand, Conversational Agents (CA) are considered non-judgmental, while people are still learning to trust these non-judgmental technologies [5]; on the other hand, journalers experience fear of being judged when it comes to someone else reading their individual journal as it is also affirmed by Hubbs and Brand [3]. We observed during the test that two participants (P2 and P3) expressed their view of the CA as a non-judgmental confidant whom they feel to talk with openly about feelings and experiences. Additionally, the prototype created a sense of safety and freedom from the feeling of being judged and participants felt directly in control of their actions and expression during the interactive journaling. Further, P2 claimed that they would never have a conversation with the journal notebook but would do that with Talkus AI-relius, which implies how the interactivity of CA would create a perception of it being present and alive. One of the challenges with reflective thinking is to act on the reflection [43], and we observed Talkus AI-relius to be seen as a confidant in this way as P2 asked Talkus AI-relius for advice on how to act on their personal reflections. The user and the system began to build a relationship that participants appreciated. P2 mentioned during the test that they felt that the interaction with CA, compared to a journal notebook, was more engaging and light-hearted when processing negative emotions. P2 also noted that it might result from the experience's novelty arising from trying the prototype for the first time.

There is a need for further exploring how interactive technology can support reflection [2, 44–46], and one way we observed our prototype to do this was through reflective prompts. All the participants appreciated the reflective prompts from Talkus AI-relius and asked for multiple extra reflective prompts to support their journaling. The value of these reflective prompts was that their contents were unexpected or not necessarily a topic the participants would have thought of themselves. These unexpected inputs enriched their reflective experiences by opening for thoughts and ideas they otherwise would not have. One participant (P3) expressed that it is easier to predict what a person they know would say in a particular situation than what Talkus AI-relius would. Although useful, the reflective prompts needed to be repeated for the participants to be able to process them and break them down for their reflection. Using reflective prompts to create a conversation between the user and CAs fosters a dialogic reflection where the user can construct knowledge and enhance meaning from the content [4]. Additionally, making journaling more collaborative gives the journaler a chance to get feedback and to practice critical thinking [3].

Power dynamics is another layer added to the non-judgmental relationship between the user and CAs–a key element provided by Deibel and Evanhoe's framework [5], which we explored. The most common approaches to designing dialogues are prescriptive and persuasive–dialogues that tell users what to do rather than guiding them to explore and reflect on themselves [2]. Our prototype did not persuade the participants to achieve any specific level of reflection; instead, the participants, as P3 put it, felt free to pursue their personal expressions and visual aesthetics and that they felt free to ask for the agent's prompts to dive deeper into their reflective thinking.

Interaction with a CA is typically seen as a support to mediate other actions [9]. Our prototype was designed for intermittent human-AI interaction where the user is in control, and the artifact only participated when spoken to [22]. We observed during the test that participants appreciated being in control of the conversation but would have also enjoyed giving more agency to Talkus AI-relius. For instance, it could have given more agency in helping with reflective prompts or even initiating the journaling activity by nudging the user to support journaling consistency. With Talkus AI-relius the interaction is mainly turn-based (intermittent) as the primary interaction is through the user's journaling activity and then supporting and answering the questions by Talkus AI-relius. Some results suggest that even if the writing moment is sacred and not to be disturbed, more continuous human-AI interaction benefits the journaling experience. In this case, Talkus AI-relius can suggest or remind the participant of previous journaling entries on similar topics, e.g., as the writing occurs. These results suggest that the user appreciates being in control in the context of reflective journaling with a CA but is open to be surprised and to more prescriptive interactions, as mentioned by Kocielnik et al.

[2] or continuous and proactive human-AI interaction as described by van Berkel et al. [22]. Further, different types of human-AI interactions affected the user's expectations of the conversation. P1 expressed uncertainty about what was expected of them in the conversation with the CA and was unsure if it was rude only to write down their thoughts and not have a conversation with Talkus AI-relius–they almost felt a moral obligation to keep a conversation going and talk about everything they wrote.

Interaction design is increasingly about forms of interaction beyond visual and tactile perception [44], and designers need to learn how to design interactions where human language is the primary way of exchanging information [5]. An example of this that we observed during the test was how to communicate written and spoken input modalities intuitively. We observed that the combination of written and spoken input was beneficial for achieving the design purpose, but it needs further exploration with users. Different reflective questions may be differently suited for different modalities [8], which we observed to be true in using reflective prompts in our prototype. We particularly observed a design challenge regarding input modality when a participant struggled with remembering and understanding the meaning of the reflective prompt only by listening to it. The use and combination of written and spoken modalities must be adapted and iterated repeatedly.

Additionally, the user's preference in the context of interactive journaling may affect the combination or use of interaction modalities. One test participant (P2) mentioned that they wanted to write down their thoughts first to have something ready to say to Talkus AI-relius. The observation opens up another layer of the discussion regarding how to approach and design for the different paradigms of human-AI interaction suggested by van Berkel [22]. Finally, another participant (P1) argued that the combination of written and verbal input would work if they could have the conversation with the agent transcribed.

The design encouraged the participants to engage in social interaction for reflection, for instance, through feedback, comments, and additional perspectives from Talkus AI-relius. We further observed that participants would ask Talkus AI-relius for reflective prompts to help them when they got stuck: *it was a comfort to have the agent as a confidant to ask every time I got stuck to ask for help* (P3). The design was able to onboard the user slowly, which supported building the relationship with Talkus AI-relius. We observed during the tests that even though the prototype onboarded the user slowly, the participants wanted to explore the agent's capacity and limits further. Furthermore, one participant (P1) expressed that they wanted to discover all options and choose among the available ones.

5.2 Conversational and Collaborative Journaling with AI

Two challenges were experienced when conducting the Wizard of Oz method with the conversational prototype. The first one was related to simulating the speed of the interaction–the human wizard could not match the performance of a functioning conversational agent. Simulating the behavior of a CA using Wizard of Oz is challenging [14, 42]. For example, the challenge became obvious when unexpected requests from the user were asked to the agent, which was not part of the pre-recorded prompts–resulting in the wizard having to think on the spot which pre-recorded prompt was the most suitable for the situation. The second challenge regards consistency with predetermined interaction protocols and prototype functionality during the test [14].

Throughout the test, participants asked questions or made requests that the prototype was not designed to handle. Therefore, the default response from the wizard had to be using the pre-recorded prompt of the agent "apologizing" for not being able to perform the action. Having to default to the apology prompt multiple times throughout the test felt uncomfortable and humorous but doing so was nonetheless critical for the test's success. Avoiding improvised responses on the spot is essential during a Wizard of Oz test [14]. Wizard of Oz is a suitable method for testing prototypes implementing AI [14] and conversational design [5, 26], and despite the uncomfortable and humorous moments, our Wizard of Oz test proved to be both fun and insightful.

6 Limitations

Our findings offer contributions towards aiding design researchers in using conversational technologies for designing interactive journaling experiences.

However, it comes with its own limitations. This study involved a small group of participants for the initial interviews and prototype tests and was conducted within a ten-week timeframe. Due to the relatively small size of the sample, the result may not be representative of a larger society. Further the design of interactions was mainly limited to the verbal interactions. We believe this study can be expanded to include other interaction modalities such as the tangible, embodied and sound interactions. To strengthen the empirical results, we invite further user research with a bigger and more diverse group of participants.

7 Concluding Discussions

We presented part of a larger project about designing interactive and reflective journaling experiences with AI and specifically with Conversational Agents. We presented the design process, a prototype (Talkus AI-relius) and the results of testing sessions.

Our findings offer insights regarding different four qualities of journaling experiences with CA, the interactive, reflective, conversational, and collaborative qualities. Although some of them might be seen as universal qualities of a successful human-CA interaction, the assemblage of all these qualities ensures a compelling journaling experience. This finding can help the design of journaling experience in variety of contexts, such as education, mindfulness, mental health and food journaling, among others. This finding has also triggered our interest regarding the quality of design materials in the context of human-CA interactions. The possibility of using words and verbal language as primary design materials, while designing for aforementioned qualities (interactive, reflective, conversational, and collaborative), is the main focus of this discussion section.

First, we reflected on our roles and approaches as interaction designers and researchers in designing human-CA interactions and experiences. The main challenge here is that as the interface is primarily built with words rather than traditional UI elements and visuals, hence instead of designing visual interfaces, a conversational interface requires ideation, prototyping, and testing of user interfaces with words, language, and conversations as design materials. Therefore, to return to Schön's famous concept, interaction designers would require to engage with words and dialogues and to have reflective conversations with them as the materials of situation [45, 46]. That reflective practice support building suitable and meaningful interactions and experiences.

Second, interaction designers typically explore graphical elements and visual communication of UI; similarly, the CA interaction designers need to explore and iterate on the choice of words, intent, utterances, and nuances to shape dialogues and conversations. The practice of choosing the right words, making dialogue, and creating conversations require a designer to both write down and listen to the choice of words and language. This practice supports interaction designers in simulating the conversation and imagining how that might play out in the real world. We anticipate that this designerly iterative and reflective process of engaging with words as design material can contribute to designing better and more transparent and just CA systems by detecting biases in language from the beginning and in a new way.

Third, we had another insight from this study on how the user interface affordances are situated in the context of interacting with CA. It is commonly recommended to design graphical user interfaces (GUI) in a way that affords only one principal way to take action for a specific purpose, for instance, using consistency as a design principle [10, 48–50]. However, designing the interaction with CA requires an understanding that people might use words and conversation in many different ways, and there are multiple ways to say something and utter an intent. In a sense, there are infinite ways a user can approach the interaction with the CA. While, designing infinite ways to interact with the CA is not realistically possible, interaction designers need to be aware of and collect the most common and appropriate words and language uttered or used in a conversation in a specific context, for example, in interactive journaling.

Forth, regarding the design methods, we found that sketching the conversational agent's personality and expressions with words was a suitable approach to imagining how the interaction would play out and how the humans related to the CA. Using words when sketching conversational interfaces was beneficial because the goal was to describe the conversation and the qualities of interactions between humans and the CA. As a result, sketches became less about visual imagery and more about written descriptions and verbal meanings (Figs. 1 and 2). To sketch-out the human-CA interaction and relationship through words, nonetheless, allowed the idea to be externalized, visualized, iterated, and improved.

In addition to words, it is beneficial for interaction designers to learn how to design with the material qualities of AI in general, such as prediction, adaptivity, and agency, in a conversational interface. These qualities impact the interaction and relationship between the user and the agent, e.g., the agency directly affects the power dynamics of the human-CA relationship as it determines the personality, amount of participation, and initiative. Hence the real design challenge here is to shape interactions with conversational agents through a reflective conversation [47] with a multiplicity of materialities of the situation: words, language, and dialogues as primary materials and predictability, adaptivity, and agency as secondary materials.

Acknowledgments. We would like to show appreciation for the people who participated in the user studies.

Appendix

Appendix A. Examples of CA'S Key Behaviors and Prompts

The situation	CA's behavior	CA's prompt
Meeting someone for the first time	Greet the user, introduce themselves, and explain a short version of what can be expected	"Hello there, my name is Talkus AI-relius, and I am your journaling companion. What's your name?"
Talking with someone familiar	Greet by name and express happiness about seeing them again	"Welcome back [name], it is good to see you again. Today it's 10th of May 2022. Would you like to journal?"
Asked to help with something it can do	Proceed to explain to the user if needed	"Ok, great. You can journal in two different ways, the first way is by using the pen to write in the journal, and the second way is to speak to me using your voice. Are you ready to start our first journaling session together?"
Asked to help with something it can't do	Apologize and inform them that it can't do it and suggest an alternative	"I apologize, this is not an action I can perform. Do you want me to suggest an alternative action?"
Interrupted	Stop what it is doing, wait, and listen to what the user is saying and act on suggested new task	"…do you want me to do [name of task recognized from user interaction]?"
Mistaken	Apologize and ask for clarification or repetition	"I am sorry, I didn't understand that. Do you mind clarifying or repeating?"

(*continued*)

(continued)

The situation	CA's behavior	CA's prompt
Correcting someone	Ask the user if they meant "x"	"Do you mean [correction]?"
Asked a question it couldn't answer	Apologize and inform the user that it is a question it can't answer	"I am sorry, I don't have answers to that question."
Asked a personal question	Explain that it itself doesn't have an opinion but that it could bring in an outside perspective if the user wants	"I don't have personal opinions. I am here to help you process your opinions, thoughts, and emptions. But if you want, I can bring in an outside perspective."
Asked an inappropriate question	Explain that this is not something it will discuss but encourages the user to explore their thoughts, feelings, and point of view	"I don't discuss these kinds of topics, but I encourage you to explore your thoughts, feelings, and point of view in your journal."

Appendix B. The Interaction Design Wheel(s) of Fortune

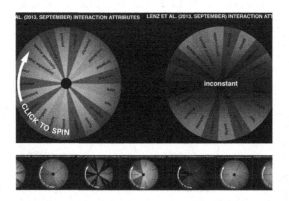

Appendix C: Combinations of Elements of Interaction

Sketch No.	Combination of elements
24	Fast, tool, continuity, control, secondary orality, R2 dialogic reflection, continuous human-ai interaction
25	Fluent, media, movement, tool use, oral culture, R3 transformative reflection, continuous human-ai interaction
26	Targeted, dialogue partner, state, embodiment, literate culture, R0 descriptive reflection, proactive human-ai interaction
27	Uniform, aesthetic experience, pace, experience, secondary orality, R1 reflective description, proactive human-ai interaction
28	Constant, tool, connectivity, embodiment, oral culture, R0 description, proactive human-ai interaction
29	Approximate, dialogue partner, movement, control, secondary orality, R4 critical reflection, intermittent human-ai interaction
30	Powerful, aesthetic experience, pace, control, literate culture, R2 reflective description (forgot to include human-ai interaction)
31	Slow, aesthetic experience, proximity, transmission, literate culture, R0 description, proactive human-ai interaction
32	Instant, aesthetic experience, continuity, optimal behavior, oral culture, R1. Reflective description, proactive human-ai interaction
33	Approximate, dialogue partner, speed, control, secondary orality, R2 dialogic reflection, intermittent human-ai interaction
34	Inconstant, system, movement, optimal behavior, literate culture, R0 description, intermittent human-ai interaction
35	Precise, system, connectivity, optimal behavior, oral culture, R2. Dialogic reflection, proactive human-ai interaction
36	Incidental, system, state, control, oral culture, R2 dialogic reflection, intermittent human-ai interaction
37	Gentle, media, time-depth, embodiment, literate culture, R4 critical reflection, proactive human-ai interaction
38	Delayed, media, directness, optimal behavior, literate culture, R0 description, continuous human-ai interaction
39	Fast, tool, continuity, control, secondary orality, R2 dialogic reflection, continuous human-ai interaction

References

1. Blake, T.K.: Journaling; an active learning technique. Int. J. Nurs. Educ. Scholarsh. **2** (2005). https://doi.org/10.2202/1548-923X.1116
2. Kocielnik, R., Xiao, L., Avrahami, D., Hsieh, G.: Reflection companion: a conversational system for engaging users in reflection on physical activity. Proc. ACM Interact. Mob. Wearable Ubiquitous Technol. **2**, 70:1–70:26 (2018). https://doi.org/10.1145/3214273
3. Hubbs, D.L., Brand, C.F.: The paper mirror: understanding reflective journaling. J. Exp. Educ. **28**, 60–71 (2005). https://doi.org/10.1177/105382590502800107
4. Hughes, H.W., Kooy, M., Kanevsky, L.: Dialogic reflection and journaling. Clearing House: J. Educ. Strat. Issues Ideas **70**, 187–190 (1997). https://doi.org/10.1080/00098655.1997.10544193
5. Deibel, D., Evanhoe, R.: Conversations with Things: UX Design for Chat and Voice. Rosenfeld Media (2021)
6. Yang, X., Aurisicchio, M., Baxter, W.: Understanding affective experiences with conversational agents. In: Proceedings of the 2019 CHI Conference on Human Factors in Computing Systems, pp. 1–12. Association for Computing Machinery, New York (2019). https://doi.org/10.1145/3290605.3300772
7. Amershi, S., et al.: Guidelines for human-AI interaction. In: Proceedings of the 2019 CHI Conference on Human Factors in Computing Systems, pp. 1–13. Association for Computing Machinery, New York (2019). https://doi.org/10.1145/3290605.3300233
8. Kocielnik, R., Avrahami, D., Marlow, J., Lu, D., Hsieh, G.: Designing for workplace reflection: a chat and voice-based conversational agent. In: Proceedings of the 2018 Designing Interactive Systems Conference, pp. 881–894 (2018)
9. Luger, E., Sellen, A.: "Like having a really bad PA" the gulf between user expectation and experience of conversational agents. In: Proceedings of the 2016 CHI Conference on Human Factors in Computing Systems, pp. 5286–5297 (2016)
10. Norman, D.A.: How might people interact with agents. Commun. ACM **37**, 68–71 (1994)
11. Rozendaal, M.C., Ghajargar, M., Pasman, G., Wiberg, M.: Giving form to smart objects: exploring intelligence as an interaction design material. In: Filimowicz, M., Tzankova, V. (eds.) New Directions in Third Wave Human-Computer Interaction: Volume 1 - Technologies. HIS, pp. 25–42. Springer, Cham (2018). https://doi.org/10.1007/978-3-319-73356-2_3
12. Wiberg, M.: The Materiality of Interaction: Notes on the Materials of Interaction Design. The MIT Press, Cambridge (2018)
13. Ghajargar, M., Bardzell, J., Lagerkvist, L.: A redhead walks into a bar: experiences of writing fiction with artificial intelligence. In: 25th International Academic Mindtrek Conference, pp. 230–241. Association for Computing Machinery, New York (2022). https://doi.org/10.1145/3569219.3569418
14. Wärnestål, P.: Design av AI-drivna tjänster. Studentlitteratur AB (2021)
15. Ghajargar, M., Wiberg, M., Stolterman, E.: Designing IoT systems that support reflective thinking: a relational approach. Int. J. Des. **12**, 21–35 (2018)
16. Pirzadeh, A., He, L., Stolterman, E.: Personal informatics and reflection: a critical examination of the nature of reflection. In: CHI'13 Extended Abstracts on Human Factors in Computing Systems, pp. 1979–1988 (2013)
17. Terzimehić, N., Schött, S.Y., Bemmann, F., Buschek, D.: MEMEories: internet memes as means for daily journaling. In: Designing Interactive Systems Conference 2021, pp. 538–548. Association for Computing Machinery, New York (2021). https://doi.org/10.1145/3461778.3462080
18. Ong, L.T.R., Pemberton, R.: Enhancing classroom learning through computer-mediated reflective writing and peer feedback. J. Mod. Lang. **19**, 99–120 (2009)

19. Tholander, J., Normark, M.: Crafting personal information - resistance, imperfection, and self-creation in bullet journaling. In: Proceedings of the 2020 CHI Conference on Human Factors in Computing Systems, pp. 1–13. Association for Computing Machinery, New York (2020)

20. Zhang, Y., Parker, A.G.: Eat4Thought: a design of food journaling. In: Extended Abstracts of the 2020 CHI Conference on Human Factors in Computing Systems, pp. 1–8. Association for Computing Machinery, New York (2020). https://doi.org/10.1145/3334480.3383044

21. Ghajargar, M., et al.: From "explainable AI" to "graspable AI." In: Proceedings of the Fifteenth International Conference on Tangible, Embedded, and Embodied Interaction, Salzburg, Austria, pp. 1–4. Association for Computing Machinery (2021). https://doi.org/10.1145/343 0524.3442704

22. van Berkel, N., Skov, M.B., Kjeldskov, J.: Human-AI interaction: intermittent, continuous, and proactive. Interactions **28**, 67–71 (2021). https://doi.org/10.1145/3486941

23. Kulesza, T., Burnett, M., Wong, W.-K., Stumpf, S.: Principles of explanatory debugging to personalize interactive machine learning. In: Proceedings of the 20th International Conference on Intelligent User Interfaces, pp. 126–137 (2015)

24. Cronholm, S., Göbel, H.: Design principles for human-centred AI. In: ECIS 2022 Research Papers (2022)

25. Angenius, M., Ghajargar, M.: Design principles for interactive and reflective journaling with AI. In: Computing Conference 2023. Springer, London (2023)

26. Hall, E.: Conversational Desigjn. A Book Apart (2018)

27. Allen, J.F., Byron, D.K., Dzikovska, M., Ferguson, G., Galescu, L., Stent, A.: Toward conversational human-computer interaction. AI Mag. **22**, 27 (2001). https://doi.org/10.1609/aimag. v22i4.1590

28. Janlert, L.-E., Stolterman, E.: Faceless Interaction—a conceptual examination of the notion of interface: past, present, and future. Hum.-Comput. Interact. **30**, 507–539 (2015). https://doi.org/10.1080/07370024.2014.944313

29. Gaver, W.: What should we expect from research through design? In: Proceedings of the SIGCHI Conference on Human Factors in Computing Systems, Austin, Texas, USA, pp. 937–946. Association for Computing Machinery (2012). https://doi.org/10.1145/2207676.220 8538

30. Angenius, M.: Talkus AI-relius: An Interactive Journaling Artifact That Supports Reflection Through Conversation (2022)

31. Lee, M., Ackermans, S., van As, N., Chang, H., Lucas, E., IJsselsteijn, W.: Caring for vincent: a chatbot for self-compassion. In: Proceedings of the 2019 CHI Conference on Human Factors in Computing Systems, pp. 1–13. Association for Computing Machinery, New York (2019). https://doi.org/10.1145/3290605.3300932

32. Sanders, E., Stappers, P.: Convivial Toolbox: Generative Research for the Front End of Design. BIS, Amsterdam (2012)

33. Lenz, E., Diefenbach, S., Hassenzahl, M.: Exploring relationships between interaction attributes and experience. In: Proceedings of the 6th International Conference on Designing Pleasurable Products and Interfaces, pp. 126–135. Association for Computing Machinery, New York (2013). https://doi.org/10.1145/2513506.2513520

34. Petersen, M.G., Iversen, O.S., Krogh, P.G., Ludvigsen, M.: Aesthetic interaction: a pragmatist's aesthetics of interactive systems. In: Proceedings of the 5th Conference on Designing Interactive Systems: Processes, Practices, Methods, and Techniques, pp. 269–276 (2004)

35. Lim, Y., Stolterman, E., Jung, H., Donaldson, J.: Interaction gestalt and the design of aesthetic interactions. In: Proceedings of the 2007 Conference on Designing Pleasurable Products and Interfaces, pp. 239–254. Association for Computing Machinery, New York (2007). https://doi.org/10.1145/1314161.1314183

36. Hornbæk, K., Oulasvirta, A.: What is interaction? In: Proceedings of the 2017 CHI Conference on Human Factors in Computing Systems, pp. 5040–5052. Association for Computing Machinery, New York (2017). https://doi.org/10.1145/3025453.3025765

37. Fleck, R., Fitzpatrick, G.: Reflecting on reflection: framing a design landscape. In: Proceedings of the 22nd Conference of the Computer-Human Interaction Special Interest Group of Australia on Computer-Human Interaction, pp. 216–223. Association for Computing Machinery, New York (2010). https://doi.org/10.1145/1952222.1952269

38. Wheel Decide. https://wheeldecide.com/. Accessed 15 Aug 2022

39. Navas, E., Gallagher, O., Burrough, X.: Keywords in Remix Studies. Routledge, Milton Park (2017)

40. Houde, S., Hill, C.: What do prototypes prototype? In: Helander, M.G., Landauer, T.K., and Prabhu, P.V. (eds.) Handbook of Human-Computer Interaction, 2nd edn, pp. 367–381. North-Holland, Amsterdam (1997). https://doi.org/10.1016/B978-044481862-1.50082-0

41. Buchenau, M., Suri, J.F.: Experience prototyping. In: Proceedings of the 3rd Conference on Designing Interactive Systems: Processes, Practices, Methods, and Techniques, pp. 424–433. Association for Computing Machinery, New York (2000). https://doi.org/10.1145/347642.347802

42. van Boeijen, A., Daalhuizen, J., Zijlstra, J.: Delft Design Guide: Perspectives, Models, Approaches, Methods. BIS Publishers, Amsterdam (2020)

43. Nakamura, K., Feng, H., Priss, S., Mei, H.: Designing for night-time reflection: how to support night-time reflection through non-digital means. In: The 39th ACM International Conference on Design of Communication, pp. 386–388 (2021)

44. Ghajargar, M., Wiberg, M.: Thinking with interactive artifacts: reflection as a concept in design outcomes. Des. Issues **34**, 48–63 (2018). https://doi.org/10.1162/DESI_a_00485

45. Ghajargar, M., De Marco, A., Montagna, F.: Wise things": when smart objects stimulate reflection. In: Proceedings of 11th International Conference on Interfaces and Human Computer Interaction, pp. 233–238 (2017)

46. Baumer, E.P.S., Khovanskaya, V., Matthews, M., Reynolds, L., Schwanda Sosik, V., Gay, G.: Reviewing reflection: on the use of reflection in interactive system design. In: Proceedings of the 2014 Conference on Designing Interactive Systems, pp. 93–102. Association for Computing Machinery, New York (2014). https://doi.org/10.1145/2598510.2598598

47. Schön, D.A.: The Reflective Practitioner : How Professionals Think in Action. Routledge, Milton Park (1983). https://doi.org/10.4324/9781315237473

48. World Leaders in Research-Based User Experience: 10 Usability Heuristics for User Interface Design, https://www.nngroup.com/articles/ten-usability-heuristics/. Accessed 09 Sept 2022

49. Hutchins, E.L., Hollan, J.D., Norman, D.A.: Direct manipulation interfaces. Hum.-Comput. Interact. **1**, 311–338 (1985). https://doi.org/10.1207/s15327051hci0104_2

50. Norman, D.: The Design of Everyday Things: Revised and Expanded. Basic Books, New York (2013)

Increasing the Coverage of Clarification Responses for a Cooking Assistant

Gina E. M. Stolwijk$^{(\boxtimes)}$ and Florian A. Kunneman📧

Vrije Universiteit Amsterdam, De Boelelaan 1105, 1081HV Amsterdam,
The Netherlands
gina.stolwijk@gmail.com, f.a.kunneman@vu.nl

Abstract. In conversation genres like instruction, clarification questions
asked by a user may either relate to the task at hand or to common-sense
knowledge about the task domain, whereas most conversational agents
focus on only one of these types. To learn more about the best approach
and feasibility of integrating both types of questions, we experimented
with different approaches for modelling and distinguishing between task-
specific and common sense questions in the context of a cooking assistant. We subsequently integrated the best ones in a conversational agent,
which we tested in a study with six users cooking a recipe. Even though
the three elements functioned well on their own and all participants completed the recipe, question-answering accuracy was relatively low (66%).
We conclude with a discussion of the aspects that need to be improved
upon to cope with the diverse information need in task-based conversational agents.

Keywords: Clarification · Cooking assistant · Natural language
processing · User study

1 Introduction

Today's task-based conversational agents have been mainly built to generate
responses to direct knowledge questions, where the context is represented by the
relevant knowledge underlying these questions and is leveraged to determine the
user goal, perform slot-filling and answer follow-up questions [25,27]. Typical
examples of such task-domains are restaurant reservations and service agents. In
contrast, in conversational genres like instruction-giving, information requests
are typically related to the task at hand, where both the task-related concepts
and status are of importance for a proper interpretation of the request. An agent
giving directions in a virtual environment, for example, would need to consider
the current location and view of the user, as well as types and features of objects
along with their spatial relation [13].

In this paper we study the challenges of modelling information seeking dialogue as part of cooking instruction, a genre where both common-sense knowledge and task-related knowledge are required by the agent to best assist the
user in its endeavour. In order to handle the diverse questions that may be

A. Følstad et al. (Eds.): CONVERSATIONS 2022, LNCS 13815, pp. 171–189, 2023.
https://doi.org/10.1007/978-3-031-25581-6_11

asked during cooking instruction dialogue, the agent would need to incorporate a vast body of recipe-related and cooking-related knowledge, recognise which of the two needs to be drawn upon when faced with an information request, and know whether a proper answer to the question is available. Such an application hence comes at a larger risk of confusing a request with a different one and giving the wrong response to a question, which is why most task-based conversational agents limit the scope of requests that can be addressed to only task-related questions (e.g.: [12,23]) or only questions about general domains (e.g.: [25]).

The studies that did apply conversational agents with both task-specific knowledge and domain-specific knowledge did not obtain insight into the quality of responses to clarification questions when such a system converses with a user. [29] created a dataset consisting of cooking recipes and annotated cooking instruction dialogue grounded in these documents, and limit evaluation to performance on this dataset. Participants in the recent Alexa Taskbot challenge [1] who integrate a diverse set of knowledge sources, like Howdy Y'all [2], Grillbot [14] and Miutsu [20], only focused on user satisfaction in their evaluation. In contrast, in our study we propose detailed heuristics to draw upon a particular information source during conversation, and conduct a user study where we evaluate the conversations on the answer accuracy and can pinpoint the nature of the mistakes that are made. We address the following research questions:

RQ1) How can a task-based conversational agent distinguish task-specific from general domain questions?

1. We deployed and evaluated a set of approaches to model general domain knowledge and task-specific knowledge in the cooking domain, divided into:
    (a) Cooking-related question answering based on question-answer pairs in a community question answering platform
    (b) Extracting knowledge from cooking recipes based on heuristics and segmenting the recipe procedure into conversational steps
    (c) Classifying given questions into task-related or common sense
2. We integrated the approaches in a conversational agent, and formulate a set of heuristics to enable the agent to draw upon the right knowledge module during the conversation

RQ2) To what extent can a task-based conversational agent distinguish task-specific from general domain questions in a real-world setting?

To answer this question, we evaluated the conversational agent through a user study where the users are actually cooking when talking with the agent. All conversations were specifically analyzed for the performance of the agent when addressing user questions.

2   Related Work

2.1   Modelling Knowledge for Conversational Agents

Disclosure of the right knowledge at the right time is a key aspect to the success of many task-based conversational agents, where the nature of the task defines the requirement of its knowledge-based capabilities. For tasks that are targeted at fulfilling a request (e.g.: transfers in a banking context, or booking a restaurant), the most common approach is to train a model on dialogues that are annotated for a pre-defined set of slots and values [25]. Another common task is conversational search, where the right answer to a user's query is coordinated with the user through conversation. Since such agents need to accommodate a wide range of questions, large datasets are typically used [33], and retrieved based on question-question similarity (i.e., example-based) [32]. For tasks that require the user or agent to perform a sequence of steps, like navigation [13], document inquiry [12] or cooking [23, 29], the agent needs to have a thorough understanding of the important concepts and their relation in separate documents. Enabling this required knowledge may be approached as a reading comprehension task [6], or by transforming documents into a dedicated meaning representation for the task at hand [7, 21]. In our approach, we adopt an example-based approach to model general domain knowledge, and parse recipes for a particular set of information units to accommodate task-based knowledge.

2.2 Distinguishing Between Different Knowledge Sources

The main challenge for conversational systems that need to accommodate a wide range of questions, is the large search space that increases the chance for confusing a posed question with a similar one. A common approach to tackle this is to deploy a module to first classify a question by its domain [2] or type [31]. A different approach is taken by [28, 29], who limited the commonsense-knowledge in their cooking agent to a set of predefined topics (e.g., replacing ingredients, use of cooking utensils, etc.) by creating databases with background information for each topic, and deployed a set of rules and custom actions to select the right knowledge source to address a question. We adopt both question type classification and a set of heuristics to query the right knowledge-module (task-specific or common sense) in our system. In contrast to [29], the commonsense database that we make use of covers a broader range of questions in the cooking domain. In addition, we conduct a user study where we zoom in on the quality of question answering, which has not been done in the studies cited above.

3   Increasing the Coverage of Clarification Responses

We distinguish two broad types of clarification questions that may be asked during cooking recipe instruction: commonsense questions and task-specific questions. For both types we set out to ensure a broad coverage in a data-driven way, and additionally studied how well the two can be distinguished to reduce the chance for confusion during conversation. In the following, for each of these three sub tasks we will describe experimentation to inquire into the best performing method. We focus our study on the Dutch language sphere, but the methods we apply are mostly applicable to other languages as well.

3.1   Commonsense Question Answering

The common-sense question-answering task is formulated as finding the best answer to a general user question in the cooking domain from a large database with QA-pairs. We experimented with two approaches to model question similarity.

Approach 1) Word2vec. The first algorithm aimed to find the sentence(s) from a database with the largest similarity to the user's query using a word2vec model [22]. For this, SpaCy's [16] Dutch pipeline nl_core_news_lg was implemented,[1]. For each sentence in the database, using word2vec, separate token embeddings were computed, which were averaged to obtain a sentence embedding. An incoming user query was represented in the same way and compared to each query in the database using cosine similarity, selecting the sentence with the highest similarity as the best match.

Approach 2) Sentence-BERT. The second algorithm consisted of finding the sentence(s) from the database with the smallest distance to the user's query, using the context-dependent sentence-BERT trained on Dutch data.[2] BERT (Bidirectional Encoder Representations from Transformers) has shown to allow for state-of-the-art performance in a wide range of tasks [10]. Sentence-BERT computes the embeddings for each sentence separately, and then compares them using a similarity metric [26]. Each sentence was mapped to a vector space of 768 dimensions, using mean pooling of the context-dependent token embeddings with an attention mask. The sentence embedding of the user query was compared to the embedding of each query in the database using cosine distance, selecting the sentence with the lowest distance as the best match.

Dataset and Pre-processing. We chose to make use of a general community question answering (CQA) platform, which aligned with our purpose of common sense cooking knowledge. We downloaded 10,000 questions from the Dutch Community Question Answering platform goeievraag.nl[3], categorised with the Food and Drinks label. Each QA-pair consisted of a user query and the most popular, or first given, answer. We pre-processed the queries in the database by applying a CNN-based part-of-speech tagger by means of SpaCy.[4] Afterwards, only (proper) nouns, verbs and adjectives were maintained, as they represent the central information to most cooking-related questions. Stop words were also removed,[5] after which each query was vectorised by either of the two approaches.

Experimental Procedure. We performed a controlled experiment by manually selecting seventy queries from the database and testing how well the two

---

[1] https://spacy.io/model/nl#nl_core_news_lg.

[2] jegorkitskerkin/bert-base-dutch-cased-snli.

[3] https://www.startpagina.nl/v/eten-drinken/.

[4] https://spacy.io/api/tagger.

[5] Using the following stopwordlist: https://github.com/explosion/spaCy/blob/master/spacy/lang/nl/stop_words.py.

Table 1. Proportion of correct answers per algorithm and ranking on retrieving the right common-sense cooking-related question-answer pair.

Rank	Algorithm	
	Word2vec	sentence-BERT
1	0.47	0.66
2	0.09 (of 53% = 0.05)	0.24 (of 34% = 0.08)
3	0.06 (of 48% = 0.03)	0.20 (of 26% = 0.05)
Total	0.55	0.79

approaches perform in retrieving any of these queries when presented with a differently worded version of it. We set the size of the database to 10,000. The manual selection was done by one of the authors. So as to ensure a variety of queries to evaluate on, the selected queries were evenly distributed across seven question categories (see Appendix A for details).

To generate seed queries for each of the 70 selected queries, we used a combination of two techniques: backtranslation [11,18] with deep-translator [3] and paraphrasing [4] with the parrot [9] library. The augmenter aimed to produce a maximum of 10 paraphrases, by collecting the input utterance and annotations (intents, slots, slot types), and augmenting these [9]. To make sure that the generated sentences covered the same meaning as the original query, but differently phrased, one of the authors manually checked each generated sentence and removed incorrect paraphrases. In the end, an average of almost four sentences per original query remained (M = 3.97, SD = 1.91), for a total of 278. Grammatically incorrect sentences were not removed, since end users could also pose incorrectly formulated queries. The seed queries were pre-processed in the same way as the queries in the database.

For the two approaches (Word2vec and Sentence-BERT) we tested how well they could retrieve the right query from the database at different database sizes. The approaches were presented with each of the 278 reformulated variants of the queries. As evaluation, the average number of correct answers (i.e., belonging to the exact original [non-paraphrased] query) was computed. To measure how close an approach was, this number was computed for the correct answer at rank 1, 2 or 3. Significant effects were measured by performing an ANOVA with a dichotomous dependent variable (correct/incorrect). The main effects as well as the interaction between the independent variables 'database size' and 'algorithm' were assessed. This was done combining all three highest ranks: if the best match was incorrect, the second best was also taken into account, if the second best match was incorrect, the third best was also taken into account.

Results. The results per approach, database size and ranking are given in Table 1. There was no significant interaction between database size and algorithm on answer correctness ($F(2) = 1.93, p = 0.15$). A second ANOVA was performed looking only at the main effects, showing that the best performing algorithm was sentence-BERT $F(1) = 177.56, p < 0.001$), and changing the size of the database did not significantly affect performance ($F(2) = 0.62, p = 0.54$).

The sentence-BERT approach manages to retrieve a correct question for around 80% of the queries when considering all three ranks. If the first retrieved question-answer pair is not correct, the chance of finding a correct answer at the second rank drops considerably to 0.24. In a conversational setting, these outcomes are not trustworthy enough for presenting the user with an alternate answer (e.g.: the second-ranked QA pair) when an initially retrieved result is not satisfactory. Sentence-BERT gave the best results, for which scores higher than 0.28 were associated with mostly incorrect answers. This approach will be implemented in the cooking assistant for answering common-sense questions in the cooking domain, using a threshold of 0.28 below which an outcome is presented.

3.2   Task-Specific Question Answering

A cooking assistant should have a sufficient number of recipes to instruct to the user, which are abundantly available on web-based cooking platforms. The approach to modelling recipe-specific knowledge is strongly related to the particular recipe to model, and more specifically to the way the recipe is formatted. We identify the following as the most important elements of a recipe: the recipe name, the number of people for whom the recipe is meant, the expected cooking time, the ingredients and quantities, the cooking utensils and the recipe procedure.

Part of what we present below incorporates heuristics that are specific to the website from which we extract recipes and their constituents (Smulweb[6]). The extraction of other types of information is more generalisable to any website with cooking recipes, namely separating quantity, unit and ingredient and dividing the recipe procedure into steps that are suitable to a conversational interface.

Heuristics. Part of the heuristics were based on numerals and grammatical information, for which we made use of SpaCy's POS-tagger and lemmatizer, trained on the Dutch pipeline nl_core_news_lg.[7] An example of the recipe lay-out and type of information that was extracted is given in Fig. 1.

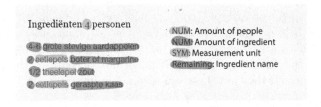

Fig. 1. Recipe ingredients split up using part-of-speech tags and heuristics.

---

[6] https://smulweb.nl/.

[7] https://spacy.io/models/nl#nl_core_news_lg.

Extracting Recipe Steps. The task of extracting recipe steps can be formulated as a segmentation task, where each segment should be suitable as a single unit of instruction in a conversational setting. In line with [17], we defined single instruction steps as instructions where a single action is performed. A difficulty is that a single sentence may include multiple actions.

To identify cooking actions and their accompanying information from a recipe instruction, it was first split up into sentences.[8] We then generated a dependency tree for each sentence using the NLTK library.[9] In parallel, the full sentence was tagged using SpaCy's POS-tagger. The assumption was made that each step (sub-tree), should contain at least a verb (i.e., cooking action) as its root, of which the children down to the leaves represented the context (ingredients, quantities, utensils, etc.). Whenever a token was indicated to be the root of a subtree, it was assessed whether this token was considered a verb as indicated by the tagged sentence. If both of these conditions were met (i.e., token is the root of a subtree, and token is a verb), the subtree was treated as a step. The root of the main tree and the remaining tokens served as a step on its own.

Since POS-tagging models are usually not trained on imperative sentences [7], which are common in cooking instructions, we retrained the tagger using a Random Forest classifier. The classifier used different features in order to find the best fitting tag for a token: the token itself, its precedent, its subsequent token, its prefix (3 first letters), its suffix (3 last letters), whether it is the beginning or the end of a sentence, whether it is a number, and whether it has capitals. For training purposes, a dataset of 284 sentences (3,851 tokens) was extracted from a variety of Dutch cooking instructions posted on Smulweb. For this dataset, the SpaCy tagger's results were used as a reference, after which the tags were manually corrected where necessary by one of the authors. The focus of this correction was on tokens that were wrongfully (not) tagged as verbs, since the verbs were used to split up the procedure.

Experimental Procedure. To evaluate the quality of recipe segmentation with and without a re-trained Pos-tagger, we extracted ten cooking recipes from Smulweb. The ten selected recipes were annotated manually by one of the authors to set a ground truth for evaluation. They were then fed into the different algorithms.[10] Apart from recipe segmentation, the information units of the recipes were also annotated. We found that this information could be identified by means of the heuristics at near-perfect accuracy for the ten recipes, which can be explained by their accommodation to the platform.

We compared the two segmentation approaches to two baselines: a baseline that consisted of selecting each sentence as a single step, and a semi-random baseline which segmented a sequence at each position with probability $1/k$ (where k is the average segment length of the ground truth). We represented the output of the four approaches by marking each token with a 0 or 1, where the latter indicated the end of a step.

---

[8] https://spacy.io/api/sentencizer.

[9] https://www.nltk.org/_modules/nltk/tree.html.

[10] See (Appendix C) for the annotation guidelines.

Results. The best performing algorithm was the dependency tree-based segmentation using POS-tagging, closely followed by the dependency tree-based segmentation using the re-trained tagger (Table 2). The Sentencizer errors were almost all false negatives (i.e., predicted not to be the end of a step, while it actually was), while the tree-based segmentations yielded some false positives as well (i.e., predicted to be the end of the step, while it actually was not).

Table 2. Confusion matrices between each approach and the ground truth segmentation.

Ground truth	Random baseline		Sentencizer baseline		Tree-based with regular POS		Tree-based with fine-tuned POS	
	0	1	0	1	0	1	0	1
0	1,058	159	1,216	1	1,200	17	1,195	22
1	152	18	63	107	25	145	27	143

3.3   Combining Question-Answering Methods

To assist a conversational agent to distinguish between task-specific and common-sense questions in the cooking domain, we set out to train a machine learning classifier to differentiate between the two.

Question Type Classification. We approached question type classification as a supervised machine learning task, aiming to detect features that distinguished both types of questions, which served as a basis for classifying new instances. Two features were created: the number of tokens and the number of characters in a query. Then, the queries were preprocessed by lemmatising, removing stop words and lower-casing. Sentence embeddings were again computed using Sentence-BERT [26], returning a total of 768 features. The five embedding positions with the highest scores on the training data were selected by using the ANOVA F-value between each feature and the label (i.e., indices 2, 112, 284, 320, 420). This resulted in seven features, when added to the two length-based features. A random forest classifier with 100 estimators was used to classify sentences as belonging to the general question type or to the recipe-specific question type.

A total of 359 queries (70% training and 30% evaluation) were selected and written to train and validate the classifier on. These consisted of 223 general cooking questions selected from the previously described Dutch food and drinks questions database, and 136 recipe-specific questions which were manually written based on the types of questions that the cooking assistant was able to answer. Ten splits were created, so that the average performance of the classifier over these different train/evaluation sets could be computed. The classifier's performance was evaluated using precision, recall and F1-score. We compared the Random Forest classifier to a majority baseline.

Results. The random forest classifier performed better on the evaluation set than the majority baseline (Table 3). The accuracy of the classifier was approximately 85% ($M = 0.85, SD = 0.01$, for ten evaluation/test splits).

Table 3. Classifier performance based on 108 test queries

	General			Specific			Macro-F1
	Precision	Recall	F1-score	Precision	Recall	F1-score	
Baseline	0.60	1.00	0.75	0.00	0.00	0.00	0.37
Random forest	0.87	0.91	0.89	0.85	0.79	0.82	0.86

4 Analyzing the Quality of Clarification Responses in Real-world Cooking Assistant Conversations

4.1 Conversational Agent Architecture

To test our question-answering models in action, we developed a conversational agent with a dialogue management component based on the Information State Update paradigm [30], connected to the Google Dialogflow conversational design interface to handle natural language understanding and interface with the user (Fig. 2). We developed Chefbot[11] to plan and manage the cooking instruction dialogue and draw upon the agent's knowledge about recipes and the cooking domain. A Django[12] application was developed to connect Chefbot to Dialogflow.[13] In Chefbot, moves of the agent are specified and linked to preconditions and effects, such as the previous intent of the user and the position in the recipe. The information state is updated based on a move's effects.

Fig. 2. Google Dialogflow interface.

The general conversation flow was modelled as follows: After an initial greeting, the agent asks the user what recipe s/he would like to cook. When a decision

---

[11] https://github.com/fkunneman/Chefbot_NCF.git.
[12] https://www.djangoproject.com/.
[13] https://github.com/fkunneman/smoothbot.

is made, the agent presents the ingredients and utensils on the screen, for the user to confirm that all preparations have been made. Then the recipe instruction starts, where at each instructed step the user has the option to ask for details or clarification, as well as to ask commonsense cooking questions. When the recipe is completed, the agent does a last topic check and closes the conversation.

4.2 Selecting Clarification Responses

Whereas answers to common-sense questions could directly be extracted from the database, recipe-specific information was stored as part of the recipe in a Json-file to be retrieved by Chefbot. Based on the heuristics and segmentation approach described in Sect. 3.2, recipes were parsed and transformed into a json-file with the following elements: Recipe title, Number of people, Cooking duration, Ingredients (including unit and amount), Cooking utensils and Recipe steps (consisting of Step description text, Ingredients used in step, Quantities of ingredients used in step, Image and More extensive step description texts).

When a user query was classified task-specific, it was matched to one of the predefined intents (Appendix B). Each of the intents required specific bits of information, which were extracted from the json-file and/or from the context of the conversation (e.g., previous steps, already used ingredients...).

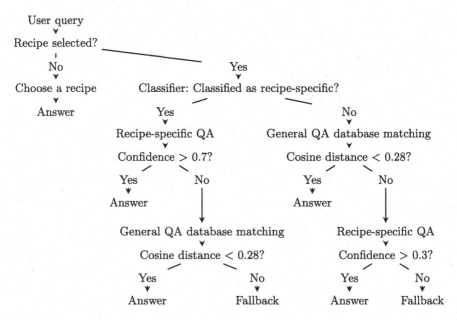

Fig. 3. Decision tree for selecting a response to the user query based on the conversation context, question type classification and answer confidence.

We defined a decision-tree by which the agent decides what knowledge source (task-specific or common-sense) to draw upon to answer a query (Fig. 3). Questions asked before selecting a recipe were answered by drawing upon the knowledge that the agent has of the available recipes and the agent's capabilities. Once a recipe had been selected, the user's query was assessed by the question type classifier (see Sect. 3.3). If the query was classified as general and the distance score was below 0.28 (which was found to be the optimal threshold in Sect. 3.1), the answer to the best matching question (based on the best-performing BERT with cosine distance approach) in the general QA database was returned to the user. If the user's query was classified as recipe-specific and the confidence of the best matched Dialogflow intent was above 0.7 (empirically determined), the best match's answer was returned to the user. If the confidence was too low, or the distance score too high, the other path was tried. If the threshold was not met, it was checked for the other response-type, now checking for a 0.3 threshold. This lower threshold than the 0.7 described previously was used since it was the value that was set for the first version of the implemented cooking assistant, and allowed to reduce the number of fallback intents. If in this case the confidence was again too low or the distance score too high, a fallback intent was triggered. Otherwise, the best matching answer was returned.

4.3   Experiment Design and Data Analysis

We conducted a user study to evaluate the quality of question answering during cooking instruction.

Participants. Six participants cooked a recipe using the cooking assistant. Their average self-reported cooking skills score was 63.5 ($M = 63.50, SD = 17.40$, [19]) out of a maximum score of 98. The participants had some prior knowledge about the study's goal: to assess the performance of a smart cooking assistant. Since the number of participants was relatively small due to the limited resources, they were encouraged to ask as many questions as they could come up with. This allowed the small number of participants to still give the researchers relevant quantitative and qualitative insights, by assessing the types of questions that might arise at the time of cooking a recipe (i.e., in a natural setting), concerning both task-specific knowledge as well as domain knowledge.

Procedure. Before using the cooking assistant, participants completed the self-reported cooking skills questionnaire, were instructed about the main goal of the study and received some information about the ingredients and cooking time needed to complete the dish. All participants cooked a spicy Mexican casserole, which was selected based on its linearity (i.e., no temporally overlapping steps) and limited complexity. Each participant cooked the dish in their own kitchen.

The experiment was done by means of a video-call, during which participants were instructed to ask as many questions as they could come up with, while preparing the given dish. The experimenter shared their screen, and entered all user queries, such that it was not necessary for participants to download any of the required software. Then, the answer given by the cooking assistant was returned to the participants. Shortly after finishing the recipe, the participant was asked to fill in the System Usability Scale [5].

Evaluation. The quality of clarification responses during the six conversations was measured by manually checking their correctness, based on which precision, recall and F1-score were computed.

Table 4. Classifier performance the 293 queries asked during recipe instruction.

Label	Precision	Recall	F1-score
General	0.53	0.70	0.61
Specific	0.92	0.85	0.88
Weighted avg.	0.85	0.82	0.83

4.4 Results

A total of 297 queries ($M = 49.50$, $SD = 16.93$) were asked. 6 of these were manually labeled as "Before classification" (i.e., before selecting a recipe), 57 as "General" and 234 as "Specific". This is a relatively small dataset. However, it serves as a first indication of the types of questions that users ask in a natural setting, on top of the more artificial setting explained above.

The results of the random forest classifier on distinguishing between general-domain and task-specific questions are reported on in Table 4. The weighted average F1-score was 0.83 for the random forest classifier. General domain questions were more difficult to identify than task-specific questions. Out of the incorrectly classified queries (18%), the heuristics (i.e., maximum distance score or minimum confidence score) corrected 29%. This means that a total of 87% of the queries ended up being correctly classified.

The influence of different components in the decision tree on returning the right answer is presented in Table 5. 66% of all questions were correctly answered, while 87% were correctly classified. This could be partly attributed to directing the wrong answer to a question answering component (21% of the questions were not correctly recognised or failed to pass the threshold-based heuristics), and for the other part to a wrongly retrieved answer by the algorithm or the absence of an answer in the database. The latter applies for a large part to the general QA database, where only for 56% of the questions an answer would be available in the database (had they correctly passed through the decision tree to be retrieved by the Sentence-BERT approach). The threshold-based heuristics accounted for 13 queries that wrongfully did not pass the threshold and 5 queries that were passed to the right question-answering module after a wrong classification.

Out of the incorrect responses, only 6% was still relevant to another part of the recipe, and used by the participant at some point later in time. In 19% of the cases where the agent could not give a correct response, a fallback intent was triggered (e.g., "Can you rephrase your question?"). The remaining 74% of non-correct answers led to confusion amongst participants, since an unexpected answer was returned. Only 25% of the general cooking questions was answered correctly. Of the remaining 75%, most mistakes were made because the posed query was not present in the database. Of the recipe-specific questions, a much higher percentage of 76% was answered correctly.

Table 5. Influence of different components in the conversational agent on returning a wrong answer.

	General		Recipe-specific		Total	
	N	P	N	P	N	P
# Questions asked	57	1.0	234	1.0	291	1.0
# Questions available in database	32	0.56	205	0.88	237	0.81
Remaining questions after question type classification	40	0.70	199	0.85	239	0.82
Remaining questions after decision tree heuristics	37	0.65	194	0.83	231	0.79
Correct answers returned by QA component	14	0.25	178	0.76	192	0.66

System Usability. The average score on the system usability scale, from 0 to 100, was 82.08 ($M = 82.08$, $SD = 4.85$). Three participants gave a score above 80, showing that they liked it and would probably recommend it to other people. The remaining participants gave a score between 68 and 79, showing that they thought the agent performed okay, but still needs some improvement.

5 Discussion

The main take-away from our study is that the approaches we took to answering general domain questions and task-specific questions show good performance in a controlled experiment, while this drops considerably when they are posed with questions asked by a user that is involved with the actual task. Our heuristics for handling user requests in combination with our detailed analysis of the conversations permits to pinpoint the two main causes for this performance gap: performance of general QA and confusion between common-sense and task-specific questions. In the following, we will provide explanations for these causes and discuss their implications for an improvement of conversational systems covering a knowledge space of similar width.

As for the first cause, a significant difference was seen in the performance on general cooking-related questions, where the F1 score dropped from 0.89 in the controlled experiment to 0.61 in the user study. This can be foremost ascribed to a mismatch between the used source for general domain questions, a CQA platform where at least part of the queries are posed out of curiosity, and the application area of users that are involved in the act of cooking when posing their questions. Improvement can be made by filtering types of queries from the database that are typically not posed during cooking instructions, and by iteratively adding queries that are not present in the database but have been posed by users. Alternatively, the use of a CQA could be discarded altogether and replaced by a dataset grounded in dialog as [29] have done, which does limit the number of questions that can be addressed.

The second cause, the confusion between common-sense and task-specific questions during the cooking instruction conversations, has led to a considerable portion (21%) of wrong answers given. Part of this can be attributed to the question type classifier, although it did yield a consistent performance on the controlled evaluation (macro F1 = 0.86) and user study (weighted F1 = 0.83). The heuristics (cosine distance <0.28 or confidence> 0.7) were another factor that led to a failed match in some cases. These failed question type categorizations were partly due to incomplete formulations of the user, that could be dealt with by using slot-filling. In addition, recipe-specific questions about the quantity of an ingredient were often mistaken for general questions, which could be improved upon by either omitting ingredient names as a feature for question type classification, or by training dedicated classifiers on particularly distinguishing different requests that include a recipe ingredient. Finally, the conversational interface itself could be used, by asking the user for a confirmation when there is confusion between particular question types, or relying on the user to perform conversational repair when a wrong response has been given. [8] show that wrong answers by a home assistant can be instrumental to move forward in a conversation. The system itself should of course be properly equipped to interpret user repair after a wrong response. A final point of discussion is the consideration to refrain from giving an answer when a question is out of scope. This option is currently only triggered in the heuristics when a threshold has not been met, but not integrated as central feature. Arguably, a system that is aimed at covering a wider knowledge space in a domain should also be knowledgeable of what it does not have the answer to. One way to identify questions that can not or should not be answered by the agent is by training a classifier on a set of unanswerable questions, as has been done in [24].

A central limitation to our study is that we only tested the system with six participants who were encouraged to ask many questions to the agent. This has been suitable as a first exploration, but in future work this number should be higher to draw strong conclusions, and participants should not be tasked with anything else than making the recipe to learn more about system performance and common questions that are asked. Apart from that, a strength of the current set-up is that participants were actually in their kitchen when talking to the assistant, and the thorough analysis of the conversations has given a clear indication of system requirements and challenges when expanding on the agent's knowledge. A question that the outcomes raise is whether a task-based conversational system should cover a long tail of questions that may someday be asked by a user, at the cost of confusing more questions with different ones. The current study shows that this cost is too significant, but the gain may be worthwhile when the rate of wrong answers can be reduced. Our study highlights a number of directions to explore further to this end.

6   Conclusion

We set out to increase the coverage of clarification responses for a cooking assistant, by drawing upon a community question answering platform for answering common sense questions related to cooking and a recipe platform for modelling recipe-specific knowledge. The approaches to answer cooking-related questions based on these data were tested in a controlled set-up and in a user study as part of a cooking assistant. The outcomes of the user study supported that having to distinguish between commonsense and task-specific questions can lead to a considerable proportion of questions that are not answered by the right module. In addition, much improvement can be made by increasing the coverage of common sense questions. Testing the quality of clarification responses in a user study has been vital to gain empirical insights into the information-seeking challenges of an instruction conversation in a broad knowledge domain.

A   General Question-Answering: Question Types

Questions in seven categories were selected:

1. Replacing ingredients: with what a certain ingredient can be replaced (e.g., with what can I substitute golden caster sugar?).
2. Meaning of ingredients: the question might rise what a certain ingredient is (e.g., what are goji berries?).
3. Difference between ingredients: what is the difference between two (similar) cooking ingredients (e.g., what is baking soda?).
4. Ingredient sustainability: how long an ingredient can be kept before it goes bad (e.g., how long is opened, organic coconut oil sustainable??).
5. Cooking time of ingredients: how long it takes to bake/cook a certain ingredient (e.g., for how long does sweet potato need to bake in the oven?)
6. Health: whether some ingredient or its usage is healthy (e.g., is it unhealthy to re-use a tea bag?)
7. Performing cooking techniques: how a certain cooking technique is performed (e.g., how do I boil water quickly in a pan?).

Table 6. Cooking domain predefined measurement units and English equivalents.

Language	Units
NL	gram, gr., gr, g., g, kilogram, kilo, kg., kg, liter, l., l, milliliter, ml., ml, centiliter, cl., cl, deciliter, dl., dl, eetlepel, eetlepels, el., el, theelepel, theelepels, tl., tl, kop, bos, zak, beetje, plak, plakken, scheut, handje, snuf, pond, ons, pint, tak, teen
EN	gram, gr., gr, g., g, kilogram, kilo, kg., kg, liter, l., l, millilitre, ml., ml, centilitre, cl., cl, decilitre, dl., dl, tablespoon, tablespoons, tbsp, tbsp, teaspoon, teaspoons, tsp, tsp, cup, bunch, bag, bit, slice, paste, dash, hand, snuff, pound, ounce, pint, branch, clove

B   Recipe-Specific Question-Answering: Intent Types

Which recipes. Ask which recipes are available for the user to cook.

Cooking recipe. Choose which recipe to cook, out of the available ones from Chefbot's database.

Confirm recipe. Confirm that they want to make the chosen recipe.

Number of people that the recipe is meant for. The user can ask the agent for how many people the recipe is intended. Users could subsequently use this information in order to adapt the quantities of the ingredients to the number of people for whom they want to cook.

Estimated preparation time. The estimated time for preparing the recipe has been added to the recipe's context. This allows the user to ask the agent how long it should take them to prepare a certain recipe.

Recipe name. Allows the user to ask what the name of the current recipe was.

Time or steps passed/left. The user can ask how far along they are with the recipe, or how much is left, in terms of time and/or in terms of steps. Such a question would lead to the answer "According to the recipe, the preparation should take around 30–60 min. You have already been cooking for 27 min. You have executed 14/20 steps".

Ingredients not used yet. The user can ask the agent about the recipe that have not been used yet in previous steps. This allows them to check whether they are still on the right track, or whether there are any ingredients that should have been used already, but have not been used yet. Additionally, this functionality can be helpful whenever a recipe step states to "add all the remaining ingredients". The user could then ask which are the remaining ingredients.

Continuation. Go to the next step after completing the current one.

Repeat. Repeat the current step.

Previous step. Go back to the previous step.

Update. Let the agent know that the current step has been executed

Elicit. Ask for some clarification whenever a step is unclear. The agent can only respond to this when a step has been written in a more detailed and a more basic way.

Accept repair: show gratitude. Thank the agent for clarifying.

Accept repair: understood. Let the agent know that the clarification is understood.

How much. Ask how much of the ingredient in the current step is needed.

How to. Ask to explain how a specific cooking technique needs to be executed. For this, the technique needs to be explicitly explained within the recipe.

Motivate. Ask why a certain step is needed.

Close recipe. Finish the recipe.

C   Recipe Annotation Guidelines: Ground Truth

Recipe name. The recipe name was the title of the recipe at the top of the page.

Number of people. The number of people for whom the recipe is intended, was indicated at the beginning of the ingredients list as follows: "Ingredients for N people".

Category. Found below the title of an individual recipe on smulweb.nl [15].

Cooking time. Found below the categories of an individual recipe on smulweb.nl [15].

Ingredients list. The ingredients were split up in three parts (if present): the amount, the measurement unit, and the name of the ingredient.

Utensils. For the cooking utensils, the list was split up depending on its format. The most frequent formatting was a list of comma-separated utensils names, however, other options also occurred, such as bullet-point lists.

Procedure. In order to split up the procedure, first of all, it was split up into sentences. If one sentence contained more than one cooking action (e.g., boil the water and put the pasta in it), this was again split up into two separate steps. Whenever there are multiple ingredients, for all of which the same action needs to be performed (e.g., add the onion and the garlic), they were kept together in one same step.

References

1. Agichtein, E., Maarek, Y., Rokhlenko, O.: Alexa prize taskbot challenge (2022)
2. Alfifi, M., et al.: Howdy y'all: an alexa taskbot (2022)
3. Baccouri, N.: Deep-translator. https://github.com/nidhaloff/deep-translator (2020)

4. Beddiar, D.R., Jahan, M.S., Oussalah, M.: Data expansion using back translation and paraphrasing for hate speech detection. Online Soc. Netw. Media **24**, 100153 (2021). https://doi.org/10.1016/j.osnem.2021.100153. https://www.sciencedirect.com/science/article/pii/S2468696421000355
5. Brooke, J.: SUS: a quick and dirty usability scale. Usability Eval. Ind. **189** (1995)
6. Burges, C.J.C.: Towards the machine comprehension of text: an essay (2013)
7. Chang, M., Guillai, L.V., Jung, H., Hare, V., Kim, J., Agrawala, M.: Recipescape: an interactive tool for analyzing cooking instructions at scale. In: Proceedings of the 2018 CHI Conference on Human Factors in Computing Systems. ACM (2018)
8. Cho, J., Rader, E.: The role of conversational grounding in supporting symbiosis between people and digital assistants. Proc. ACM Hum.-Comput. Interact. **4**(CSCW1), 1–28 (2020)
9. Damodaran, P.: Parrot: paraphrase generation for NLU (2021)
10. Devlin, J., Chang, M.W., Lee, K., Toutanova, K.: Bert: pre-training of deep bidirectional transformers for language understanding. arXiv preprint arXiv:1810.04805 (2018)
11. Edunov, S., Ott, M., Auli, M., Grangier, D.: Understanding back-translation at scale. In: Proceedings of the 2018 Conference on Empirical Methods in Natural Language Processing, pp. 489–500 (2018). https://doi.org/10.18653/v1/D18-1045
12. Feng, S., Wan, H., Gunasekara, C., Patel, S., Joshi, S., Lastras, L.: doc2dial: a goal-oriented document-grounded dialogue dataset. In: Proceedings of the 2020 Conference on Empirical Methods in Natural Language Processing (EMNLP), pp. 8118–8128. Association for Computational Linguistics (2020). https://doi.org/10.18653/v1/2020.emnlp-main.652. https://aclanthology.org/2020.emnlp-main.652
13. Gargett, A., Garoufi, K., Koller, A., Striegnitz, K.: The give-2 corpus of giving instructions in virtual environments. In: Proceedings of the Seventh International Conference on Language Resources and Evaluation (LREC 2010) (2010)
14. Gemmell, C., Fischer, S., Mackie, I., Owoicho, P., Rossetto, F., Dalton, J.: GRILL-Bot: a flexible conversational agent for solving complex real-world tasks. In: 1st Proceedings of the Alexa Prize Taskbot (2022)
15. Groep, J.: Gelegenheid recepten (2021). https://smulweb.nl/recepten/gelegenheid
16. Honnibal, M., Montani, I., Van Landeghem, S., Boyd, A.: spaCy: Industrial-strength Natural Language Processing in Python (2020). https://doi.org/10.5281/zenodo.1212303
17. Jian, Y., Zaporojets, K., Deleu, J., Demeester, T., Develder, C.: Extracting structured data from recipes using conditional random fields. In: Proceedings of the 1st Conference of the Asia-Pacific Chapter of the Association for Computational Linguistics and the 10th International Joint Conference on Natural Language Processing, pp. 821–826 (2020)
18. Lample, G., Conneau, A.: Cross-lingual language model pretraining. In: 33rd Conference on Neural Information Processing Systems (2019)
19. Lavelle, F., et al.: The development and validation of measures to assess cooking skills and food skills. Int. J. Behav. Nutr. Phys. Act. **14**(1), 118 (2017)
20. Lin, Y.T., et al.: Miutsu: NTU's taskbot for the alexa prize. arXiv preprint arXiv:2205.07446 (2022)
21. Maeta, H., Mori, S., Sasada, T.: A framework for recipe text interpretation. In: Proceedings of the 1st Conference of the Asia-Pacific Chapter of the Association for Computational Linguistics and the 10th International Joint Conference on Natural Language Processing, pp. 553–558 (2014)
22. Mikolov, T., Chen, K., Corrado, G., Dean, J.: Efficient estimation of word representations in vector space. arXiv preprint arXiv:1301.3781 (2013)

23. Neumann, N., Wachsmuth, S.: Recipe enrichment: knowledge required for a cooking assistant (2021). https://doi.org/10.5220/0010250908220829

24. Rajpurkar, P., Jia, R., Liang, P.: Know what you don't know: unanswerable questions for squad. In: Proceedings of the 56th Annual Meeting of the Association for Computational Linguistics (Volume 2: Short Papers), pp. 784–789 (2018)

25. Rastogi, A., Zang, X., Sunkara, S., Gupta, R., Khaitan, P.: Towards scalable multi-domain conversational agents: the schema-guided dialogue dataset. In: Proceedings of the AAAI Conference on Artificial Intelligence, vol. 34, no. 5, pp. 8689–8696 (2020)

26. Reimers, N., Gurevych, I.: Sentence-BERT: sentence embeddings using Siamese BERT-networks. EMNLP (2019)

27. Stoyanchev, S., Keizer, S., Doddipatla, R.: Action state update approach to dialogue management. In: ICASSP 2021-2021 IEEE International Conference on Acoustics, Speech and Signal Processing (ICASSP), pp. 7398–7402 (2021)

28. Strathearn, C., Gkatzia, D.: Chefbot: a novel framework for the generation of commonsense-enhanced responses for task-based dialogue systems. J. ACM 46–47 (2021)

29. Strathearn, C., Gkatzia, D.: Task2Dial: a novel task and dataset for commonsense enhanced task-based dialogue grounded in documents (2022)

30. Traum, D.R., Larsson, S.: The information state approach to dialogue management. In: van Kuppevelt, J., Smith, R.W. (eds.) Current and New Directions in Discourse and Dialogue, pp. 325–353. Springer, Dordrecht (2003). https://doi.org/10.1007/978-94-010-0019-2_15

31. Van-Tu, N., Anh-Cuong, L.: Improving question classification by feature extraction and selection. Indian J. Sci. Technol. 9, 1–8 (2016)

32. Xue, X., Jeon, J., Croft, W.: Retrieval models for question and answer archives, pp. 475–482 (2008). https://doi.org/10.1145/1390334.1390416

33. Zaib, M., Zhang, W.E., Sheng, Q.Z., Mahmood, A., Zhang, Y.: Conversational question answering: a survey. Knowl. Inf. Syst. 1–45 (2022)

Designing Context-Aware Chatbots for Product Configuration

Tom Niederer[1] , Daniel Schloss[1($\boxtimes$)] , and Noemi Christensen[2]

[1] Karlsruhe Institute of Technology, Kaiserstraße 12, 76131 Karlsruhe, Germany
daniel.schloss@kit.edu
[2] CAS Software AG, CAS-Weg 1 - 5, 76131 Karlsruhe, Germany

Abstract. Product configurators provide an interface for customizing complex products. However, large form-based configurators overwhelm many end users and are often considered expert tools. This paper therefore addresses the problem of the complexity of current product configurators. Since chatbots can respond flexibly to queries and offer a natural language interface, they have the potential to simplify the configuration process. In this paper, we present a chatbot for product configuration that we developed using the design science research approach and in collaboration with an industrial partner. We derive design principles for configurator chatbots from user interviews that relate in particular to the flexibility of the chatbot compared to a static process. These design principles were implemented in our chatbot artifact which was evaluated in an online experiment (N = 12) and compared to a baseline chatbot with an inflexible configuration process. Our results indicate that the proposed design increased dependability and configuration performance, and overall had positive effects on participants' engagement. Thus, this study contributes prescriptive knowledge on the design of context-aware chatbots for product configuration and a novel artifact in the form of a context-aware configurator chatbot prototype.

Keywords: Chatbots · Product configuration · Context-awareness

1 Introduction

Product configurators emerged in the course of digitalization, when the demand for customized products grew, and "Mass Customization" became a phenomenon [1]. For companies, product configurators offer a good opportunity to organize the increasing demand for tailored products. The industry partner of the research project presented in this paper, CAS Software AG, offers product configurators for this purpose. Although CAS has been successfully developing Configure, Price, Quote (CPQ) solutions for midsize and large customers for 35 years, product configurators present a major design challenge due to the high number of configuration items and variants. Due to their specificity, software-based product configurators are often considered expert tools and cannot be easily used by customers and sales staff. The term "Mass Confusion" [2] describes a major issue occurring in complex customization settings. Customers can be overwhelmed by the

© The Author(s), under exclusive license to Springer Nature Switzerland AG 2023
A. Følstad et al. (Eds.): CONVERSATIONS 2022, LNCS 13815, pp. 190–210, 2023.
https://doi.org/10.1007/978-3-031-25581-6_12

number of available options and the complexity of the product structure. Information overload can deter users from choosing at all. Even small-scale configuration problems often have complex knowledge bases, e.g. when a product consists of components that can have sub-components or similar. Component interdependencies, restrictions, and rules introduce additional complexity [3]. In such settings, users are exposed to a multi-layered configuration process that involves many steps, many options to select from, and hard-to-track product domain restrictions. Researchers from the domain of product configuration as well as the CAS Software AG are constantly looking for ways to reduce complexity for end-users.

Studies in various information system domains have shown that natural language interaction can reduce complexity for end-users (e.g. [4, 5]). Natural language interfaces provide even inexperienced users with the capabilities to formulate requests in areas where they lack proficiency. They can reduce the need for experts to translate queries into domain-specific technical terms. For these reasons, natural language interfaces are also of interest for the special application of product configuration where managing complexity is the central challenge. Due to their ability to engage in natural language, chatbots could be a suitable tool to facilitate complex and lengthy processes like product configuration for the user.

However, while a configuration process is usually mapped to a stringent and linear scenario, a conversation is not. It can consist of contextual queries, surprising turns, interim questions, and even uncooperative behavior. Within a configuration dialogue, several scenarios might occur where the bot needs context to react appropriately. A customer might ask "What are my options?" or "Why not green?" instead of specifying the desired color. Here the proposed chatbot should be able to connect this follow-up question to the narrow context. End-users might also reference the broad context or change their mind: "Actually, I prefer red" at any moment during the configuration. Finally, modern chatbots possess the ability to extract multiple pieces of information within a single request [6]. The process could thus be accelerated, if users know their preferences beforehand: "I want a blue sportscar with high-end hi-fi interior". Due to the outlined characteristics of product configuration and natural language communication, a chatbot as a product configurator must have a high degree of flexibility.

Context-aware chatbots are intelligent agents that can consider contextual knowledge to simplify the human-machine interaction. This work sees the concept of context-awareness as a tool to provide the required adaptability and a fit between task and information presentation. A context-aware chatbot holds the potential to ultimately lead to a higher task performance for users [7, 8]. This work therefore investigates the design of a context-aware chatbot for product configuration. Our research project, conducted as a Design Science Research (DSR) project, aims to answer the following research questions:

- RQ1: How to design a context-aware chatbot for product configuration to facilitate the configuration process for the user?
- RQ2: How does a context-aware configuration chatbot compare to a basic question-answer chatbot regarding usefulness, ease of use, and cognitive load?

2   Theoretical Background and Related Work

2.1   Product Configurators

Since product configurators offer valuable opportunities for companies on the one hand, but also pose challenges, product configuration research has been devoted to the problems of configurators and addresses them with design proposals. To address the "Mass Confusion" [2] concern, product configurator research suggests teaching the customer about product attributes and their mapping to design parameters [6]. They also stress the importance of identifying customer needs. Customers might not be interested in exploiting all possible alternatives [6]. Furthermore, customers differ in their knowledge about the product to configure. For these reasons the configuration process can lead to a cognitive overload of information. Since a too high cognitive load can negatively influence task performance, in this case on the configuration task [7], an adequate representation format is crucial for the cognitive fit and the performance in a configuration process [2].

So far, only few technologies for assisting a configuration process have been tested. Most software based-configuration interfaces are available to customers as web forms [3, 5, 8]. However, they come with problems like limited flexibility and intuitiveness as well as complexity, which will be discussed in more detail in the subsequent section. For this reason, we are testing a chatbot as a new technology for product configuration, which reflects chatbot-specific but also configuration-specific design principles, as we outline in the following sections.

2.2   Conversational Interfaces for Complexity Reduction

Chatbots are a popular, but novel technological possibility to display a configuration process [9]. Due to the intuitiveness and possible efficiency of natural language, chatbots hold the potential to solve and facilitate complex tasks like product configuration. Therefore, the technology has already been tested in related areas with high complexity like e-commerce and recommendations, with the focus on assisting users in purchase decisions. Several studies use chatbots to query product databases based on communicated user preferences [10–12]. Natural language interfaces have also been applied to complex data scenarios. In recommender systems, conversational interfaces have been used to avoid information overload [5, 13]. Since it is very common for people to ask other people for recommendations (e.g. restaurants, movies) they are very familiar with formulating recommendation requests in natural language [13]. This also holds true for configuration, as the most intuitive process would be a product configuration in form of a consultation with a product expert or a sales representative.

2.3   Context-Awareness in Chatbots

A simple question-answer form would not be sufficient to facilitate configuration as this approach solely moves cognitive efforts from clicking to typing. The provision of an intuitive configuration interface is achieved by equipping the chatbot with context-aware capabilities. Context is needed where a statement relates not only to a single question but to the entire dialogue. Context-awareness enables a more natural conversational flow, which supports the call for integrating more social features in conversational agents [14]. Product configuration is context-dependent per se, since a single step is meaningless without reference to the others. In chatbot research context has been defined as extracted information from the conversation between user and chatbot [15]. There are also other derivations known, e.g. when someone does not provide requested information and context is needed to react appropriately: Corrections, references to the broad context, and references to the narrow context [16].

For a configuration bot to offer contextual knowledge, it must be connected to a memory and knowledge base. This is the case with our chatbot, which is connected to the configuration interface of CAS in order to map the hierarchical configuration steps and the respective configurations. Furthermore, modeled configuration restrictions can be used to inform the user about available options. Modeled additional information on specific product characteristics can be retrieved to answer follow-up questions. Furthermore, the bot could offer the possibility to skip certain options and apply default configuration values. Finally, product experts could formulate several desired configuration properties within a single request, while less sophisticated users are guided step by step through the process.

3   Research Approach

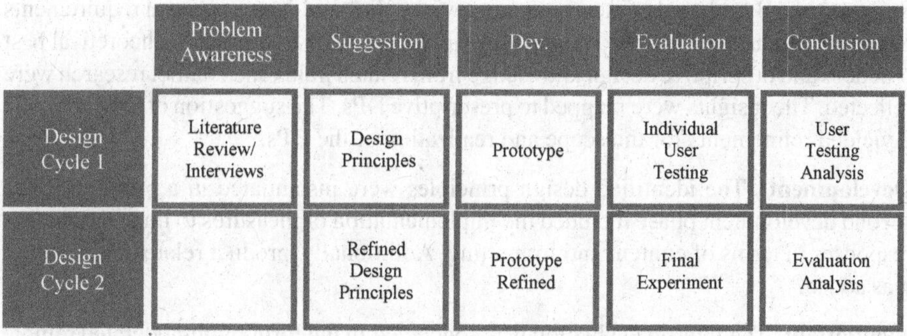

	Problem Awareness	Suggestion	Dev.	Evaluation	Conclusion
Design Cycle 1	Literature Review/ Interviews	Design Principles	Prototype	Individual User Testing	User Testing Analysis
Design Cycle 2		Refined Design Principles	Prototype Refined	Final Experiment	Evaluation Analysis

Fig. 1. Design science research approach for this project.

We consider the DSR approach to be particularly suited for gaining insights about the design of context-aware chatbots for product configuration as it involves iterative development and evaluation phases to ensure pertinence and validity [17]. Our DSR project follows the five established phases of problem awareness, suggestion, development, evaluation, and conclusion [18]. The following sections give an overview of the main steps of the implemented procedure, while Sect. 4 describes each step in detail. Our research project consisted of two cycles including an interim evaluation with first qualitative feedback and a more extensive final evaluation. The involved steps of the research project are illustrated in Fig. 1. As the interim evaluation demonstrated that the initial problem was sufficiently understood but indicated a slight adjustment of the design principles (DPs), the second iteration started with the suggestion phase after the interim evaluation.

Awareness of the Problem: To improve problem understanding, company employees with access to customer feedback (e.g. sales representatives, product managers) were interviewed to identify actual problems end-users are facing using product configuration interfaces. For this, seven semi-structured interviews were conducted. In total, seven employees (2 female, 5 male; average age $= 34.14$ years, SD $= 6.87$; working experience $= 15.57$ years, SD $= 7.69$; product configuration experience $= 5.71$ years, SD $= 2.77$) were interviewed. For the interviews, a semi-structured interview catalog was developed consisting of questions regarding demographics and professional background, as well as twelve pre-formulated questions concerning product configuration. The interview ranged from questions addressing the status quo of product configuration (e.g. "How often is the product configurator used by which user groups?") to questions addressing problems with product configuration (e.g. "Why do users cancel the configuration?") to customer requirements (e.g. "What are commonly expressed customer requirements?"). The interviews were transcribed using Microsoft Teams Live-Transcription and lasted on average 23,39 min (SD $= 2,77$). We hand-labelled sentences from the interviews and grouped them by topic. Agreement on the final clusters and classification of labelled information was reached in discussions. As we illustrate in the upcoming Sect. 4.2, the expert interview results were in line with related literature on product configuration focusing on requirements from a user perspective.

Suggestion: Based on the interviews and reviews, key end-user goals and requirements regarding product configuration interfaces were identified. Additionally, theoretical best practices and descriptive design knowledge from related fields and chatbot research were reflected. The insights were mapped to prescriptive DPs. The suggestion of Design Cycle 2 yielded refinements for the scope and realization of the DPs.

Development: The identified design principles were instantiated in a prototype. The second development phase included the implementation of measures to improve chatbot responses in terms of content and formatting. Additionally, product related information was added.

Evaluation: The interim evaluation was conducted in the form of unmoderated remote usability testing [19]. The final evaluation in Design Cycle 2 investigated whether the chatbot was able to facilitate the configuration process for end-users compared to a baseline chatbot, which only offered a step-by-step inflexible configuration process. Central evaluation criteria for the final evaluation were usefulness, ease of use, and cognitive load. These were measured by observing a user's configuration task performance and conducting a post-experiment survey.

4 Designing Context-Aware Chatbots for Product Configuration

4.1 Awareness of the Problem

The transcribed documents were analyzed to extract information addressing problems of existing product configurators, as well as the goals and requirements of end-users.

The analysis of interviews and literature resulted in five major groups of identified issues which are described in the subsequent paragraphs.

Limited Flexibility: The heterogeneity of consumers using product configuration interfaces is addressed by several authors [3, 20]. However, usually product configurators offer a single standard form for the customization experience. Users with extensive product knowledge go through the same process steps as novice customers and are exposed to the same level of detail and information [6]. Additionally, standard forms emphasize a strict order of the configuration which may differ substantially from actual user preferences: "I am relatively bound to the order, while that does not necessarily correspond to the things that are important to me" (Interviewee 7). Every selection of product characteristics can limit further selectable options. As a result, following the strict linear order of the configuration process can easily lead to suboptimal results.

Insufficient Information: Lack of information becomes apparent concerning several stages within a configuration process. First, many customers might not have detailed technical product domain knowledge at their disposal [3]. Therefore, they are not able to select specific characteristics to fulfill their needs [6]. This can be due to very domain-specific terminology. For this reason the major challenge of designing product configuration interfaces often also is conflict resolution [21]. Configuration conflicts appear when components selected by the customer do not fit together. Interviewee 7 reports frustrated customers, who "[...] could not click on what they wanted and also did not understand why".

Complexity/Confusion: High variant products are complex by nature and the central challenge of a product configuration interface is the reduction of complexity. For example at many car manufacturers often only a few product experts have a full overview of the product range [21]. Configuration interfaces presenting too many options at once do overwhelm customers [2, 3]. Interview participant 5 also reports that "[...] you simply don't see through how to do what [...]".

Limited Intuitivity/Guidance: Limited intuitivity is reported by several interview participants, as the configuration is often "[...] not self-explanatory" (Interviewee 4). Even if user guidance in the form of explanatory texts exists, it is still perceived as "problematic" (Interviewee 2). Users also fail "[...] to click on the information to find out by myself" (Interviewee 7) due to limited intuitiveness of the information representation.

Duration: The process of configuring a customized product is a "cognitively challenging task" [6]. Often customers are "not [..] interested in fully exploiting the potential of customization" [6]. Such users have some preferences in mind and after those are fulfilled further options are not particularly relevant. However, often it still "[...] takes a lot of clicks to even get to a result" (Interviewee 5).

4.2 Suggestion

Deriving Design Requirements: Having gained a deeper understanding of problems associated with product configuration interfaces, in the next step, we derived requirements addressing those issues. First, the interface should help both novice and experienced users. Therefore, the chatbot must have a flexibility that ensures the right level of efficiency and assistance for experts as well as novice users. Customers should be able to decide on their own which level of detail they need, and in which order they configure their product. Furthermore, economic and psychological studies also show that human preferences change depending on the alternatives available [22]. Thus, a product configuration interface must always support easy and flexible changes during the customization procedure. The resulting design requirement (DR) was stated as: a product configurator must offer flexibility (DR1) to support customers differing vastly in their goals, knowledge, and configuration procedure.

Second, the interface must overcome the gap of missing information. It needs to support customers who use the configurator as a tool to research what is possible with the given product. Thus, the proposed design must allow one to learn more about the product, as well as its features and characteristics. Allowing for this case comes with a high level of transparency: What happens to my configuration if I choose a certain option? How does this affect my end product regarding my preferences? Are certain options combinable? In short, a product configurator must allow exploration (DR2).

Thirdly, a product configurator must address the issue of complexity and confusion. Therefore, a crucial challenge lies in the provision of an adequate amount of information at the right place at the right time and not all at once. Interviewees suggest reducing the required mental effort by employing intuitivity and facilitation: The product configurator should be clear, easy to navigate and as easy to understand as possible. Respectively, the proposed solution should be as self-explanatory and as easy to learn as possible. Thus, it must reduce cognitive effort (DR3).

Customers usually do not want to spend hours configuring the end product, they want to configure their desired products "as quickly [...] as possible" (Interviewee 3). Therefore, a suitable configuration tool should implement mechanisms to configure quickly (DR4).

Translating Design Requirements into Design Principles: To define guidelines of how the DRs can be fulfilled in a chatbot interface, they were translated into DPs. The mapping is explained in the subsequent paragraphs and depicted in Fig. 2.

To increase flexibility (DR1) and opportunities for exploration (DR2), the chatbot design must provide conversational flexibility (DP1). The design must reflect that natural language input is of much higher variety than input in graphical user interfaces [23, 24]. The desired goal is to understand the needs of users and how they are best served [24]. It must offer users a way to directly formulate their preferences in natural language, as well as to start a configuration process by querying about the process itself for specific product properties. Furthermore, the chatbot needs to provide flexibility at any time during the configuration - it must allow for (contextual) queries, corrections, undoing of previous steps, and deviations from a standard configuration proceeding.

To increase opportunities for exploration (DR2) and to decrease required cognitive effort (DR3), the chatbot must provide relevant information before, during, and after the configuration process (DP2). Relevant information does include general (static) information about the product, the process, possibilities, and limitations. During the configuration, dynamic (context-dependent) information provision becomes particularly relevant. Furthermore, the chatbot must make use of NLU capabilities during the configuration to support users with vague or unclear request formulations. Context-dependent information is needed during the configuration: The chatbot should be able to name conflicting features and provides solutions about how a conflicting characteristic can be selected and what effects the selection would have. Ideally, the chatbot is also able to explain why different options cannot be combined. During the configuration, relevant information must also be available in the form of intermediate states and transparency regarding changes in the configuration.

To decrease required cognitive effort (DR3) and accelerate the configuration procedure (DR4) the chatbot must offer a clear structure (DP3). The design must reflect that contents and features of a text-based interface are to a much greater degree hidden from the user compared to a graphical interface [24]. Several authors implicate the necessity to reveal the system's capabilities throughout and during the interaction to form expectations and provide guidance [23–26]. Researchers have found that conversational guidance can be achieved by proposing users' responses [23], providing clickable buttons to generate text [27], and clarifying conversational flow using instructional messages [28]. For the domain of product configuration, the chatbot must present cues on how customers can reach their goals. Guidance can be enhanced by offering next steps during the configuration process. Finally, a guided mode could be offered where the chatbot asks questions, e.g. what characteristic of a certain feature the user wants to select. The implementation of DP3, however, must take DP1 into account. The clear structure must be an optional offer, that does not force users into a mechanical procedure.

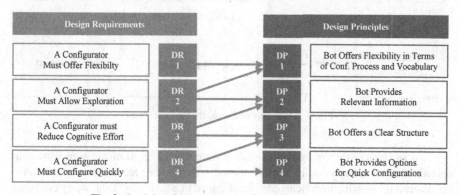

Fig. 2. Deriving design principles from design requirements

Acceleration mechanisms can be simple, for example by using default values (e.g. always choose the most often selected characteristic of available options). Configuration researchers also extensively investigate options to incorporate recommendations into product configuration [3, 29, 30]. Another suggestion from the interviews (Interviewee

5, 7) was to optimize the end-product according to a goal specified by the user (e.g. price or performance.).

4.3 Development

For chatbot development the conversational AI framework RASA was used. The primary criterion for selecting the framework was to satisfy technical requirements regarding the instantiation of the DPs. RASA is available open-source and performs well in comparison to other NLU services for chatbot development [31]. It contains NLU components for intent classification, entity extraction, and response retrieval, as well as a dialogue management component, deciding on the next action the chatbot should perform. For the implementation of the context-aware chatbot the component pipeline included the whitespace tokenizer, RASA's built-in RegexFeaturizer, LexicalSyntacticFeaturizer, its CountVectorsFeaturizer, as well as RASA's Dual Intent Entity Transformer (DIET) and RegexEntityExtractor. The Regex Entity Extractor was used to extract all the defined characteristics and features, the DIET Entity Extractor is able to identify entities that are not explicitly defined in the training data by using machine learning techniques. Furthermore, it offers a scalable architecture with easy integration of APIs and databases. Figure 3 shows the principal architecture of the chatbot:

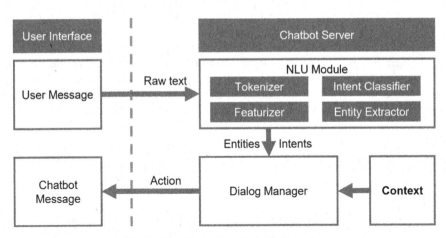

Fig. 3. Overview of the chatbot architecture

Two versions of the configuration chatbot were developed. Both versions were connected to the company's configuration backend. It determines feasible product variants, i.e. determines which components can be combined in which way. Thus, every customer request must be checked by calling the product domain database. Moreover, the backend can be consulted to retrieve additional information about the product, its properties, and their relationship to each other.

The baseline chatbot is based on simple question-answer mechanisms to configure step by step, as also realized in the standard web form. During the configuration process, the chatbot follows the same arranged order of features, and users are asked feature by feature for desired characteristics. Users can select characteristics by typing the string of the desired one or by the number. It can only provide context-independent information and does not implement the proposed design. When users with the baseline design query for specific features, the chatbot always answers with the same static response indicating which characteristics the feature contains. The proposed design, depicted on the right in Fig. 4, however, generates the response dependent on previous steps (e.g. highlighting selectable characteristics based on previous configuration steps). The context-aware chatbot was designed according to the suggested guidelines.

Context-awareness was realized using entity recognition to populate the chatbot's memory of the conversation. The conversational memory was used to provide dynamic, context-dependent responses, based on previous user utterances. The chatbot memory consists of slots storing information about all selected product characteristics and the procedural configuration stage. It was used to resolve and communicate configuration conflicts, provide information and assistance depending on the stage of configuration, as well as to assist with autocompletion resulting in a valid configuration. To react flexibly (DP1) to multiple directions of dialog the chatbot makes use of NLU modules to understand various user intents in all stages of the configuration process. Important user intents are for example to configure (i.e. to select characteristics), to request information, to request more guidance, or to ask for autocompletion.

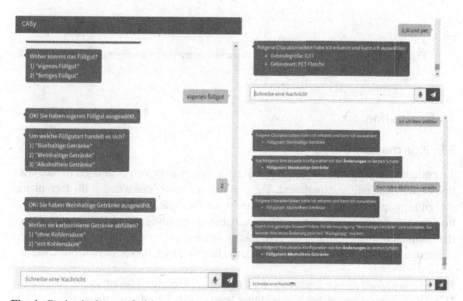

Fig. 4. Basic chatbot configuring step by step (left) and context-aware chatbot recognizing two characteristics at once (top right) or resolving conflicts (bottom right)

The results of the interim evaluation mainly addressed shortcomings of the instantiation of providing relevant information (DP2) and offering a clear structure (DP3). Thus, the second development phase added product and process related information to the chatbot responses (e.g. how many features have to be configured, what are the next configuration steps). To enhance structure and clarity the usage of emojis and mark-down formatting to demarcate information was applied. Finally, to reveal the chatbot capabilities more transparently, the chatbot provides example utterances for all its func-tionalities. Figure 5 portrays exemplarily how the warning sign emoji is used to indicate conflicts, the light bulb icon to mark instructional information, the arrow icon to offer next steps, quotation marks to point out preformulated responses and bold formatting to highlight configuration changes.

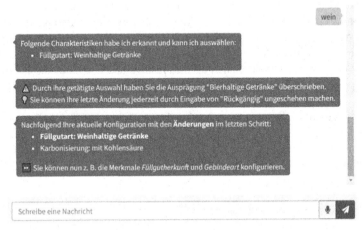

Fig. 5. Implementation of advices for the communication of configuration conflicts

5   Evaluation

5.1   Experimental Design

To evaluate the proposed design, the context-aware chatbot was compared to the base-line design in an online experiment. The evaluation investigated whether the formulated design principles could be instantiated in an artifact that did facilitate the configura-tion process for end-users. The artifact is assessed regarding its capabilities to address the outlined problems and to achieve added value to end-users. Based on established constructs of technology acceptance [32], the first two hypotheses were formulated as:

H1: The proposed design leads to a higher level of perceived ease of use.
H2: The proposed design leads to a higher level of (perceived) usefulness.

Based on the cognitive load theory, the third hypothesis was stated as:

H3: The proposed design leads to a reduction in perceived cognitive load.

To evaluate the proposed design, a controlled between-subject design online exper-iment was conducted. On the one hand, a control group of users performed a specific product configuration task with the baseline question-answer chatbot. The treatment group worked on the same task using the context-aware chatbot implementing the proposed design principles. Both groups answered a survey after the practical execution. The tasks included querying product related information and configuring according to desired product attributes. During the configuration task, participants had to resolve conflicts and to apply corrections.

Participants were mainly company employees from a different domain than product configuration who might have used a configurator lately (e.g. to configure a car). Those are considered potential end-users. Table 3 in the appendix overviews the demographics and controls of the participants.

5.2   Measurement Instruments

Perceived Ease of Use (PEOU) has been captured using a variety of subjective measures such as questionnaires [33–36]. Research has found PEOU to be related to the usability criteria perspicuity and dependability [36]. Perspicuity captures the degree to which it is easy to familiarize yourself with the product and to learn how to use it. A user feeling in control of the interaction experiences a high degree of dependability. Due to its ease of application and proven expressiveness, the User Experience Questionnaire (UEQ) is used to assess those dimensions [37, 38]. The questionnaire consists of 26 items in the form of semantic differentials (i.e. adjectives with the opposite meaning). It also captures the overall attractiveness, efficiency, and hedonic attributes (stimulation and novelty) which are associated directly or indirectly with the behavioral intention to use a system [36]. Perceived Usefulness (PU) evaluates an information system on a performance and output level [34]. To subjectively assess usefulness, scales were defined on the relevant task domains, which are information acquisition and configuration within the use case [34, 35]. As prescribed by the DRs, the main steps involved in a configuration process are information retrieval and customizing a product. Thus, the questionnaire contains two items where participants are asked to rate the prototype's usefulness regarding each process step. Applied user-related constructs are listed in Table 4.

The subjective assessment is complemented by measuring the user's task performance. The user performance was objectively assessed by logging the user's behavior during the interaction and by evaluating the participants' responses to the information retrieval task. In the appendix, Table 5 provides an overview of the obtained measurements. The *durations* and *number of messages* indicate the depth of the interaction and allow quantitative inferences regarding participants' proceedings and their investment in the task. Based on the responses, an *information retrieval score* was calculated, which is the share of correctly answered questions. From the logs, the performance criteria *interaction time* and the *number of messages* sent to the chatbot could be read out. As the configuration task specified several desired characteristics uniquely, a *configuration performance score* was calculated. The score was calculated as the share of correctly selected characteristics of all uniquely specified characteristics. Consequential errors (e.g. selecting a wrong characteristic which prevented the selection of further characteristics) were excluded from the score. Finally, the logs made traceable whether users adjusted incorrect characteristics and how much time they invested to do so.

This work hypothesizes that compared to a basic chatbot, a context-sensitive chatbot achieves higher task performances, higher PU, and higher PEOU due to a reduction in cognitive load and a higher fit between problem representation and task. Accordingly, measures to assess PU, PEOU, and cognitive load were defined and included in the experiment.

5.3 Evaluation Results

Users of the context-aware chatbot invested more time overall (on average 163.5 s more). Participants of both treatment groups invested about half of their time in the configuration task. To acquire the requested information, about the same amount of time was invested. To perform the configuration task users with the context-aware chatbot spent on average 111.5s more, which is significant ($df = 10$, $t = 1.855$, $p = 0.047$). To do a correction required significantly less time (on average about a minute) with the context-aware chatbot ($df = 8$, $t = 2.845$, $p = 0.011$). Two participants using the baseline chatbot did not perform the correction and were excluded from the configuration time measurement. The findings of more interaction investment with the context-aware design are supported by the observed number of sent messages. On average users of the baseline bot sent 37.5 messages (SD = 4.93) to the chatbot, while the test group sent 44.5 (SD = 13.28) messages on average.

Perceived Ease of Use: Participants reported a higher perspicuity, as well as higher dependability if they were using the context-aware chatbot (see Table 1). Despite the small group size (6 each) of our exploratory experiment, a significant difference between baseline and context-aware chatbot was already found for dependability.

Table 1. Descriptive statistics for perspicuity and dependability

Treatment	Baseline (n = 6)	Context-aware (n = 6)
Perspicuity		
Mean	1.00	1.67
SD	1.11	0.96
Dependability		
Mean	1.08	1.58
SD	0.52	0.41

Perceived Usefulness: The context-aware chatbot was on average perceived as more useful both for information retrieval (Mean context-aware = 2.17 (SD = 1.17) vs. Mean baseline = 1.17 (SD = 1.47) and configuration (Mean context-aware = 2.00 (SD = 0.63) vs. Mean baseline = 1.50 (SD = 1.64). In Table 2 the results for task performances are illustrated. For the information retrieval task, differences in performance scores are marginal, while the configuration scores differ significantly. The small variances in both tasks allow for the observation of behavior patterns that can be verified in the chat logs.

Table 2. Descriptive statistics for task performance

Treatment	Baseline (n = 6)	Context-aware (n = 6)
Inf.retrieval score		
Mean	0.67	0.71
SD	0.13	0.10
Conf. score		
Mean	0.79	0.93
SD	0.52	0.41

Cognitive Load: The measures on cognitive load suggest that participants experience on average rather low cognitive load, as both measured means are positive. Participants in the baseline design experienced less overall cognitive load (Mean context-aware = 0.82 (SD = 1.97) vs. Mean baseline = 1.33 (SD = 0.82)), while there is a high variance in the findings corresponding to the context-aware chatbot. The second scale, focusing rather on the medium to solve the task ("how easy or difficult was it to solve the tasks using the chatbot") favors the proposed design (Mean context-aware = 2.17 (SD = 10.75) vs. Mean baseline = 1.67 (SD = 0.82)).

Qualitative Results: Qualitatively, participants in the baseline design did miss flexibility: "It would also be nice if you didn't have to undo each step individually but jump to the desired point" (Participant 5). Participant 3 found it obstructive to "have to think about what is the next best thing". Five out of six participants using the baseline design found the step-by-step approach difficult to do corrections during the configuration.

Participants with the context-aware design criticized that not all their questions could be answered satisfactorily and they "had to rephrase the questions" (Participant 6). Here, the chatbot can be improved regarding its natural language understanding, as well as regarding the information it can provide (e.g. additional information about specific features).

Most participants highlighted the ease and intuitivity of selecting characteristics for both designs. For the baseline, the selection of characteristics was very fast due to the possibility of just typing in a number. However, the linear mechanic configuration comes at the cost of flexibility and control. All participants using the context-aware chatbot found it easy to configure. They acknowledged that typing in "buzzwords" (Participant 4) led to meaningful information or was sufficient to select characteristics. Participant 10 also appreciated the auto-complete option.

6 Discussion

6.1 Contribution

This work presents a novel approach addressing the known challenge of designing product configuration interfaces. Founded on prescriptive knowledge from product configuration and chatbot research, this work aims to facilitate the configuration process for end-users by providing an intuitive and easy to use interface. It synthesizes expert interviews and existing literature to address the main issues of existing solutions which are limited adaptiveness [6], information overload [2], and limited transparency [3, 6]. The formulated DRs are independent of the specific design of the interface and can guide the design of systems addressing the limitations of current solutions. Derived DPs reflect chatbot capabilities in terms of perceiving the conversation as the object of design. Developers can use the prescriptive knowledge to conceptualize chatbots as product configuration interfaces. The derived DPs of a chatbot for product configuration show the need for context-awareness for these kind of chatbots in order to provide flexibility (DP1), relevant information (DP2), structure (DP3), and quick configuration options (DP4). These principles can serve as the basis of a design theory for configuration bots.

From a practical perspective, the main deliverables are two chatbot prototypes (baseline and context-aware), as well as the evaluation insights. The results of the evaluation suggest that the proposed DPs did have an impact on participants' configuration experience and configuration outcome. Although the sample size was limited to 12 test persons, participants experienced significantly higher dependability and performed significantly better in the configuration with the context-aware chatbot. On average the evaluation showed that participants with the proposed design invested more time and sent more messages to the chatbot. By doing so, they used context-aware features to resolve configuration conflicts, select and reselect flexibly, and complete their configuration. They configured rather according to their preferences than to the order suggested by the bot. Although participants configuring with the baseline design knew better-suited alternatives exist and conflicts are part of the task, they made no effort to revise already selected characteristics. Participants stated qualitatively that the chatbot step-by-step approach made it hard to do corrections. Especially, the possibility to perform corrections flexibly yielded value to the test group. Participants in the test group were more successful and quicker in applying changes to their configuration. The control group confirmed this observation, as five out of six participants requested more flexibility for doing corrections.

For both designs, the self-reported overall mental effort was rather low, while it was even lower with the baseline design. The chat logs and evaluation results suggest that this low perceived mental workload is a result of the unsuitability of the baseline chatbot for the task at hand, as it did not lead the participants to reconsider their decisions. Accordingly, a reduction in perceived cognitive load (H3) could not be verified. However, the chatlogs suggest that the proposed design lead to higher engagement (e.g. more messages sent, more time invested to configure). The results indicate that the context-aware chatbot was perceived as easier to use than the baseline (H1), while the results were significant for the dimension dependability.

Significant differences in task performance results indicate that the proposed design was more useful than the baseline (H2), which was also inclined by queried perceived usefulness. A reduction in cognitive load due to the treatment could not be verified. Participants with the proposed design invested more mental effort, which was needed to complete the task at hand successfully. In conclusion, the context-aware chatbot is particularly suitable in an iterative configuration process involving changes and exploration.

The baseline can serve as a fallback when users want to quickly select characteristics manually.

6.2 Limitations and Future Works

This research project comes with five main limitations which offer opportunities for further studies on chatbots for product configuration. First, only the company's employees took part in the expert interviews. Future works could integrate a more diverse set of end-users. However, the interviewed experts did have access to customer feedback, some of them over years. Thus, they were able to produce generalizable insights from different product domains, while feedback from end-users might be subject to individual experience and the individual product domain.

Second, the evaluation was based on a sample size of 12 participants. Mainly participants without extensive product configuration experience were recruited, who were considered potential end-users. The evaluation results could be strengthened by increasing the sample size and targeting real end-users from the domain of application.

Third, the task participants had to perform during the evaluation was designed according to the DRs. To measure performance in terms of correctly selected characteristics objectively, the task's scenario specified preferences. Configuration conflicts were integrated into the task design, as their presence in configuration processes was confirmed by the interviewees and literature [21]. Further research must examine the proposed design's impact on the configuration experience of real end-users with their preferences. However, such an approach makes it difficult to apply objective performance measures, as the results are subject to individual preferences.

Fourth, the measures of perceived usefulness and cognitive load consisted of two items each. The small sample size and high variance in those measures do not permit the deduction of generally valid statements that have been quantitatively proven. However, the measurements allow to observe trends that could be reinforced by observing the participants' configuration proceedings, as well as their qualitative responses. Further research can extend evaluation metrics and sample sizes.

Fifth, by delimitation in the stated research questions, the proposed design principles are evaluated against a baseline without context-aware abilities. A comparison to a classical web form was not in the scope of this project. Due to their ability to reduce complexity for end-users and to provide flexibility in the configuration process, this work attributes added value to the usage of natural language, which has not been evaluated in a between-subjects comparison. On the one hand, participants qualitatively acknowledged the ease of selecting and changing product characteristics flexibly. On the other hand, web forms offer more flexibility regarding information representation than a chat interface. Further research can build on our contribution and compare different configuration modes.

7 Conclusion

Chatbots can reduce complexity and facilitate request formulation for end-users by allowing them to interact in natural language. Product configuration is an application where customers can be overwhelmed by the mass and complexity of the product features in current solutions. Existing interfaces often do not differentiate between novice and expert users and emphasize an order of configuration for end-users.

As we could show in a small-scale evaluation, a context-aware chatbot for product configuration provides flexibility in terms of possible conversation paths and vocabulary used. Drawing from expert interviews and literature, DRs were compiled from which general DPs were formulated. Those can serve as a blueprint to guide the development of chatbots or natural interfaces for product configuration. The instantiation of the proposed design was evaluated against a baseline design in a between-subjects comparison. Users with the proposed design invested on average more time and messages for the configuration and ended up with a better output in terms of task performance. Furthermore, participants attributed higher usefulness and higher usability to the proposed design. For both designs, the reported mental workload was rather low, indicating low perceived complexity. The instantiation of the DPs proved to be especially beneficial for quickly selecting and revising product attributes in an iterative process, flexibly in terms of order and vocabulary used. In use-cases with a higher number of variable product attributes, the visual possibilities offered by a chat window appear to be limited and might be supported by a web-form representation.

Further researchers are invited to apply, evaluate, and extend the proposed design and design theory on a chatbot for product configuration facilitating the user configuration process. Since the results of this project suggests high potential for combined approaches, a combination of a chatbot and a classical configuration interface could be an idea for future work to build on.

Appendix

Questions Asked in the Semi-structured Interviews

Status Quo

- "How often is the product configurator used by which user groups?"
- "What are the goals of a customer when configuring the product?"
- "What proportion of the configurations that have been started will be completed?"

Problem identification

- "For what reasons do users cancel a product configuration?"
- "How is the feedback on the product configurator?"
- "What complaints or negative feedback about the configurator are there?"
- "What are the hurdles in the current configuration process?"

Requirements
Abstract requirements

- "What are frequently expressed customer requirements?"
- "What are the relevant properties for you that a configurator has to implement?"

- "How can intuitive operation or a pleasant process flow be achieved?"

  Concrete requirements for configuration chatbot

- "In your opinion, how would a text-based chatbot have to proceed in order to to enable a pleasant configuration process?"
- "What abilities of the chatbot would be desirable"
- Opt.: negative questions in cases of insufficient feedback

  (translated from German).

Final Evaluation

Table 3. Final experiment groups

Condition	N	Age	Gender	Product configuration experience*	Chatbot usage**
Control (baseline design)	6	Mean = 29.5 (SD = 4.14)	Female = 4 Male = 2	Non-Expert = 4 Expert = 2	Mean = 3.00 (SD = 1.41)
Context-Aware (proposed design)	6	Mean = 30.17 (SD = 10.34)	Female = 2 Male = 4	Non-Expert = 4 Expert = 2	Mean = 3.33 (SD = 1.21)

*Measured on a five-point Likert scale
**Measured on a seven-point Likert scale

Table 4. User-related constructs

Construct	Reference	Measurement	Items
User experience questionnaire	Laugwitz et al. (2008)	7-point likert scale	26
Perceived usefulness	Lund (2001)	7-point likert scale	2
Cognitive load	Paas (1992), Eysink et al. (2009)	7-point likert scale	2

Table 5. Performance related metrics

Measurement	Description
Interaction duration	Duration to complete all tasks
Information retrieval duration	Duration to complete task one
Configuration duration	Duration to complete task two
Correction retrieval duration	Duration to complete task three
Number of messages 0000000	Total number of messages sent to the chatbot
Information retrieval score	Performance score in the information retrieval task
Configuration score	Performance score in the configuration task

References

1. Pine, B.J., II., Victor, B., Boynton, A.C.: Making mass customization work. Harv. Bus. Rev. **71**, 108–111 (1993)
2. Huffman, C., Kahn, B.E.: Variety for sale: mass customization or mass confusion? J. Retail. **74**, 491–513 (1998). https://doi.org/10.1016/S0022-4359(99)80105-5
3. Felfernig, A. (ed.): Knowledge-Based Configuration from Research to Business Cases. Morgan Kaufmann is an Imprint of Elsevier, Amsterdam (2014)
4. Li, F., Jagadish, H.V.: Constructing an interactive natural language interface for relational databases. Proc. VLDB Endow. **8**, 73–84 (2014). https://doi.org/10.14778/2735461.2735468
5. Sun, Y., Zhang, Y.: Conversational recommender system. In: The 41st International ACM SIGIR Conference on Research & Development in Information Retrieval. ACM, New York (2018)
6. Randall, T., Terwiesch, C., Ulrich, K.T.: Principles for user design of customized products. Calif. Manag. Rev. **47**, 68–85 (2005). https://doi.org/10.2307/41166317
7. Sweller, J.: Cognitive load during problem solving: effects on learning. Cogn. Sci. **12**, 257–285 (1988). https://doi.org/10.1016/0364-0213(88)90023-7
8. Blecker, T., Abdelkafi, N., Kreutler, G., et al.: Product configuration systems: state of the art, conceptualization and extensions (2004)
9. Dale, R.: The return of the chatbots. Nat. Lang. Eng. **22**, 811–817 (2016). https://doi.org/10.1017/s1351324916000243
10. Gupta, S., Borkar, D., de Mello, C., et al.: An e-commerce website based chatbot. Int. J. Comput. Sci. Inf. Technol. **6**, 1483–1485 (2015)
11. Cui, L., Huang, S., Wei, F., et al.: SuperAgent: a customer service chatbot for e-commerce websites. In: Proceedings of ACL 2017, System Demonstrations, Stroudsburg, PA, USA. Association for Computational Linguistics (2017)
12. Nica, I., Tazl, O.A., Wotawa, F.: Chatbot-based tourist recommendations using model-based reasoning. In: ConfWS, pp. 25–30 (2018)
13. Christakopoulou, K., Radlinski, F., Hofmann, K.: Towards conversational recommender systems. In: Proceedings of the 22nd ACM SIGKDD International Conference on Knowledge Discovery and Data Mining. ACM, New York (2016)
14. Clark, L., Pantida, N., Cooney, O., et al.: What makes a good conversation? Challenges in designing truly conversational agents. In: Proceedings of the 2019 CHI Conference on Human Factors in Computing Systems (2019)

15. Jain, M., Kumar, P., Kota, R., et al.: Evaluating and informing the design of chatbots. In: Proceedings of the 2018 Designing Interactive Systems Conference. ACM, New York (2018)
16. Vlasov, V., Drissner-Schmid, A., Nichol, A.: Few-shot generalization across dialogue tasks (2018)
17. Hevner, A.R.: A three cycle view of design science research. Scand. J. Inf. Syst. **19**, 4 (2007)
18. Kuechler, B., Vaishnavi, V.: On theory development in design science research: anatomy of a research project. Eur. J. Inf. Syst. **17**, 489–504 (2008). https://doi.org/10.1057/ejis.2008.40
19. Barnum, C.M.: Usability Testing Essentials: Ready, Set… Test!, 2nd edn. Morgan Kaufmann, Amsterdam (2020)
20. Ardissono, L., Felfernig, A., Friedrich, G., et al.: A framework for the development of personalized, distributed web-based configuration systems. AI Mag. **24**, 93 (2003). https://doi.org/10.1609/aimag.v24i3.1721
21. Drews, M.: Interaction Patterns für Produktkonfiguratoren. In: Mensch & Computer 2008, pp. 367–376. Oldenbourg Wissenschaftsverlag GmbH (2008)
22. Kahneman, D., Tversky, A.: Prospect theory: an analysis of decision under risk. In: Handbook of the Fundamentals of Financial Decision Making, pp. 99–127. World Scientific (2013)
23. Diederich, S., Brendel, A.B., Kolbe, L.M.: Designing anthropomorphic enterprise conversational agents. Bus. Inf. Syst. Eng. **62**(3), 193–209 (2020). https://doi.org/10.1007/s12599-020-00639-y
24. Følstad, A., Brandtzæg, P.B.: Chatbots and the new world of HCI. Interactions **24**, 38–42 (2017). https://doi.org/10.1145/3085558
25. Dzindolet, M.T., Peterson, S.A., Pomranky, R.A., et al.: The role of trust in automation reliance. Int. J. Hum. Comput. Stud. **58**, 697–718 (2003). https://doi.org/10.1016/S1071-5819(03)00038-7
26. Luger, E., Sellen, A.: "Like having a really bad PA" the gulf between user expectation and experience of conversational agents. In: Proceedings of the 2016 CHI Conference on Human Factors in Computing System, pp. 5286–5297 (2016)
27. Jain, M., Kota, R., Kumar, P., et al.: Convey: exploring the use of a context view for chatbots. In: Proceedings of the 2018 CHI Conference on Human Factors in Computing Systems, pp. 1–6 (2018)
28. Gnewuch, U., Morana, S., Maedche, A.: Towards designing cooperative and social conversational agents for customer service (2017)
29. Cöster, R., Gustavsson, A., Olsson, T., et al.: Enhancing web-based configuration with recommendations and cluster-based help. In: 2002 Workshop on Recommendation and Personalization in eCommerce (2002)
30. Tiihonen, J., Felfernig, A.: An introduction to personalization and mass customization. J. Intell. Inf. Syst. **49**(1), 1–7 (2017). https://doi.org/10.1007/s10844-017-0465-4
31. Braun, D., Hernandez-Mendez, A., Matthes, F., et al.: Evaluating natural language understanding services for conversational question answering systems. In: Proceedings of the 18th Annual SIGdial Meeting on Discourse and Dialogue, Stroudsburg, PA, USA. Association for Computational Linguistics (2017)
32. Davis, F.D., Bagozzi, R.P., Warshaw, P.R.: User acceptance of computer technology: a comparison of two theoretical models. Manag. Sci. **35**, 982–1003 (1989). https://doi.org/10.1287/mnsc.35.8.982
33. Aladwani, A.M.: The development of two tools for measuring the easiness and usefulness of transactional Web sites. Eur. J. Inf. Syst. **11**, 223–234 (2002). https://doi.org/10.1057/palgrave.ejis.3000432
34. Freeman, L.A., Jessup, L.M.: The power and benefits of concept mapping: measuring use, usefulness, ease of use, and satisfaction. Int. J. Sci. Educ. **26**, 151–169 (2004). https://doi.org/10.1080/0950069032000097361

35. Lund, A.: Measuring usability with the USE questionnaire. Usability Interface **8**(2), 3–6 (2001)
36. Mlekus, L., Bentler, D., Paruzel, A., et al.: How to raise technology acceptance: user experience characteristics as technology-inherent determinants. Gr. Interakt. Org. **51,** 273–283 (2020). https://doi.org/10.1007/s11612-020-00529-7
37. Laugwitz, B., Held, T., Schrepp, M.: Construction and evaluation of a user experience questionnaire. In: Holzinger, A. (ed.) USAB 2008. LNCS, vol. 5298, pp. 63–76. Springer, Heidelberg (2008). https://doi.org/10.1007/978-3-540-89350-9_6
38. Schrepp, M., Hinderks, A., Thomaschewski, J.: Construction of a Benchmark for the User Experience Questionnaire (UEQ), vol. 4, p. 40 (2017) https://doi.org/10.9781/ijimai.2017.445

Author Index

Printed in the United States
by Baker & Taylor Publisher Services